COLUMBIA COLLEGE CHICAGO
3 2711 00204 6872

A TOAST TO ECLIPSE

CLIP
EXTRA

A TOAST TO ECLIPSE

ARPAD HARASZTHY
AND THE SPARKLING WINE OF OLD SAN FRANCISCO

BRIAN McGINTY

UNIVERSITY OF OKLAHOMA PRESS : NORMAN

Also by Brian McGinty

Strong Wine: The Life and Legend of Agoston Haraszthy (Palo Alto, Calif., 1998)
The Oatman Massacre: A Tale of Desert Captivity and Survival (Norman, Okla., 2005)
Lincoln and the Court (Cambridge, Mass., 2008)
John Brown's Trial (Cambridge, Mass., 2009)
The Body of John Merryman: Abraham Lincoln and the Suspension of Habeas Corpus (Cambridge, Mass., 2011)

This book is published with the generous assistance of the Kerr Foundation, Inc.

Still Life of Fruit and Champagne by Samuel Marsden Brookes (1816–1892). Brookes was a Bohemian Club friend of Arpad Haraszthy and the premier still life painter of late-nineteenth-century San Francisco. This painting shows a bottle of Eclipse, a glass, and an arrangement of fruit. Oil on canvas, 28" × 22", before 1880. Private collection.

LIBRARY OF CONGRESS CATALOGING-IN-PUBLICATION DATA

McGinty, Brian.
A toast to Eclipse : Arpad Haraszthy and the sparkling wine of old San Francisco / Brian McGinty.
p. cm.
Includes bibliographical references and index.
ISBN 978-0-8061-4248-7 (hardcover : alk. paper) 1. Sparkling wines—California—San Francisco. 2. Haraszthy, Arpad, 1840–1900. 3. Arpad Haraszthy & Company. I. Title.
TP548.6.S65M34 2012
641.2'2—dc23

2011034655

The paper in this book meets the guidelines for permanence and durability of the Committee on Production Guidelines for Book Longevity of the Council on Library Resources, Inc. ∞

1 2 3 4 5 6 7 8 9 10

To the memory of my grandfather
Agoston F. Haraszthy (1869–1943)

For the Christmas season of 1891, J. C. Fitzgerald, a San Francisco journalist, composed this "Christmas Ode," in the form of an acrostic, to Arpad Haraszthy and his Eclipse Champagne:

A drink of really good champagne
Rolls down one's throat, like timely rain
Preparing soil for Autumn's grain;
A man of taste need ne'er complain
Drinks he but dry Eclipse Champagne.

Headache to him will be unknown,
As fresh he'll look as rose just blown.
Rich, delicate with flavor fine,
A man need wish no better wine,
So each good judge of wine declares,
Zealously, too, the judge prepares
The palate, so that with a test—
Haraszthy's wine it may well test—
You drink ECLIPSE—and find it BEST!

Europe herself cannot produce,
Clearer, better or purer juice;
Like all good things it grows with use,
Imperial above excuse,
Proudly its claims we recognize
So none can wonder that we prize
Eclipse Champagne,—for we are wise.

Connoisseurs all with one accord
High praises to this brand award;
As good as gold or honor'd check
Most men declare is ECLIPSE SEC.
Perhaps at Xmas time we all
Across a glass would like to fall,
Good cheer at Christmas goes right well
No one has any need to tell,
Eclipse Champagne no head will swell.

From the *Pacific Wine and Spirit Review*,
February 5, 1892

CONTENTS

ILLUSTRATIONS

A TOAST TO ECLIPSE

INTRODUCTION

I have always believed that history should tell a story, and that good history should tell a good story. This book tells the story of Eclipse champagne and of the man who conceived it, produced it, and made it famous in the closing years of the nineteenth century. Much of the action of the story takes place in San Francisco, in a time when it was the largest, most dynamic city in the American West. But the story strays here and there to other venues: the peaceful vineyards of the Sonoma Valley, north of San Francisco; the banks of the San Diego River in Southern California; the foothills at the western edge of the Sacramento Valley in Northern California's Yolo County; and the labyrinth of tunnels that underlies the ancient city of Épernay in the Champagne country of northeastern France.

Eclipse was a sparkling wine created by Arpad Haraszthy,[1] one of the most prominent winemakers of California in his time, a man whose reputation rested on his own accomplishments as a vineyardist, wine producer, writer, speaker, and leader of the viticultural industry of his state, but whose fame derived in large part from that of his father, Agoston Haraszthy. Often called the "Father of California Viticulture,"[2] Agoston Haraszthy died when Arpad was only twenty-nine years old, but Agoston's extraordinary career as an international traveler, writer, town builder, legislator, metallurgist, pioneer vineyardist, and winemaker left an indelible impression on his son.

Arpad Haraszthy was inspired by his father's dream of making California one of the greatest wine-producing regions in the world. He began to pursue that goal when California winemaking was still in its infancy—when the best grapes for making California wine had yet to be discovered and proven, when the best locations for planting vineyards had not yet been established, and when popular tastes were offended by the idea that good wine could be made in a primitive country overrun with gold miners and desperados. Arpad Haraszthy devoted his adult life to the idea, inculcated in him by his father, that good sparkling wine could be made in California and that California's sparkling wine would one day compete with the finest products of the French Champagne country. That he did not fully achieve his goal does not detract from his compelling story. For he was the first Californian to produce sparkling wine on a sustained basis, the first to adhere throughout a long career to the strict standards of the *méthode champenoise,* and the first to pursue standards of the highest quality even in the face of commercial failure. The fact that Eclipse faltered in the great economic depression of the 1890s and that Arpad's sudden death in 1900 prevented him from reviving its production, speaks more to the difficulties of his quest than his own failures.

To understand the story of Eclipse, it may be helpful at the outset to sketch some of the background against which the story must be told. The first wine in California was made by the Franciscan friars, who built their chain of twenty-one missions stretching north from San Diego to Sonoma in the closing years of the eighteenth and the early years of the nineteenth centuries. The mission wines were made principally for sacramental use and domestic consumption (a priestly dinner table without at least a little wine was a poor table indeed), although small quantities were shipped to consumers outside the state. Winemaking expanded to private ranchos and pueblos (towns) in the early years of the nineteenth century. The pueblos of Los Angeles (in Southern California) and San Jose (in Northern California) became winegrowing centers where table wines, liqueurs, and spirits were produced. Most of these productions were consumed locally (drunkenness was often commented on by visitors), although small quantities found their way onto the trading ships that plied the California coast and were eventually transported to such distant destinations as Hawaii, South America, and even New York and

Boston. Some of the early winemakers experimented (as the mission fathers may have done before them) with the manufacture of sparkling wine, although for short periods and in limited quantities.

Efforts to produce wine along the Atlantic Coast of North America had begun in the seventeenth century, possibly even earlier, when European settlers (the Spanish in Florida and the English to the north) sought to cultivate fine European grapes of the species *Vitis vinifera*. But the climate and native diseases conspired against them. As settlers did in the nineteenth-century north and west of the Ohio River, they were also able to make some wines from American grapes, which were well-adapted to the bone-chilling winters, insects, and molds that menaced the vines. But the wines were harsh and unpleasant to palates trained to the delights of European wines. California, with its sunny hillsides, mild winters, and long, dry summers, gave promise of providing a new American homeland for *vinifera* grapes and fine, European-style wines. It was with the goal of producing such wines that Agoston Haraszthy came to California in 1849. And it was with the hope of producing a fine sparkling wine on the model of French Champagne that Arpad Haraszthy began his work in San Francisco in the 1860s.

Arpad worked in the days of cable cars and horse-drawn trolleys, when gaslights illuminated the warehouses and cellars of San Francisco, when electric lights and telephones were still novelties, and when most of the work of making wine and imbuing it with the effervescence that is the hallmark of sparkling wine was done by hand, by craftsmen trained in the exacting skills of the Champagne method. In those days, cases of the bottled wine were loaded onto horse-drawn wagons and taken to San Francisco's waterfront for transport by ship to distant ports in California and other countries. Many ocean-going ships were powered by steam, but many others were still powered by sail, so the city's crowded wharves and piers were lined with the masts of vessels from around the world. The common laborers of late-nineteenth-century California were mostly Chinese immigrants—scorned by many of the white settlers of the state, but valued by employers like Arpad Haraszthy who required dependable workers who could master delicate skills and perform them conscientiously day in and day out—and at low wages.[3] The railroad arrived in San Francisco early in the era of Eclipse, and quickly came to dominate the transportation needs of the city and the nation. By the 1870s, it was possible to send cases of the San Francisco sparkling wine by rail over the Sierra Nevada and the Rockies to cities in the Middle West and along the Atlantic Coast. But much of the transportation was still done by ship. Thus it was possible for Arpad Haraszthy to send his wines across the oceans, to Central and South America, to Australia and the islands of the South Pacific, to Japan, and to England.

Sparkling wine is made in California today with the aid of modern machinery and technology. Electrically powered pumps and filters, robotic disgorging and riddling machines, and automated bottling and corking and labeling devices have taken the place of the laborious handwork of the 1880s and 1890s. The result is, in many ways, a better wine, produced on a more reliable basis, with less waste, and with a better chance for producing a profit for the winery owners. But the skills of the cellar masters of today still owe much to those of their long-ago predecessors. The base wines that are to be transformed into sparkling liquids must still be chosen with the skills of an artist; wines must still be blended to produce the delicate flavors, aromas, and bouquets that delight discriminating consumers. The finished products must be reliable, predictable, but also desirable. The high quality that Arpad Haraszthy pursued in his time is still the goal of the finest sparkling wine producers of the twenty-first century, although they seek to attain those goals in ways that would cause Arpad Haraszthy to blink his eyes and shake his head were he alive today.

An important difference between sparkling wine production in the modern era and that of the nineteenth century lies in the name (or designation) that can be applied to the product that is sent to market. In California in the nineteenth century, and in many other countries as well, it was entirely acceptable for winemakers to label their sparkling wines as "champagne."[4] If it was wine—the fermented juice of the grape—and if it was charged with bubbles produced by carbon dioxide trapped in the bottles, it could be called "champagne" wherever it was made.[5] If it was produced in Australia, for example, it might be called "champagne" or "Australian champagne." If in Argentina, it could be "champagne" or "Argentine champagne." The first reported use of the word "champagne" in America was in the 1830s.[6] Its use continued in California in the 1850s and 1860s, and in California it was so well accepted by the 1890s that the French commissioner of agriculture himself used it to describe California sparkling wine. On a visit to the state in 1893, he said that the "champagne manufactured here, I must admit, I have found very fair," adding, "I think that there is a possibility of the exportation of California champagne to France, but it will be under very trying circumstances."[7] As late as 1962, the great French-born wine author, André L. Simon, could write that "in the U.S.A., . . . by traditional usage, the makers of American sparkling wines have long used the name Champagne [*sic*]."[8] But Champagne makers in France objected to the use of "champagne" on any wines not produced in the Champagne region of France. It was their position, and ultimately that of the French government, that "Champagne" could only be produced in the Champagne region of France, that "Champagne" was a designation of geographic significance, not a mere class or type of wine, and that any use of the name in other geographic areas, even in other areas of France, was false and misleading. (French producers made similar claims about wines named for other French regions, such as Burgundy and Chablis, and winemakers in other countries made like claims with respect to wines designated as Port, Malaga, Marsala, Chianti, Madeira, and Tokay).

The laws applicable to this issue in both Europe and the United States evolved during the twentieth century, eventually arriving at a point where, in the United States, a wine could be sold as "champagne" if its true place of origin was disclosed to consumers (if, for example, it was labeled as "California champagne" or "Australian champagne"), while in Europe, and especially in France, the law became more insistent that "Champagne" could be used only for sparkling wines produced in the Champagne region. The law moved gradually in the direction of accommodating the French demands, although significant exceptions were recognized. In the United States, for example, sparkling wine producers were forbidden to use the name "champagne" after March 10, 2006 (the date of an international agreement between the United States and the European Union), unless they had previously received Certificate of Label Approvals (COLAS) from the federal government permitting them to do just that.[9] This was called the "grandfather clause," and it authorized some very large producers to continue to label their wines "California champagne," even wines produced in bulk rather than in individual bottles, because they had traditionally done so before the applicable date. New producers, however, were forbidden to initiate the practice.

In Arpad Haraszthy's time, there were no laws directly governing the labeling of sparkling wine (or any other wine, for that matter), although internal revenue laws did briefly discourage producers from calling their wines "champagne" by imposing an oppressively high tax on wines "made in imitation of sparkling wine or champagne." This law was quickly amended, however, to limit it to wines "not made from grapes grown in the United States," thus exempting domestic producers from the tax.[10] Eclipse, and the other sparkling wines that Arpad produced, were called "champagne" because it was legal, usual, and customary to call them that—and further, because Arpad was convinced that his wines were made by the same methods and to the same standards as the sparkling wines produced in the Champagne region.

It is interesting to observe, however, that he did not use the word "champagne" on his labels. So far as I have been able to determine, no bottle of Eclipse, or any other Haraszthy sparkling wine, was ever labeled as "champagne," although they were so described in advertising. But it was never really necessary to put the word itself on the labels. Champagne consumers can recognize a sparkling wine bottle by its distinctive size and shape, by the color and thickness of the glass of which it is made, by its gently sloping shoulders, by the wire-wrapped cork that protrudes from its throat, and by the foil capsule that encloses the cork, the wire, and the neck like holiday gift wrapping. The name of the producer, the brand name, the type and class of the wine, and (in appropriate cases) the vintage year, may be added. But it is obvious at a glance that it is a bottle of sparkling wine without the necessity of spelling out the words, or designating it as "champagne." It was thus in the time of Arpad Haraszthy, when a typical label stated only:

Arpad Haraszthy & Co.
Eclipse Extra Dry

Arpad Haraszthy's production was not limited to sparkling wine. Over his long career, he produced many other types of wine, including dry table wines (both red and white), sweet wines (including Port and Sherry), and varietally labeled wines (notably Zinfandel). Many, perhaps even most, of his wines were sold in bulk, delivered to consumers in barrels, and never bottled. This was a common method of delivering still (non-sparkling) wines to consumers throughout the nineteenth century. A barrel of wine would be delivered to a store, and individual buyers would fill their own bottles from the barrel. His sparkling wines, of course, were always bottled, for the essence of sparkling wine produced according to the méthode champenoise is the effervescence that is trapped in the wine during the secondary fermentation, and this would be impossible without a strong enclosure and an air-tight cork to protect the effervescence from the surrounding atmosphere.

The bottles were hand blown, imported from France at considerable cost.[11] Because they were hand blown, the strength of their sides and bottoms, with their characteristic punts or push-ups, varied from bottle to bottle. Similarly, the pressure of the carbon dioxide trapped inside the bottles varied from one lot of wine (or *cuvée*)[12] to another, so a considerable percentage exploded during the secondary fermentation.[13] The sound of the bursting bottles was sometimes likened to the report of artillery fire on a battlefield,[14] and the cellar workers, whose duties required them to turn the bottles daily, wore wire masks to protect their faces from flying glass. The loss of bottles (and wine) through breakage was never welcome, but it was an inevitability of the méthode champenoise.

Throughout his winemaking career, Arpad Haraszthy faced challenges. The first, and perhaps most difficult, was to translate the time-honored techniques of the French Champagne country into practical methods that would produce reliable results in California. California was different in many ways from the Champagne district. The California soil and climate, the grapes grown in California's vineyards, the progress of the seasons through the growing cycle of the vines, the temperatures and atmospheric conditions that prevailed during the months of crushing, fermenting, racking, bottling, and finishing the sparkling wines, varied from those of Champagne in sometimes subtle but often startling ways. It was not easy for Arpad to adapt the techniques he learned in Épernay into practical California methods, and his early efforts to do so were failures. By persistence and determination, however, he finally succeeded in achieving predictable results. Within a few years after he produced his first successful sparkling wines, they won general praise. But he did not rest on his laurels, and he continued his efforts to improve his wines (both still and sparkling) throughout his career.

Financial challenges were real and constant in Arpad Haraszthy's time. The production of sparkling wine was laborious and expensive, and fluctuations in economic conditions only added to these problems. The California wine industry expanded throughout his years as a winemaker, but not in predictable ways. There were starts and stops, periods of almost euphoric expansion followed by intervals of retrenchment that caused many vineyardists and winemakers to despair, close their cellars, pull up their vines, and replace them with more prosaic plantings of fruit orchards or grain fields.

The financial vicissitudes of the wine industry were exacerbated from the 1870s on by the phylloxera, the minute but voracious root louse that sucked the life out of the fine European vines that Agoston Haraszthy and others had brought into the state in the 1850s and 1860s. The phylloxera was first identified in California vineyards in the 1870s, though it had infested them even earlier. Before the nineteenth century drew to a close, the tiny insect devastated most of the vineyards of France, and laid bare tens of thousands of acres of California's vine lands. Countless methods of combating the scourge were tried and found wanting before it was ultimately proven that grafting the European vines onto phylloxera-resistant North American rootstocks would save the vineyards. It was in part because of the phylloxera that the California Legislature created the Board of State Viticultural Commissioners in 1880 and that Arpad Haraszthy was elected as its president. For eight years, he led the state board, seeking not only to combat the phylloxera but also to find solutions to the economic woes that beset the wine industry. During the eight years of his presidency, he traveled throughout the state, attending conventions, giving speeches, inspecting vineyards, conferring with winemakers, and writing articles that appeared in newspapers and trade journals.

Competition from European producers was a constant concern for California winemakers, for there was widespread public prejudice against wines produced in California—evidenced not only among wine consumers in Eastern cities, but even among Californians. Arpad joined other California winemakers in an effort, first, to improve the quality of California wines, and second, to convince the wine-consuming public that California wines were constantly improving—that some were the equals of their European competitors, and some were demonstrably better. It was a fact in the nineteenth century, as it is in the twenty-first, that a French, German, or Italian label on a bottle of wine is no guarantee that the contents of the bottle are good, or even drinkable. Yet the public learns slowly, and those who seek to educate it have a hard task. Arpad Haraszthy was one of those who sought to educate the public, and he contributed in no small measure to the gradual improvement in the reputation of California wines in general—and its sparkling wine in particular.

Another challenge to the winemaking industry was the temperance movement. Born in the early years of the nineteenth century as a righteous reaction to the excessive consumption of distilled liquors, it gradually came to include the fermented juice of the grape as one of its targets. Wine had traditionally been praised as a temperance agent—as a moderate beverage that, consumed judiciously and in moderate amounts, would help to combat rather than exacerbate the problem of drunkenness. But temperance crusaders gradually came to regard all alcoholic beverages as social and moral scourges. While Arpad Haraszthy and his fellow winemakers were striving to obtain the passage of "pure wine" laws that would improve the healthfulness of their products and assure consumers that wines were not contaminated with chemicals, dyes, or vegetable juices, temperance crusaders were laboring mightily to ban all wines, along with beers, whiskeys, and gins—and their iconic bête noir, "demon rum."[15] By 1919, the temperance crusaders succeeded in gaining ratification of the Eighteenth Amendment to the U.S. Constitution, which initiated a twelve-year-long experiment with national prohibition. The danger that the temperance movement posed to the wine industry was only vaguely felt during Arpad Haraszthy's lifetime, but it was real and constantly growing, and when prohibition arrived it was catastrophic. Production of wine became almost totally illegal (there were exceptions, notably for sacramental wines, medicinal wines, and wine tonics), and California's fine wine vineyards were devastated.[16] During Arpad Haraszthy's lifetime, the growing power and fervor of the temperance movement was a Sword of Damocles that hung precariously over the lives and careers of all California winemakers.

I have tried in this book to convey an accurate history of Arpad Haraszthy's sparkling wines; how their reputation grew from the first experiments he made at his father's Buena Vista wine estate in the Sonoma Valley in 1862; and how the wines were conceived, developed, and sold. The characteristics of the Haraszthy sparkling wines, and especially of Eclipse champagne are described, insofar as it is possible to recreate the characteristics of any beverage that has not been tasted for more than a century. In the absence of tasting, we must resort to the written record left behind in books and newspaper articles, in speeches and journals, in the medals won at competitions, and in the formal and informal recollections of men and women who knew the wine and drank it in the waning years of the nineteenth century.

I have also tried to convey the essential qualities of Arpad Haraszthy, to discern his character, explore his faults, and assess his accomplishments. He was, if nothing else, an interesting man. Charles Wetmore, a journalist and winemaker who was also a good friend, described him as "tall" and "well-proportioned."[17] The passport application he filled out on his way to France in 1857 tells us that his hair and eyes were black, his nose large, and his complexion dark.[18] In his mature years, he wore a bushy mustache and a small beard, much in the style of the French Emperor Napoleon III. He was a hard worker, noted for his attention to detail. Wetmore wrote in 1891 that Arpad's sparkling wine cellars in San Francisco were so well managed that, "within three minutes time," he could "give you full particulars of every cuvée he has made since 1868, including where he bought the grapes or wine, the condition of the same, the proportion of the blending, the place where the bottles and corks were purchased, and every other item concerning the manufacture, including the date of each separate operation."[19]

Arpad could, on occasion, be stern and opinionated. He admitted that his nature was "hasty and impetuous" and that he was easily angered.[20] When his oft-repeated assertion that his father was the first man to bring the celebrated Zinfandel grapevine to California was challenged in the press, he marshaled his evidence (thin though it was) and pressed his assertion with what some thought unseemly vigor. The result was a controversy that flared for a while, but soon died down, only to be revived by historians nearly a hundred years later.[21]

Arpad was, by most accounts, a well-liked man, respected and admired by his fellow winemakers. Wetmore said that he was "a splendid talker" and that he almost invariably "had something to say worth listening to." He was at his best, possibly, "when relating some of the earlier experiences of the viticulturists of the State, or in telling a story of California in the Spanish days, gained from his marriage into one of the most noted families of the State."[22]

He was, in other words, a good storyteller. But stories may be told *about* storytellers as well as *by* them. If, as I believe, good history should tell a good story, it may be appropriate that the subject of this book was himself a good storyteller. Whether the story of his life, and the history of Eclipse that is inseparable from it, is good history, readers may decide for themselves. That it is a good story, I think few will deny.

CHAPTER ONE

THE SON OF HIS FATHER

If it is impossible to tell the story of Eclipse without telling the story of Arpad Haraszthy, it is impossible to tell the story of Arpad Haraszthy without telling the story of his father, Agoston Haraszthy. Charles Wetmore wrote a biographical sketch of Arpad in 1891 for the *Pacific Wine and Spirit Review,* then the leading trade journal of the California wine industry. In it Wetmore wrote that one of Arpad's chief distinctions was "the recognition he receives for being the 'Son of his Father,' for in him and his work are seen the work of patient industry and persistent endeavor, guided by prospective zeal of three generations of Haraszthys. His connection with our industry is in no sense fortuitous or accidental; his name can scarcely be mentioned without bringing to mind Agoston Haraszthy, his father, and Charles Haraszthy, his grandfather, so much have their purposes been unified."[1]

Wetmore himself was one of the leaders of the California wine industry in 1891, former chief executive officer of the Board of State Viticultural Commissioners, the founder and proprietor of a highly admired vineyard and winery in the Livermore Valley, and a frequent and high-profile writer and speaker on California wine. He had been working with Arpad for almost twenty years on issues that confronted California's winemakers. Wetmore knew Arpad well, and he liked him. In Wetmore's estimation, Agoston Haraszthy's meteoric career as a leader of California's wine industry was a key to understanding Arpad's career in the same industry. "The father has been the anchor of the son's mind so far as fixed purpose is concerned," Wetmore wrote, "and the companion of his course so far as the progress of a life's work may be seen."[2]

For his own part, Arpad never forgot his father's winemaking legacy, nor lost an opportunity to remind winemakers and wine consumers of it. Agoston Haraszthy's memory was, Arpad stated, "sacred" to him.[3] It was one of the treasures, not only of his own life and heritage, but of the history of California, and he was prickly when anyone sought to detract from it. When, in 1885, an old vine grower in the Napa Valley asserted that Agoston was not the man who brought the celebrated Zinfandel vine to California (as most winemakers then understood he was), Arpad was quick to correct him, not as he said, "to rob anyone of the just merit of his achievements," but to "preserve the justly earned reputation" of his father.[4] It was, of course, good business for Arpad Haraszthy, the proprietor of one of the busiest winemaking establishments in the state, the state's leading producer of sparkling wines, and a major vine grower as well, to extol the virtues of Agoston Haraszthy as a California wine pioneer. But Arpad needed no special inducements to do that. Whatever his critics might say of him, Agoston Haraszthy was a trailblazing vine grower and winemaker and an enthusiastic spokesman for the future of California wine. That fact, coupled with a record of accomplishments on two continents and in scores of business enterprises, marked him as one of history's most fascinating characters. If he was Arpad Haraszthy's hero, so be it. Other men had had lesser heroes, and had defended them with less justification.

Both Agoston and Arpad Haraszthy were Hungarians born and bred. Agoston was born on August 30, 1812, in the city of Pest, on the south bank of the Danube River, facing the royal stronghold of Buda across the river (Buda and Pest were not united until 1873), the only son of Charles (originally Károly) Haraszthy and his wife, Anna Mária Fischer.[5] Charles Haraszthy had been born in 1789 in Szeged, an important market town in southern Hungary, though he was the scion of an old and noble family from the far northeastern corner of the country.[6] There, at a place called Mokcsa in the County of Ung, his Haraszthy forbears had acquired estates that entitled them to be known as the Mokcsai Haraszthy family. By the time Agoston Haraszthy was born in Pest in 1812, Charles and Anna Mária had settled in the Terézváros (Theresatown) parish of Pest. Before he grew to manhood, however, they relocated to southern Hungary, in the neighborhood of Futak, a large estate that hugged the Danube a few miles west of the Serbian city of Novi Sad.

In Hungary, nobles of Agoston Haraszthy's class were treated with respect by their fellow nobles and deference by the vast population of peasants. Since Latin was the official language of government, Agoston was entitled to be addressed in that language as *Spectabilis Dominus* and in Magyar (the tongue of the ethnic Hungarians) as *Tekintetes Úr*, both of which translated to the English equivalents of Honorable Sir or Noble Lord.[7] As a Hungarian nobleman, Tekintetes Úr Agoston Haraszthy attended the General Assemblies of the nobles of Bács County and served in local offices. Most of his time, however, was left free for his own affairs.

Agoston Haraszthy was twenty years old when, on January 6, 1833, he married Eleonora Dedinsky, the seventeen-year-old daughter of Ferencz Dedinsky, superintendent of the 34,000-acre Futak estate.[8] The Dedinszkys were a family of Polish origin though they had resided in the Kingdom of Hungary for centuries and long been members of the Hungarian nobility. Futak was a sprawling agricultural domain that included a large manor house, a Roman Catholic church, and vineyards that spread along the Danube. There and elsewhere in Hungary, the Haraszthys were dedicated to the cultivation of the grapes that formed the basis of Hungary's estimable wine industry. Years later, Charles Haraszthy wrote an article for a San Francisco newspaper in which he stated that he had spent most of his adult life in the wine business, that he had traveled through all of the important wine-producing countries of Europe (except Spain and Portugal), and that he had cultivated extensive vineyards over a period of thirty-one years with what he called "an unparalleled success."[9] If this recollection smacks of boasting, it should surprise no one who knew Agoston or Arpad Haraszthy in later years, for neither ever hid his light under a bushel.

The Haraszthys were active in vineyard cultivation in and around Futak, and may even have taken charge of the vineyards of the Futak estate, which was owned by the absentee Count József Brunswick, the Lord Chief Justice of Hungary. Like his fellow nobles, Agoston was an enthusiastic farmer and an avid hunter. He was also the master of an estate where he raised silkworms and cultivated vineyards. Eleonora presented him with two sons named for Hungarian heroes, Géza (later called Gaza) on December 27, 1833,[10] and Attila on April 16, 1835.[11] But life in Hungary seemed stultifying to him. Business activity was nearly nonexistent, for a man who sought to establish a new enterprise had to obtain royal permits and negotiate a maze of royal regulations. Agoston traveled when he could and made efforts to export Hungarian products to neighboring countries. Sometime in the middle of 1839, he visited Mehádia, a fashionable resort at the base of the Transylvanian Alps, where he met some English and American tourists who convinced him that he should visit their countries. They gave him letters of introduction with which he departed at the end of 1839 on a long journey that took him through Vienna and the German states to England, thence across the Atlantic to New York City.[12]

Years after his arrival in the United States, Agoston told tall tales about the circumstances of his departure for the United States, claiming that he had been involved in political scheming against the Hapsburgs, who then occupied the Hungarian throne, and had incurred official wrath by trying to rescue a Hungarian poet "whose only offense was that he had dared to sing of freedom and the rights of man."[13] He came to America, he said, as a political exile. In fact, he was not involved in any unusual political activity in Hungary. Agoston was a young man who brimmed over with ideas for commercial and agricultural enterprises, and he knew that the United States was a land of economic freedom. The truth was that he came to the United States in search of economic opportunity rather than to escape oppression. As he admitted in a remarkable book published only four years later, "I had come to America for one reason only—namely, to see this blessed country for myself."[14]

Traveling with a cousin named Károly Fischer, Agoston began a whirlwind tour through the United States, first admiring the wonders of New York City, then following the Hudson River and the Erie Canal to the Great Lakes and the raw and undeveloped territory of Wisconsin. There the cousins were struck by the beauty of the Sauk Prairie, a broad expanse of flowers and grass on the Wisconsin River about twenty-five miles west of Madison. Agoston bought some land, laid out streets and put up houses, and gave birth to a town called Haraszthy.[15] With an English business partner, he dammed a creek, erected grist and saw mills, established a ferry across the Wisconsin River, and operated a brickyard and a store. He bought a newly launched steamboat, named it the *Rock River,* and put it into service on the Wisconsin and Mississippi Rivers.[16] In Wisconsin, he farmed his land with enthusiasm, raising corn to supply a U.S. Army post nearby, keeping sheep and pigs, and planting vines on hillsides overlooking the Wisconsin River. He tunneled wine cellars into the hillside to provide proper storage for his vintages. But his vines did not thrive in the cold Wisconsin winters. When his almost frantic business activities permitted him to steal time away from Haraszthy, he embarked on a tour of the United States, taking notes for a book he was writing about the country for Hungarian readers.[17]

Two years after his arrival on the Sauk Prairie, Agoston Haraszthy returned to Hungary. He had decided that his trip to the United States would not just be an adventure but a new chapter in a new life, and he wanted his family to share it with him. When he arrived home in 1842, he met for the first time his third son, who was born at Futak on June 28, 1840, and named Arpad, for the legendary chieftain who led the Magyars into Hungary in A.D. 896.[18] While the family made arrangements for their journey to Wisconsin, Agoston contracted with a Hungarian publisher to bring out his book about the United States. Called *Utazás Éjszakmerikában* (*Travels in North America*), it was issued in two volumes at Pest in 1844. Only the second book about the United States to be published in the Hungarian language, it struck a chord with Hungarian readers, and a second edition was published in 1850.[19]

The extended Haraszthy family—Agoston and Eleonora, his father Charles and his mother Anna Mária, and his sons Gaza, Attila, and Arpad—crossed the Atlantic at the end of 1842, then hurried to their new home in Wisconsin. The settlers there greeted them warmly, and Agoston resumed his leadership of the frontier community. He was a man who commanded attention, a little above medium height, slim, with a handsome face that was adorned with a mustache and beard and crowned with a tousled mop of black hair. The settlers knew that he was a nobleman, but they did not understand the Spectabilis Dominus and Tekintetes Úr titles that he answered to in Hungary, and they called him "Count" Haraszthy.[20] That was not his Hungarian title, but it seemed to fit him in his New World home. His sons were the "Little Counts" and his father was the "General." Both of the Haraszthy men were cultured, affable, and inventive, but the "General" had a scholarly turn of mind while the "Count" was impetuous and daring. One of their family friends later commented on the difference between Charles and Agoston, telling Arpad: "There is the greatest difference between your father and your grandfather. Your grandfather has a thousand ideas and never puts one of them in practical motion. Your father has a thousand ideas and the trouble with him is that he puts them all in motion."[21]

Time after time, Agoston demonstrated his reckless delight in defying danger. On one of his many hunting expeditions onto the Sauk Prairie, he invaded a wolf's den in an attempt to steal a cub and was surprised by the outraged mother. Unarmed, he met the wolf's attack head on and strangled it with his bare hands. The encounter soon became a legend among the settlers on the Sauk Prairie.[22]

In business, Agoston seemed to be equally daring. He started to build a handsome new home overlooking the Wisconsin River, and he acquired large tracts of land in a neighboring valley, while continuing to operate his ferry, brickyard, store, and mills, and pilot his steamboat on the Wisconsin and Mississippi Rivers. One year, he piloted the boat all the way down the river to New Orleans (his mother died on this voyage and was buried somewhere along the river bank).[23] He gave property to the archbishop of Milwaukee to establish a Roman Catholic parish and set aside another tract of land for a Catholic mission. He made provisions for his sons' educations, donating land for a local school, and sending his youngest son Arpad to live with an American family so he would have a good grounding in the English language. The Haraszthy family grew with the addition of two daughters, Ida born in 1843[24] and Otelia in 1848,[25] and a son Béla (later spelled Bela) in 1846.[26]

In 1848, Agoston hit on the idea of building a great bridge across the Wisconsin River. He organized a joint stock company for the purpose and got the approval of the Wisconsin legislature, but before the bridge could be built he heard news that electrified the nation: amazing deposits of gold had been discovered in far-off California. He formed an emigrant company, of which he was elected captain, fitted up a large covered wagon, and set out across the plains to California. For nine months, he and his family trudged along the Santa Fe and Gila trails to San Diego, where they arrived at the end of 1849.[27]

Agoston Haraszthy was a Forty-Niner, but he had not come to California for gold. He told another emigrant that he had come there "to settle, not for the gold," and that he intended to plant a vineyard near San Diego.[28] Now a pioneer on the far western frontier of the United States, he seemed vaguely embarrassed to be called "Count" and preferred the more democratic "Colonel," an honorific title that hinted more at his standing as a gentleman than a military officer.[29]

Arpad Haraszthy reached his tenth birthday in San Diego in 1850. He was Agoston's third son, but old enough to appreciate his father's seemingly endless energy and to help him some in carrying out his many projects. The two years that the Haraszthys spent in San Diego were frantic, with Agoston throwing himself into the commercial, agricultural, and even political life of the mission town. He planted trees and vines, both at the Mission of San Luis Rey north of San Diego and in San Diego itself. He acquired land, planted a vineyard on the banks of the San Diego River, and sent away for vine cuttings with which to enhance his vine stock.[30] He formed a business partnership with one of the leading Spanish citizens of the town and organized a syndicate of prominent men that subdivided a section of the San Diego Bay shore (the new development was formally called Middle San Diego but informally known as Haraszthyville).[31] He was elected marshal of San Diego, then sheriff of San Diego County, and finally California State Assemblyman for the San Diego district.[32]

Agoston's six children were quickly growing up. His oldest son, Gaza, had left the family's wagon train in Albuquerque, New Mexico, to join the United States dragoons, with which he was still serving somewhere in the desert Southwest. His second son, Attila, now sixteen, was a faithful assistant on his father's many commercial and agricultural projects. Arpad was eleven years old, soon to turn twelve, while the younger children were Ida, eight, Bela, five, and Otelia, three. Educational opportunities in California were nearly nonexistent, so Eleonora Haraszthy decided to leave San Diego by ship, taking her four youngest children to the East Coast, where they could attend good schools. Attila would remain with Agoston, and Gaza would continue his service with the dragoons.

Some time toward the end of 1851, Agoston took his family to the wharf outside San Diego and put them on an ocean steamer bound for New York. Traveling by way of Panama, the Haraszthys arrived in New York late in 1851 or early 1852. They were in the city when Lajos Kossuth, leader of the abortive Hungarian uprising of 1848, was welcomed there as a hero.[33] After a few months, they moved about twenty-five miles west to the town of Plainfield, New Jersey, where Eleonora settled while her children attended school. They were still in Plainfield in 1853 when a Hungarian exile named Lázár Mészáros settled on a farm in the village of Scotch Plains, just a few minutes away.[34] Mészáros had been minister of war in Kossuth's government, but after the Austrians and Russians combined to drive Kossuth and his cabinet out of Hungary, he became a fugitive from Hapsburg justice, eventually coming to live in the United States. Mészáros was, among other things, an enthusiastic horticulturist. On his Scotch Plains farm, he started a commercial nursery, which he stocked with trees, shrubs, and a good supply of grapevines. Eleonora and her children became close friends of the Hungarian exile, visiting often at his farm and nursery, where they exchanged recollections of Hungary and indulged their mutual interest in horticulture.[35]

When Arpad was not attending school or visiting the Mészáros farm and nursery, he traveled widely over the United States. His father supplied him with the funds for his travels, believing that a well-rounded education should include a familiarity with distant places and people. One of his trips took him through the states of the North and Middle West, and even into Canada. Another took him through all of the states of the Old South.[36] He was nearly seventeen years old when, in the spring of 1857, he returned to California, arriving in San Francisco on April 30 of that year on the steamship *Golden Gate*.[37] He had, of course, kept abreast of his father's busy life during the years he was on the East Coast, but his return enabled him to see firsthand much of what Agoston had done in his absence.

After he served out his term in the California Legislature, Agoston decided to abandon San Diego and set down roots in San Francisco, the commercial center of the Gold Rush state. In the spring of 1852, he bought two hundred acres of land near the old Spanish mission of Dolores.[38] There he raised vegetables, fruits, and flowers, and imported grapes from Southern California for resale in San Francisco. With Attila working at his side, he developed a nursery and horticultural garden stocked with flowers, shrubs, trees, and grapevines. He bought some vine cuttings from local vineyardists and sent away for others, for he knew that there was a wealth of choice grapevines on the East Coast and in Europe, and he was convinced that if he brought them to California he could make some really good wines. But San Francisco was too cold and foggy for grapes to ripen, so he turned south, acquiring several hundred acres of rolling land at a place called Crystal Springs in the vicinity of San Mateo.[39] There he built a house and barns and began to lay out a vineyard that covered thirty acres and included more than twenty thousand vines.[40]

While Agoston was developing his new property, he joined some Hungarian friends in San Francisco in the operation of a gold refining business, and in the spring of 1854 he obtained an appointment from President Franklin Pierce as assayer of the new United States Branch Mint in San Francisco.[41] He worked feverishly at his new job and at his private refinery nearby, but officials became alarmed when one of his mint accounts revealed a major deficiency, and San Francisco newspapers reported the shocking news that he had been indicted for embezzlement. As investigations continued, the case dragged on for five years, at the end of which a federal jury cleared him of all charges.[42]

While awaiting the jury's verdict, Agoston had turned his attention back to his vineyards. He soon realized that Crystal Springs, like San Francisco, was too cold for grapes to ripen, so late in 1856 he traveled north of San Francisco to the Sonoma Valley, where he found a small but promising vineyard that had been started in the 1830s by a Christianized Indian. The first vineyards in Sonoma had been planted by the Spanish priests, who established the Mission San Francisco Solano de Sonoma in 1823. A young Spanish soldier named Mariano Guadalupe Vallejo (afterwards the comandante general of California) had come to Sonoma in the 1830s to lay out a town and garrison a barracks to protect California's northern frontier from the threat posed by the Russians at nearby Fort Ross. Vallejo, in 1856, was the patriarch of Sonoma and the owner of vineyards and producer of wines that had attained some note in Northern California. He had about sixteen acres of vines, while the Indian's property (which had since passed through the hands of a half-dozen owners) covered another sixteen acres, and five or six smaller vineyards were scattered here and there on the valley floor and in the surrounding foothills.[43] Agoston tasted some of the wine from the Indian's property and, toward the end of 1856, made arrangements to buy the vineyard and adjoining land, which he named Buena Vista. He quickly added to his property, soon assembling a tract of five thousand acres of valley and hillside land that he believed could be turned into a spectacular vineyard.[44] It would be the largest in California and, if he had his way, the finest.

Arpad's return to California came at an opportune time, for in the spring of 1857 his father and older brothers (Gaza had returned from his service with the dragoons) were busy moving vines from Crystal Springs to Sonoma, digging up rooted plants and gathering cuttings in baskets, then taking them in wagons either to San Francisco or to the nearby San Francisco Bay shore, where they were loaded in boats and floated across the bay to Sonoma.[45] Arpad had the opportunity to visit both Crystal Springs and Buena Vista and to observe the vines that were being moved across the bay. Years later he remembered some of the vines that were transported that spring.[46] Many were "native" California (i.e., Mission) vines, but a good number were "foreign" (i.e., European) vines that his father had first begun importing in San Diego. Arpad's recollections of the vines that were moved from Crystal Springs to Sonoma in 1857 would eventually prove to be controversial.[47]

At the end of his two months in California, Arpad returned to the East Coast, where he helped his younger brother Bela enroll in school, and then set out across the Atlantic. He and his father had decided that he would pursue his higher education in France. From New York, he crossed the Atlantic on the steamer *Cornelius Vanderbilt* and reached Paris in the latter part of 1857.[48] He enrolled in the École Centrale, Civile Polytechnique, where he pursued a course in engineering. After a couple of years, however, letters from his father persuaded him to turn his attention to winemaking, in his own words, "to learn practically the management of wines and the manufacture of champagne."[49] He left Paris in the latter part of 1860 and went north to the city of Épernay in Champagne, carrying with him letters of introduction from the Master of the Household of Emperor Napoleon III and the promise of generous tuition payments from his father in far-off California.[50]

Épernay was one of the two most important towns in the Champagne district (the other was Reims). It stood on the site of an old Roman settlement, straddling the River Marne about ninety miles northeast of Paris. The chalky rock beneath the town's streets was honeycombed with caves and tunnels in which the sparkling wine for which Champagne was famous was bottled and stored in almost perfect conditions of temperature and humidity. The legend was that Champagne was invented about 1708 by the Benedictine monk Dom Pérignon, cellar master of the nearby Abbey of Hautvillers, although in fact the techniques necessary to make wine sparkle had been discovered years earlier and Pérignon had merely improved them. The Champagne district was once famous for its still wines, both red and white (they, like the sparkling wines, went to market as "Champagne"), but the production of sparkling wine gained popularity at the end of the eighteenth century and assumed commercial importance in the nineteenth.

Arpad presented himself at the house of De Venoge, an important Champagne firm established in the 1830s by a Swiss family. He remained there nearly two years, studying all aspects of the manufacture of sparkling wine—the blending, the tasting, the bottle management, the machinery used in the wine's production, and, as he later wrote, "the carrying through of all the different processes necessary to the perfection of champagne."[51] He took copious notes and illustrations that eventually filled three volumes. By early 1861, his studies had progressed to the point that he was able to translate a long passage from one of his French textbooks into English and send it to San Francisco, where it was published in the *Daily Alta California* of May 20, 1861. Titled "The Manner in Which Champagne Is Made," the passage consisted of a fascinating description taken from Victor Rendu's *Ampélographie Française* (published in Paris in 1854 and 1857) detailing the complex and exacting French process for making sparkling wine.[52]

Arpad's studies at Épernay were interrupted in the early summer of 1861 when his father arrived in Paris, traveling with his mother and his eighteen-year-old sister, Ida, and Arpad went down to the capital city to greet them.[53] Flush with the success of his first four years in Sonoma, Agoston was now embarked on a great new adventure—a mission authorized by a resolution of the California Legislature and an appointment from Governor John G. Downey to go to Europe to gather vines and report back to the legislature "upon the ways and means best adapted to promote the improvement and growth of the grape vine in California."[54]

Since Arpad last saw him in 1857, Agoston had developed his Buena Vista vineyard into the largest in California. He had covered the foothill slopes of the Mayacamas Mountains with hundreds of acres of vines and had persuaded dozens of new vineyardists to buy land in Sonoma, where he planted vineyards for them and instructed them in the techniques of vine culture.[55] He had entered his wines in competitions in state and county fairs and won awards for their excellence. In 1858, he had written a practical guide to vine planting and winemaking, titled a "Report on Grapes and Wines of California," that was published by the California State Agricultural Society and distributed to would-be winemakers throughout the state.[56] He had extended his tunnels into the mountains at Buena Vista and built cellars and distilleries furnished with the latest winemaking equipment. He had, in the words of San Francisco's *Daily Alta California,* earned recognition as "the first grape grower of California."[57] Agoston's vineyard was not only the state's largest, but his collection of foreign (i.e., European) vines was the most extensive ever yet assembled. He had, the *Alta* told its readers, "done more than any other person to encourage the cultivation of the grape, particularly of the foreign varieties."[58] But he still hungered for more and better varieties, and he had set out on an ambitious journey to visit the most famous wine-producing centers of Europe, inspect their vineyards and cellars, and gather up as many cuttings as he could ship back to San Francisco, there to be planted, tested, and distributed throughout the state.

Arpad was delighted to be reunited with his loved ones and grateful for the opportunity to help his father on his new mission. "My son," Agoston later wrote, "had been four years in school in Paris, and latterly in the Champagne districts, where he is now learning the manufacture of Champagne and other wines. He proved a great assistance to us during our stay in Europe; he acted as my secretary, my correspondence with scientific societies increasing daily, as well as with prominent officers of different governments."[59]

The Haraszthys left Paris early in August for the Burgundy district of northeastern France. They reached the Rhine at Cologne, followed the great river south into Switzerland, crossed the Alps to Italy, traveled by boat to Marseille, crossed southern France to Bordeaux, went south into Spain, and then returned by ship to France. All along the way, they gathered vines from vineyards and horticultural gardens, conversed with practical vine growers and winemakers, and interviewed learned professors. Many of the vines the Haraszthys collected were grown in the vineyards they visited, but some were sent to them from Hungary and others from exotic lands such as Greece and Smyrna and Egypt. Arpad acted as his father's assistant on the whole trip. By the middle of October, Agoston was ready to head back to California, for he had promised the legislature a written report on his journey, and he had contracted with Harper and Brothers in New York to deliver the manuscript of a book about his trip. He made arrangements with a United States consul to ship his collection of vine cuttings to San Francisco, then boarded a ship for his return trip. Leaving Eleonora and Ida behind to enjoy Paris, and Arpad to return to his studies in Épernay, Agoston was back in California in early December.[60]

Agoston's vines arrived in San Francisco at the end of January, 1862. He brought them up to Sonoma, where he calculated that there were more than 100,000 cuttings. With a touch of Haraszthyan exaggeration, he estimated that they represented 1,400 different varieties. Upon careful examination, it was found that there were only 350 varieties—but it was still an impressive number.[61] He asked the legislature to reimburse him for the expenses of his trip—$12,000—and promised in return to turn the vines over to the state. Agoston thought the state government should establish a central viticultural nursery, where the cuttings could be planted, propagated, tested, and made available to would-be vineyardists. "The sum thus expended will be a trifle to the real value of said vines, . . ." he wrote in his report, "but to the people of this State it will in time be worth as many millions."[62] The *Alta* agreed, telling its readers that the expense to the state "would be as nothing" compared to the benefits that the people would derive from Agoston's vines.[63] But the legislature was of a different mind and declined the offer.[64] Agoston then took it upon himself to distribute the vines, preparing a catalog and placing advertisements in newspapers. He offered to send collections of vines to farmers, asking them to inform him if they wanted grapes for fresh fruit or for winemaking. "Wine growers must bear in mind that generous wines, with the desired bouquet, can only be made from proper foreign vines," he said, "and it costs no more to plant and cultivate one acre of foreign vines than of native."[65]

The legislature's rebuff did little to dampen Agoston's enthusiasm, or the confidence that vine growers and winemakers around the state seemed to have in him. On April 23, 1862, just a week after the California Senate refused to purchase his European vines, the California State Agricultural Society met in Sacramento and elected him as its president.[66] The Society was an influential group, and its presidency offered him a pulpit from which to preach the gospel of California wine. He took full advantage of it, traveling around the state, delivering speeches, giving demonstrations, and offering cuttings from his European collections. California wine, he said, had a great future, and it remained only for Californians to work diligently—and intelligently—to bring it about.

The book that Agoston had promised to write for Harper was ready for the presses in the spring. Titled *Grape Culture, Wines, and Wine-Making, with Notes upon Agriculture and Horticulture*, it was a handsomely printed volume of slightly more than 400 pages, consisting of 140 pages devoted to a journal of Agoston's European tour, the text of his report to the legislature, an updated version of his 1858 "Report on Grapes and Wines of California," and English translations of technical essays on winemaking and related subjects by European authorities.[67] The book was widely distributed in California and other parts of the United States, where it received good press. The *Alta* said the book was "substantial" and "full of the most valuable information upon all the branches of wine-growing," while the *New York Times* said it contained much that would interest "the general reader, and indeed all persons of *taste*."[68]

If *Grape Culture, Wines, and Wine-Making* provided additional evidence of Agoston Haraszthy's talent for writing clear and entertaining prose in a language he had not mastered until after his thirtieth birthday (in Hungary he had spoken Magyar and German), Arpad was demonstrating a similar talent in a series of letters he began writing to the editor of the *California Farmer* while he was in Épernay. The *California Farmer* was a pioneering agricultural journal, published in

San Francisco by a one-time nurseryman from Boston named James Lloyd Lafayette Warren. Like Agoston Haraszthy, Warren believed in the gospel of California wines and was only too pleased to print the observations of a precocious young man who was studying winemaking in the Champagne country.

Arpad's first contribution to the *California Farmer* was a letter written from Paris, published in June 1861.[69] It was followed by other letters from Paris, from Ems (Arpad was then traveling with his father), Montpelier, Châlons-sur-Marne, Épernay, and Reims.[70] In the letters, Arpad discussed a variety of topics related to wine. He described different kinds of wine presses, problems arising from frost in vineyards, and European wine locales of special interest, such as the Castle of Johannisberg on the Rhine and the Clos de Vougeot in Burgundy. Warren welcomed the young contributor to his pages, noting that Arpad's style was "clear, comprehensive, and pleasing," and that it "gave evidence of a close and candid observer of things—the sure evidence of a thoughtful mind." "It will be remembered," Warren added, "that the writer is a son of our distinguished citizen, Col. Haraszthy, of Sonoma, who has done so much for the Cultivation of the Vine in this State."[71]

Arpad's thirteenth letter to the *California Farmer,* written from Épernay on April 4, 1862, was published in San Francisco on July 18 of that year.[72] By that time, Arpad had begun preparations for his journey home to California, for his studies at De Venoge were completed. Leaving Épernay for Paris, he crossed the English Channel to England, where he visited the London International Exhibition on Industry and Art, then headed west across the Atlantic and on to California, where he arrived as the harvest of 1862 was in preparation.

Agoston was delighted to welcome his son to Sonoma, as were his brothers and sisters. Gaza, Attila, and Bela were all at work at Buena Vista by now—Attila as the vineyard master, directing the crews of Chinese workmen who tended the sprawling vineyards, and Gaza and Bela working in the press house and distillery—while Ida and Otelia were ensconced with Eleonora in the white Pompeian-style villa Agoston had built on a knoll in the middle of his vineyards. Arpad was promptly installed as the cellar master in the press house and given responsibility for transforming the grapes brought in from the vineyards into wine. Years later, he remembered that one of his first tasks that year was to make two casks of claret (a dry, red table wine, finished in the style of Bordeaux). He recalled that the claret was made from Zinfandel grapes.[73]

But Agoston had not sent Arpad to the Champagne district to make claret. One of his principal goals at Buena Vista from the outset had been the production of a good sparkling wine. In his 1858 "Report on Grapes and Wines of California," Agoston had included a short description of the traditional processes by which effervescence was induced in bottled wines, with the bubbles creating the "sparkling" effect, though he cautioned that "a well-practiced hand is needed" and that "in large establishments, where they make the champagne, every man has his own duty or office to perform."[74] He had himself attempted to make sparkling wine at Buena Vista, though with uneven success, for the process was difficult and fraught with pitfalls. Fresh from the cellars of De Venoge, Arpad now qualified as a sparkling wine expert of sorts—though his expertise had not yet been put to a practical test.

Arpad began his first attempts to make sparkling wine at Buena Vista in the fall and winter of 1862–63.[75] Acknowledging the difficulties that he encountered, he later called these attempts "experiments," but they were not the earliest efforts to make sparkling wine in California. If the mission padres were not the first to produce sparkling wine in the Golden State (Arpad hinted in his own writing that they may have been),[76] an American pioneer named Benjamin D. Wilson is generally accorded that honor. Wilson was a Tennessee-born fur trapper who came to California in 1841, married into one of the prominent Spanish families near Los Angeles, and as "Don Benito" Wilson became one of the state's largest landholders.[77] Wilson is best remembered today for Mt. Wilson, the 5,710-foot peak that rises from the San Gabriel Mountains above Pasadena. In his own lifetime, however, he was noted as a politician (he was at one time the mayor of Los Angeles and a state senator), an enterprising businessman, and a pioneer vine grower and winemaker. In 1855 and 1856, at his vineyards near the San Gabriel Mission east of Los Angeles, Wilson produced some sparkling wine that earned good reports in the local press. By 1858, however, his sparkling wine efforts came to a stop, suggesting that he had met with more failures than successes.[78]

In 1857, a pair of brothers named Sainsevain took up the effort where Wilson left off, producing a wine they called "Sparkling California" in their San Francisco cellars. Pierre and Jean Louis Sainsevain were nephews of Jean Louis Vignes, a Frenchman who arrived in Los Angeles in the 1830s and began California's first commercial wine production near the old Los Angeles plaza. The brothers took over their uncle's Los Angeles business in the early 1850s and expanded it into San Francisco cellars a few years later. With the aid of Pierre Debanne, a Champagne maker they brought to California from France, they bottled 50,000 bottles of sparkling wine in 1857 and another 150,000 in 1858. Pierre Sainsevain later moved to San Jose, where he continued sparkling wine production on a sporadic basis, but eventually abandoned it.[79]

Arpad began tentatively at Buena Vista, producing what he later called a "few experimentary dozens" (sparkling wine was traditionally counted in dozens of bottles). This gave what he later remembered was "a very satisfactory result." A second effort was "equally satisfactory." Pleased with his son's efforts, Agoston gave him orders to proceed to a larger bottling. This amounted to some nine or ten thousand bottles which, Arpad later admitted, "were a total failure," for the wine did not sparkle as it should have, and the bottles all had to be uncorked and emptied. Arpad attributed this failure to improper temperatures in the fermenting room (he knew that sparkling wine would ferment properly only if the air around it was not too cold). So he built fires in the cellars and, for three months, "took his blankets and slept in the fermenting room and kept the fires going himself during the night." But to no avail. This effort also ended in failure.[80]

While Arpad struggled with his sparkling wine, Agoston devised an ambitious plan to expand his Sonoma operations. He went to San Francisco in the spring of 1863 and enlisted the support of a group of prominent capitalists to organize the Buena Vista Vinicultural Society

(BVVS), a joint stock company (or corporation) with a capital stock of $600,000 and a board of nine trustees. It required a special act of the California Legislature to complete the organization of the new company (the laws of most states were distrustful of corporations, and many forbade them from engaging in agriculture). Agoston received 2,600 of the total of 6,000 shares and agreed to run the BVVS as its superintendent.[81]

The spring and early summer of 1863 was a happy time in Sonoma, for both Arpad and his brother Attila had fallen in love and made plans to marry. Their intended brides were daughters of General Vallejo, their friendly crosstown competitor in the wine business. It was on June 1, 1863, in the parlor of Vallejo's Sonoma home that Arpad Haraszthy married Jovita Francisca Vallejo and Attila Haraszthy married Natalia Veneranda Vallejo. The wedding was performed by Father Peter Deyaert, a Catholic priest from Napa. Jovita was nineteen years old and Arpad two months short of his twenty-third birthday. Natalia was twenty-five years old and Attila twenty-eight. Arpad and Jovita took up residence in a little house she called a "shanty" in a ravine above the Buena Vista vineyards, while Attila and Natalia settled themselves into a house they called "Champagne" in the center of one of the vineyards at Buena Vista.[82] Both brothers continued to work on the great wine estate.

In the month following the double Haraszthy-Vallejo wedding, a correspondent for the *Alta California* came to Sonoma to survey the vineyards and wine cellars around the town (the number of vineyardists and winemakers there had expanded dramatically since Agoston first arrived in 1856). Arriving at Buena Vista, he was greeted by Agoston, who brought out two of his saddle horses and led the correspondent in a ride over the hills and valleys of the property. East of the main vineyards, the riders encountered Attila, working with a crew of thirty Chinese laborers, grubbing oaks on a steep hill and preparing the slopes for planting. On the same hill, Agoston pointed out a vineyard he had planted two years earlier. "The vines are all foreign varieties," the correspondent later wrote in his *Alta* article, "and were placed here for trial. Many of the vines have grapes on them, and are much more advanced than those planted in the valley at the same time." Agoston and the correspondent proceeded to the Buena Vista press house, where they were greeted by the "Master of Cellars, Mr. Arpad Haraszthy." He led the men into the spacious second story of the building. "A sight here met our wonder-struck eyes," the correspondent wrote. "All along the walls were thousands upon thousands of bottles, so beautifully stacked that one would almost imagine that the large ceiling was supported by these walls of bottles, and yet they are so piled that any one of them may be taken out for inspection without at all disarranging the others. Upon inquiry, we ascertained that the Master of Cellars was just directing the filling up of Champagne, which has been made in large quantities this year."[83]

From the second floor, the correspondent was taken down to a lower level, where eleven large fermenting vats, all made of California redwood, stood ready to receive the coming season's grapes. Nearby, four Chinese workers were busy filling, corking, and wiring sparkling wine bottles, while young Bela Haraszthy provided them with the corks and bottles for their work. From the fermenting vats, the visitor proceeded to the cellars, where wine was tasted, and Arpad offered him a tour of the aging barrels. "Every second barrel had a lighted candle placed on it," the correspondent wrote, "and as we looked into the depths of these well-lined and better tasting vaults, we mentally ejaculated, 'who would not belong to the votaries of Bacchus, if they resided so near one of his finest temples?'"[84]

The *Alta*'s correspondent returned to Buena Vista in September for another report. "The estate is worthy of a long notice," the correspondent wrote, "for various reasons; among others, because it has the largest vineyard in the world, and because the business of winemaking has here reached a higher development—in so far as the application of machinery is concerned—than in any other vineyard. There are a greater variety of grapes, a greater variety of production here, than in any other vineyard of the State." Arpad, still in charge of the manufacture of the "Sparkling Sonoma," greeted the correspondent again. "My impression, from what little I saw of him," the correspondent wrote, "is that he is a modest, industrious young man, who understands his business, takes pride in it, attends to it, and does not bother himself about other affairs."[85]

Not long after the *Alta*'s correspondent left Buena Vista, a writer for another San Francisco–based journal appeared in Sonoma. The *California Wine, Wool, and Stock Journal* was a monthly magazine of agricultural information edited and published by John Quincy Adams Warren, son of the editor and publisher of the *California Farmer*. Agoston was in San Francisco at the time the younger Warren's representative arrived at Buena Vista, and Arpad escorted him through the premises. In the stone press house, the journalist seemed to be most impressed by the elaborate machinery for making sparkling wine, which included a corking machine, a "cork stringer," a "cork mollifier," a "wire worker," and a "wire twister." "We tasted champagne from the rack," the correspondent later wrote, "which was of an excellent quality, and very adroitly opened by Mr. H. in order to let the sediment escape, which in itself is quite an art. They will make some 5,000 bottles of 'Sparkling Buena Vista Champagne.'"[86]

Arpad devoted a good part of his time at Sonoma to writing. His letters to the *California Farmer* had revealed him to have a talent for written expression much like his father's, and although he was still in his early twenties he had a wealth of practical knowledge about winemaking and vineyard cultivation that he was willing to pass on to others. In the spring of 1863 he began to write a series of articles for the *California Wine, Wool and Stock Journal*. He discussed practical subjects like fermenting vats, wine presses, wine cellars, grape harvesting, choosing grapes for both red and white wine, making dessert wines, and operating a distillery. He also reviewed more purely business-related topics, such as legal efforts to prevent the adulteration of wine (both he and his father were concerned about unscrupulous producers who adulterated their wine with various non-vinous substances) and taxes on wine (not surprisingly, they were strong advocates of a light tax burden on all wines and brandies). In all, he contributed twelve articles to the *California Wine, Wool and Stock Journal*, the first of which appeared in June 1863 and the last in September 1864.[87]

Early in 1864, he contributed a long article titled "Wine-Making in California" to *Harper's New Monthly Magazine.* Much of the information contained in the article applied generally to vineyard cultivation and wine-production in California, though most of it focused on Buena Vista and his father's efforts to make it the foremost wine estate in California—in fact in the whole United States. *Harper's* was one of the most prestigious and widely read popular magazines in the United States, and its pages offered Arpad—and, through him, Agoston—a good opportunity to trumpet the virtues of California wine (and, not incidentally, their own accomplishments at Sonoma). The article was illustrated with engravings showing the stone cellars Agoston had built at Buena Vista (one large building finished, the other under construction), the tunnels Chinese laborers had dug into the hillside, the huge fermenting tanks, the storage rooms filled with racks of sparkling wine, and the white Pompeian-style villa sitting in the middle of the vineyards. There were also practical drawings of techniques for propagating vines by cuttings and for pruning the growing plants. A section on the production of sparkling wine revealed some of the insights Arpad had gained in France and in his first sparkling wine efforts at Buena Vista.[88]

Just before the *Harper's* article appeared, Jovita Vallejo Haraszthy gave birth to her first child, a daughter named Agostine in honor of her grandfather Haraszthy.[89] It was a happy event for mother and father and all of her Sonoma grandparents. But the happiness was short-lived, for soon after Agostine's birth the mood at Buena Vista turned somber. Arpad's latest sparkling wine was a disappointment. Some of the bottles refused to sparkle, while others were excessively effervescent and burst, sending shards of glass flying through the cellars. The young cellar master was not sure what he had done wrong. His father was not sure. Nor were the trustees of the Buena Vista Vinicultural Society, who were growing more and more dissatisfied with the Haraszthys' management of the great wine estate, in which they, not the Haraszthys, were now the majority owners.

The sparkling wine production was expensive, and Agoston had run up big debts. He seemed to be spending less and less time in

Sonoma, more and more time traveling or tending to his personal enterprises. Sometime in the summer of 1864 Arpad resigned his position as cellar master at Buena Vista and retired to his "shanty" in the ravine above the vineyards. Was his resignation asked for—or demanded—by the trustees? Or did he simply realize that his sparkling wine work had embarrassed his father and possibly endangered his father's position as superintendent of the estate he had worked for years to build into a viticultural showplace? Years later, Arpad himself stated tersely that he was not "able to effect satisfactory terms with the directors of the Society" and thus "tendered his resignation."[90]

Soon after he left Buena Vista he went to the other side of the valley to begin a new enterprise. It was a partnership with a Swiss-Italian winemaker named Pietro Giovanari, the overseer of General Vallejo's vineyards of late.[91] Arpad's position in the new firm of Haraszthy and Giovanari was hardly comparable to his position as cellar master at Buena Vista, but he resolved to make the best of it. His father had done the same dozens of times—giving up one seemingly promising enterprise to begin another and yet another—although not always with great success. Once again, Arpad was following in his father's footsteps. Once again, he was demonstrating—as Charles Wetmore would affirm thirty-five years later—that he was "the son of his father."

CHAPTER TWO

TO MAKE THE WINE SPARKLE

There were lots of grapes in Sonoma in 1864, for the modest collection of a half-dozen or so vineyards that Agoston Haraszthy found there in 1856 had, in the ensuing eight years, expanded almost exponentially. Much of the growth was due to increased awareness throughout California of the value of grapes and wines as items of commerce. Much was frankly due to Agoston's efforts, not only to publicize California's wine-growing potential, but also to attract winegrowers to Sonoma, where he sold small parcels of land to enterprising vineyardists, gave them instructions in the principles of cultivating vineyards and making wine, and supplied them with vine cuttings appropriate for their use.[1]

Writing in 1888, Arpad was able to reconstruct a list of the men who had vineyards in the valley in 1863, and the same number may be taken as a good figure for 1864. Arpad's list contained the names of more than 50 vineyardists and almost 3,000 acres of vineyards, representing an increase of almost 60 times that of the infant industry of 1856. Agoston Haraszthy's Buena Vista was now the largest single property, with 350 acres under cultivation, but other large vineyards were owned by the firm of Dresel and Gundlach, with 130 acres, and A. J. Butler and William Hood, with 100 acres each. Arpad's brother Attila had a vineyard of 32 acres, and his brother Gaza had 25 acres.[2] (Gaza, however, was an absentee vine grower in 1864, for he had volunteered to fight with the

Union Army in the great Civil War then raging in the East, and in May of that year he and the company he commanded were captured by Confederate troops and taken to a prison in Texas.)[3] Some of the Sonoma Valley vine growers of 1864 made their own wine, while others sold their grapes to vintners, and yet others shipped them to San Francisco to be sold as table fruit. With so many acres of vines under cultivation in Sonoma, the new firm of Haraszthy and Giovanari had plenty of grapes to turn into wine.

Pietro Giovanari and his brother Gotardo had leased some land along the Sonoma Creek from Arpad's father-in-law, General Vallejo, and it was here that the new firm of Haraszthy and Giovanari began its work. There was a grist mill on the property and a small wine cellar and distillery.[4] Some grapes grew nearby, but more were purchased from independent vine growers, some from Vallejo himself. When the firm contracted for a grower's yield, they went into the vineyards, picking the grapes and loading wagons for the trip to their creekside cellars, where they processed the grapes into wine.[5]

In addition to crushing grapes and fermenting wine, Haraszthy and Giovanari acted as wine merchants, buying bulk wine on commission and selling it in the wholesale market.[6] They also bottled wine. By October, they exhibited twelve bottles of still wine and three bottles of brandy at the Napa County Fair; and, in the same month, they entered a large exhibit in the annual Mechanics' Institute Fair in San Francisco.[7]

T. Hart Hyatt, editor of the *California Rural Home Journal,* visited Sonoma while Arpad was working with Giovanari and commented on the grapes used there. The old Mission grapes of the padres were still widely used in the production of white wines, Hyatt said, although Royal Muscadine and White Riesling (also called Johannisberg Riesling, or just Riesling) were also used to some extent. But Hyatt thought that Riesling, one of the finest white wine grapes in the world, was "too shy a bearer in Sonoma to be considered a profitable wine grape, *in that locality.*" Red table wines were also made from the Mission grape, Hyatt said, but "also from the Zinfidel [*sic*], the Black

St. Peter's, and a grape called Chagres Heneling, of which we have no particular history."[8]

In the spring of 1865, Haraszthy and Giovanari advertised both red and white wines in the San Francisco newspapers. Their "Sonoma Burgundy" was described as a superior red wine made with grapes from "General Vallejo's celebrated vineyards" in Sonoma. In San Francisco, they were represented by agents Thomas E. Finley on Leidesdorff Street and James Behrens on Battery Street.[9] While his business with Giovanari continued, Arpad cultivated some smaller vineyards in and around Sonoma, and he planted vines of his own in the mountains adjoining Buena Vista.[10]

Arpad was a busy man in Sonoma, and a prosperous one as well.[11] But he was not making sparkling wine, and he did not see any immediate prospect of doing so. The Buena Vista Vinicultural Society had hired Pierre Debanne, the French Champagne maker who previously worked for the Sainsevain Brothers, to take Arpad's place, and Debanne was continuing his efforts to produce a good BVVS sparkling wine.[12] When a new business opportunity presented itself, Arpad was pleased to consider it.

He was probably acquainted with Isidor Landsberger before the two began their discussions in the spring of 1865, for Landsberger was a financial backer of the BVVS and one of the original trustees of the corporation. Born in Berlin in 1824, he had come to San Francisco in the early 1850s, first operating a successful baking business and then a commission firm. In 1856, he went to New York, where he married and remained for two years. Returning to California in 1858, he became an importer and wine broker, eventually acting as a sales agent for BVVS in San Francisco.[13] Whether the idea for a new business originated with Landsberger or Arpad, it seemed to suit the purposes of both men, and sometime in 1866 they formed the firm called I. Landsberger (but soon expanded to I. Landsberger & Co.). Landsberger seems always to have been the financial manager of the business, and probably provided the initial capital as well, while Arpad provided the winemaking expertise and the promise (or at least the hope) of producing a commercially successful sparkling wine. As Arpad left Haraszthy & Giovanari for his new duties with Landsberger, he and Jovita and little Agostine moved from Sonoma to their new home in San Francisco.

At the outset, I. Landsberger & Co. probably acted only as wine merchants. They held an agency for the sale of BVVS wines in San Francisco and could not compete directly with it in the production of wine.[14] By January of 1867, however, they were free of their connections with BVVS, as was Agoston, who left Buena Vista sometime in late 1866 or early 1867.

It was a sorry departure for the man who had devoted ten years of his life to making Buena Vista the leading vineyard in all of California, if not the nation. But his future was all but sealed when a handful of the BVVS directors charged him with "unfaithfulness and extravagance" in the discharge of his duties (other directors stoutly defended him against the charges), and he left for a nearby Sonoma vineyard owned by Eleonora. He was on his wife's property in December 1866, when a steam tank in a distillery exploded and he was forced to jump from the second story onto a pile of lumber and boxes, where he suffered serious internal injuries.[15] He eventually recovered, but his connections with Buena Vista were irretrievably severed.

It was shortly after Agoston's fall that Arpad made his first effort to produce sparkling wine with Landsberger. He later recalled that this was at the end of 1866.[16] An article published a few months later in the *San Francisco Daily Evening Bulletin* put the date at January 1867.[17] In either case, it was an auspicious event, and one that would change the future course of Arpad's life.

Arpad was an optimistic man, but it is hard to believe his later recollections that his first sparkling wine efforts with I. Landsberger & Co. "proved a complete success."[18] He knew as well as any man in San Francisco that making wine in the style of French Champagne was not easy. It was an involved and exacting process that had developed over centuries and acquired a host of customs and traditions that clung to it with the tenacity of moss to rocks.

To produce sparkling wine, a still wine first had to be made from carefully chosen grapes (or, more accurately, several still wines had to be made, for a blend of wines, called a cuvée, was always necessary). The grapes, and the wines made from them, had to be selected not only for their flavor, body, and color but also for their alcoholic content and a proper balance of sugar and acid. The wines were made by crushing and pressing, fermenting and racking, much as other wines were made. If red (often called black or blue) grapes were used, the crushing stage was omitted, so the pigments in the skins would not color the wine, and a shallow, gentle pressing was substituted.

After the wines had finished their initial fermentation, they were carefully blended in vats, and a specially prepared solution of sugar candy and still wine, sometimes mixed with yeast, was added. This solution (called the *liqueur de tirage*) was stirred into the wine to ensure even distribution of the sugar and yeast. The wine was then siphoned from the vats into bottles, which were sealed with specially made corks and laid on their sides in racks. The sugar and yeast induced a second (or bottle) fermentation, during which carbon dioxide was trapped inside the bottles.

In the weeks and months that followed, the bottles rested on their sides, as the sugar in the wine fermented and the pressure of the carbon dioxide inside them increased. After an additional several months of aging, the bottles were placed in racks and turned at regular intervals, each time giving them a deft twist or shake while simultaneously inclining them downward toward their necks. This process, called riddling (or *remuage*), caused the residue left by the expired yeast to slide down the sides of the bottles, ultimately depositing itself on the corks. When the bottles were in a perfectly vertical position (*mise sur pointe*), a skilled cellar worker took each one in hand, quickly removed the cork, and allowed the residue to be expelled (or disgorged) in a small but noisy blast of carbon dioxide.[19] The space left in the neck of the bottle was then filled with a syrup prepared especially for the purpose (called the *dosage*), and the cork was quickly replaced, tied, and wired to make sure that no more carbon dioxide escaped.

Realizing the pitfalls that lay ahead, Arpad began tentatively to produce his new sparkling wine, bottling small lots and carefully watching to see if any of the bottles were defective. A reporter for the *Bulletin* visited Landsberger's San Francisco cellars late in 1867 and reported that Arpad began his serious sparkling wine work in May of that year with a lot of sixty-five bottles. Up to the first of October, he had put up twelve separate lots, with uneven results. The first lot failed to sparkle and had to be uncorked. The second, third, and fourth lots progressed, but slowly, and a large portion had to be uncorked for want of sparkle. The fifth lot fermented too violently, and about forty percent of the bottles exploded. Arpad removed the contents of the remaining bottles to save them from similar fates.[20]

Years later, Horatio P. Stoll, an early day wine journalist and chronicler of California's wine history, left a more colorful recollection of Arpad's first efforts to make sparkling wine in San Francisco. According to Stoll, Arpad conducted preliminary experiments in the home he shared with Jovita, which he had converted into "a veritable laboratory." "His kitchen walls were lined with racks to hold champagne bottles." Emboldened by his experiments, Arpad told Landsberger that he wanted to make some commercial "champagne." Landsberger objected, but finally, "to get rid of importunity," permitted Arpad to convert one cask of still wine into sparkling wine. This conversion was made in Arpad's parlor, Stoll said, "the carpet having been taken up—and was a success."[21]

If Stoll's account is correct, Landsberger did not share Arpad's early enthusiasm for sparkling wine production and was unwilling to let him do the necessary work in the firm's business premises. But Arpad's "parlor success" won Landsberger over, and he moved the firm's offices to Jackson Street near Montgomery, where Arpad had room enough to continue his work.[22] The new location was a good one, for it was in the city's business district, one block north of the Montgomery Block, a massive four-story structure erected in 1853 by Henry Wager Halleck, then a busy San Francisco lawyer but later famous as Lincoln's Civil War general-in-chief. The Montgomery Block was the largest building in San Francisco when it opened, and it housed some storied businesses, among them the Bank Exchange Saloon, where some of the most serious drinking in the city was done. Beneath its main floor was a maze of underground vaults where wine was stored, gold was refined, and other enterprises necessary to the business life of the biggest city on the Pacific Coast were conducted. Landsberger's quarters were in a stout brick building. Above ground, the structure rose to a height of two stories, while cellars beneath the street provided ample space for storage and aging of wines.

Though Arpad had been trained in the traditional méthode champenoise, he knew that some variations in the process would be necessary in San Francisco. The city's climate was cool and moist. There were rarely any hot days, or any cold ones, for the presence nearby of San Francisco Bay and, beyond that, the Pacific Ocean, insured a uniformity of temperature and humidity. To accelerate the bottle fermentation of his wines, he built fires in wood stoves to heat the fermenting room. A label with the date of stacking was placed on the different bottle piles. After resting a few days, the bottles began to burst, and Arpad examined them carefully. If the explosions were violent, he removed the remaining bottles to the cellar beneath the fermenting room to mitigate the fermentation. If the fermentation seemed to be progressing well, he allowed it to go on. When the wine was clear and the sediment left by the yeast rested on the sides of the bottles, he determined that the fermentation had stopped, and he moved the bottles to racks, with their necks pointing downward. Each bottle was marked with a daub of whitewash on one side, to show which side should remain uppermost, and the riddling began. When the corks were removed to disgorge the sediment, the sediment was caught in tubs and a small dosage was added to each bottle. The corks were then replaced and secured with wire. This work was done as quickly as possible, to minimize the small amounts of wine that were lost in the process. The bottles were then washed and placed on racks. The corks and wires were covered with foil, labels were affixed, and the bottles were wrapped with thin paper, collected in baskets, and taken to the wooden boxes in which they would be shipped to market.

The first Landsberger sparkling wine went on sale on September 10, 1867.[23] Samples were sent to the state fair in Sacramento and to the San Joaquin County Fair in Stockton, where they were awarded the top premiums. Still wines from the Landsberger cellars were also sent to the fairs, where they won awards. Cases of the sparkling wine were shipped to New York, Liverpool, Japan, and Alaska.[24] The sparkling wine arrived in New York, as Landsberger himself later reported, "in perfect order," and was "diamond-bright, and sparkled long and continuously." In a report to the state agricultural society, Landsberger boasted that, despite thirteen years of unsuccessful efforts to make sparkling wine in California, he was "the first and only one who has successfully delivered to the market a good, pure wine, sparkling equally as much if not more than the imported French champagnes. And this I have done in a legitimate way, through natural fermentation in the bottle." (Landsberger's hubris notwithstanding, Arpad deserved the credit for this accomplishment.)

In his report, Landsberger scolded the manufacturers who sold artificially carbonated wine under the name of "champagne," charging that they "brought into the worst repute the California sparkling wines. The liquid they make, when new, foams, but never sparkles; and even its foam holds but a couple of weeks, and the wine becomes cloudy and dull."[25] Artificial carbonation was often accomplished by mixing sulphuric acid with marble dust to produce carbon dioxide and then injecting the carbon dioxide directly into the still wine. It was an unsavory but a widespread practice. The sparkling wine that Arpad made for Isidor Landsberger would never be tainted in this way, for it was carefully made according to the méthode champenoise Arpad had learned in Épernay.

As soon as Arpad's new sparkling wine was ready for market, the question arose as to how it should be labeled. It would bear the name of I. Landsberger, of course, but could it properly be called "champagne"? Arpad never doubted that his wine was made in the same style and by the same methods as its French model. Fermentation in the bottle was the sine qua non of the champagne method, the distinguishing characteristic that, in Arpad's mind, separated it from other wines that merely "imitated" the French wine. Despite this, however, a law recently passed by the U.S. Congress made it risky to call the new Landsberger wine "champagne." Part of the Internal Revenue Law of 1866, the new law imposed a tax of six dollars per dozen on wine "made in imitation of sparkling wine or champagne, and put up in bottles in imitation of any imported wine, or with the pretence of being imported wine, or wine of foreign growth or manufacture."[26] Six dollars was an oppressively high rate of taxation on a product that was designed to be sold for not much more than ten or twelve dollars per dozen, and it was not one that the makers could lightly disregard. The *Bulletin* reporter who visited Landsberger's San Francisco cellars in the fall of 1867 described the federal tax and observed that, because of it, "our manufacturers have to use the term 'sparkling wine' when the product of their skill is synonymous with that of producers in France. In the latter country champagne is made by natural fermentation of young still wine in bottle, and this practice is the only one by which a good healthy effervescing wine can be produced."[27]

Was Arpad's sparkling wine made in "imitation" of champagne? He did not think it was—he believed it was real "champagne." But neither he nor Landsberger cared to test the reach of the new law, and they labeled their new product "sparkling wine."[28] An advertisement in the *Alta* on November 20, 1867, advised readers:

> ALL THE CHAMPAGNE MADE AND SOLD by the undersigned, and which has gained a reputation for superiority, bears the following label, printed in gold:
>
> SPARKLING CALIFORNIA
>
> I. LANDSBERGER,
>
> SAN FRANCISCO,
>
> Copyright Secured.
>
> And every cork is branded with the name of the Manufacturer, ARPAD HARASZTHY.
>
> My wine is always packed in new cases.
>
> My factory is open to everybody who wishes to see the process of manufacture. All can convince themselves that only the best and

purest California Wines are used, and that I do not even add Brandy, Alcohol, or Tannin—always used in the manufacture of foreign Champagne.

I. LANDSBERGER[29]

Newspaper reporters were welcomed into the Landsberger cellars, where the proprietors delighted in explaining how they made their wines and, what was most fascinating, how they made them sparkle. A reporter for the *Alta* came early in the first year of Landsberger's sparkling wine production and marveled at the mechanical devices that adorned the premises. There was a powerful corking machine, which "squeezes the cork from four sides to the proper smallness, then drives it partly into the bottle." There was "a new kind of shaking table, invented in the establishment, with more convenience for the workmen." The tables were arranged along the middle and the sides of the cellars, three high, and pierced with holes, into which the bottles were placed after they were shaken. The new tables were more convenient for the workmen and saved valuable space on the cellar floors, which were already crowded with thousands of bottles. The reporter was told that none of the workmen employed in the cellars had ever been in the French Champagne country. They were taught all they knew about the sparkling wine process in the Landsberger cellars, and Landsberger boasted that French workers would never be needed because "Californians can learn just as fast and do just as well as any other people; they only require to be properly shown." The *Alta* reporter seemed convinced. He noted that some of the previous attempts to make sparkling wine in California had produced good wine, but not on a regular basis. Landsberger's cellars had proved at last that the elusive goals of high quality and dependable production could both be met. "The system in which it is carried on cannot be better," the *Alta* reporter informed his readers, "while the careful analysis of the wines and the application of all the lately discovered facts of science preclude any and every chance of failure."[30]

Though sparkling wine was the star of the Landsberger cellars, the firm did not neglect its still wine business. By 1868, Landsberger was advertising a full line of wines and brandies, including whites, reds, Ports, and Angelicas. (Port, of course was a sweet, fortified wine made in the style of similar wines in Portugal, and Angelica was a sweet, almost syrupy liqueur made from Mission grapes in a style pioneered by Los Angeles winemakers.)[31] Landsberger had a "depot" (store) at 429 Jackson Street in which Sonoma wines and brandies were sold, and he boasted that his wines had won a host of awards, including a gold medal for the best sparkling wine issued by the California State Board of Agriculture in June 1868.[32] Landsberger also obtained an endorsement from the California State Assembly Committee on the Culture of the Grape Vine: "Your Committee carefully tested some of Mr. Landsberger's Sparkling Wine made from California Wine of the vintage of 1867, and we pronounce it a superior article of good and pure Wine."[33]

Despite his work in San Francisco, Arpad retained strong ties with Sonoma, which were documented in a long article he wrote for the *Alta* in November 1868. Titled "The Vintage in Sonoma," the piece derived from a trip he made to the Sonoma Valley during the fall harvest of that year. It described the buzz of activity that enveloped the town of Sonoma as the newly picked grapes were brought in from the vineyards, crushed, pressed, and deposited in fermenting vats. "As the visitor nears the cellars," Arpad wrote, "he is struck by the universal activity, and by the decided business air that every face assumes."[34] Arpad's brother Attila was making wine in two different places, one for his own account and another for the estate of General Charles Williams (one of the prominent men Agoston had induced to plant vineyards in Sonoma a few years before).[35] Some of San Francisco's most enterprising wine dealers contracted for the purchase of entire crops in Sonoma. "The engagements of I. Landsberger for this valley are, I believe, the heaviest," Arpad wrote, "amounting to something over 50,000 gallons. Over 25,000 gallons of this amount he will make into champagne or sparkling wine."[36] The wine Attila made for his own account in 1868 was sold to Landsberger for the production of Landsberger sparkling wine. As Arpad later reported to the legislature's Committee on the Culture of the Grape, Landsberger's 1868 sparkling wine was made from "a combination of the Riesling, the Chasselas, the Gutedel and a few White Frontignan, and about one half of the Mission grape. The combination, though occurring almost accidentally, has been found to bring out the individual perfections of these different grapes, and produce the harmonious whole which was submitted to the committee."[37] This blending of wines from different varieties was in keeping with the French practice of combining wines from different grapes to produce a cuvée suitable for the year's production. The first fermentation of 1868 was carried out in Sonoma, after which the still wines were shipped to the Landsberger cellars in San Francisco, where they were transformed into sparkling wine.

In March 1869, the *Alta* published a long article titled "Sparkling California," which described the large quantities of "Champagne" consumed in California, most of which was imported from France. "But California aspires to produce the sparkling wine needed for home consumption," the *Alta* wrote, "and to have besides a surplus for exportation." For a dozen years or so, California winemakers had been frustrated in their attempts to make good sparkling wine. "Still they have been confident of ultimate success, and the attempts have continued until at last their confidence is justified, or at least certain of justification. The Sparkling California now made in this city compares very favorably with the good qualities of champagne; and the steady improvement for several years past implies a considerable improvement for the future." Most of the wine transformed into sparkling wine in San Francisco originated in the Sonoma Valley, where the wine was "lighter, livelier, purer in flavor, and has more of the peculiar qualities needed than the wine of any other part of the State yet tried." The *Alta* thought that the best sparkling wine came from high ground in Sonoma, where the vineyards were not irrigated and the soil was light, and added: "The best, in the opinion of Arpad Haraszthy, whose judgment in this matter is entitled to much weight, is the Zinfindel [*sic*], and next to that is the Black Pineau [*sic*]. The Riesling is good; but at present these varieties are not abundant enough, so the main reliance is [on] the Mission grape, which is flavored with White Frontignan. . . . It is one of the advantages of the Zinfindel [*sic*] that it does not contain so much sugar as the Mission grape."[38] (Many of the early commentators on Zinfandel were unable to agree on a standard spelling for the grape, and "Pineau" was a common rendering of the name we know today as "Pinot.")

Zinfandel is, of course, a red grape, and "Champagne" is always a white wine.[39] But much of the sparkling wine produced in France came from Pinot Noir, a deeply tinted red grape often described as "black" or "midnight blue."[40] The trick was to avoid crushing grapes of this kind, and to press them lightly, so that none, or very little, of the pigment in the skins found its way into the wine. French Champagnes made exclusively from dark grapes like Pinot Noir and Meunier (another dark grape grown in the Champagne region) are sometimes called *blancs de noirs* (white from black) while those made from exclusively white grapes such as Chardonnay are *blancs de blancs* (white from white). Both Arpad and Attila knew this, of course, and both presumably followed the French model for light pressing of the Zinfandel grapes. Zinfandel thus became an important element in Arpad's typical sparkling wine cuvée. His reliance on Mission grapes as late as 1868 reveals, however, that the old vines of the padres were still widely planted in California in that year, and that superior foreign varieties like Zinfandel were still the exception, rather than the rule, in the state's vineyards. These questions aside, the *Alta* found much to praise in California sparkling wine, and concluded its article with the emphatic statement that "the production of California sparkling wine equal to very good champagne is no longer doubtful."[41]

Landsberger wines were obviously getting good coverage in the *Alta,* San Francisco's biggest and most influential newspaper, but other journals were also commenting on them. In June, the *California Farmer* paid the new sparkling winemakers attention, writing: "Among several large and well known dealers in California wines who export largely, none stand higher than the house of Landsberger & Co., of our city. . . . Recently this House have [*sic*] enlarged their warehouses, adding other spacious rooms, extending from 423 to 429 Jackson St., and the present firm is now composed of I. Landsberger, Arpad Haraszthy and Oscar Schlesinger. Mr. Haraszthy is widely known as of the Sonoma Family, all wine dealers and experts in the knowledge of wines; Mr. Haraszthy has made himself master of the art of wine making, by extensive travels and researches in Europe. . . . Mr. Schlesinger is a well known merchant of experience now in this firm." The *Farmer* said that Landsberger & Co. was "a strong house, and having the knowledge, capital and the control of many of the very best wines of the state, will secure and deservedly so, a large share of the wine business."[42]

Landsberger had competition, of course. A. Finke & Co., Eberhardt & Lachman, and the Buena Vista Vinicultural Society, were all California winemaking companies that had San Francisco cellars, and all produced varying quantities of sparkling wine.[43] Arpad had begun the serious sparkling wine efforts of the BVVS in 1862, and the corporation had continued them with French winemakers after his departure. They had had some success, too, producing a wine they called "Sparkling Sonoma" and another called "Pearl of California" (a *perlwein* is, in Germany, a wine that is slightly sparkling but lacks the full effervescence of French Champagne). Finke produced a so-called "champagne" by means of the artificial carbonation that Landsberger deplored, but its sales were good. Adolph Eberhardt and Samuel Lachman were reputable still winemakers (a few years later, Lachman would buy out Eberhardt and make the surviving firm of S. Lachman & Co. into one of the largest in San Francisco). BVVS won some prestigious awards in the late 1860s and early 1870s: its "Sparkling Sonoma" won an honorable mention at the Paris Exposition of 1867, the highest prize awarded to any American wine at that event.[44]

Landsberger & Co. continued to produce a full line of still wines, red and white, sweet and dry, but their sparkling wines outshone the rest. A correspondent for the *California Farmer* was on hand when Orville Grant, brother of President Ulysses S. Grant, came to Jackson Street in the summer of 1869 to inspect the Landsberger cellars. Arpad, as articulate in person as he was in print, greeted Grant and his entourage and conducted them on a tour of the premises. "This now celebrated Wine House commenced two years ago with the intention of producing only 100 dozen Champagne per month," the *Farmer* reported, "and thinking that if the above was regularly sold per month, the business would be a good one, but by reason of the public approval of their Champagne, were forced to increase their business gradually to 200, 300, 400 cases per month, and are now producing at the rate of 800 dozen monthly, and with the future intention of increasing it to 1,000 dozen monthly and at no distant day. . . . The above does not include their still wine business, of which they are putting up 400 cases per month of the different kinds, and which they are now forced by demand for it to increase largely." Seventeen workmen, mostly Chinese, were employed in the cellars. As the *Farmer* correspondent accompanied Orville Grant through the sparkling wine works, he "noted the expressed opinion of our newcomers on several occasions, and it was this—we are not only greatly *delighted,* but greatly *surprised.*"[45]

In the spring of 1871, Landsberger & Co. celebrated the expansion of their cellars from Jackson Street south along Jones Alley to Washington Street. The new space was required by a healthy increase in the firm's sparkling wine business, and they chose to share the occasion with the people of San Francisco. Between five and six hundred guests were treated to a sumptuous lunch and an interesting explanation of the winemaking operations of the firm. As Arpad led his visitors through the cellars, he pointed out the appliances used in the manufacture of sparkling wine, stressing that Landsberger's sparkling wine was all made by natural fermentation in the bottles and without the addition of any artificial chemicals. The *San Francisco Call* reported that the visitors were "entirely convinced that the representations made to them on this head were true, as they discovered neither acids, marble dust nor injecting soda fountains; but had the bottles from which they drank taken down from the racks, where they were deposited, to undergo the last stages of manipulation towards maturity." After the guests had finished their repast, the cellar workmen were brought to the table and, in the words of the *Call*, "bountifully furnished with edibles, which they washed down with the generous wines they had themselves assisted to make." When the masters of the cellar congratulated the workmen for their contributions to the firm's success, the workmen responded "with toasts and cheers to their employers."[46]

Arpad had reason to feel satisfied in 1871. His business with Landsberger was going well. His sparkling wine was winning a good reputation, not only in California but in other states and countries. Jovita had presented him with a second child, a son named Carlos John Haraszthy, born in San Francisco on June 2, 1867.[47] And, though he was still only thirty-one years old, he was receiving recognition through his writings as one of the most knowledgeable wine men in the state.

Beginning in 1871, San Francisco's *Overland Monthly* published four long articles by Arpad under the title of "Wine-Making in California." Founded in 1865 as a Pacific Coast counterpart of Boston's prestigious *Atlantic Monthly,* the *Overland* showcased the literary talents of Californians, publishing some of the most famous stories of Bret Harte, who was its editor for several years, as well as works by Clarence King, Prentice Mulford, and Charles Warren Stoddard. In later years, the same journal would feature even more distinguished works by Jack London and Frank Norris.

"Wine-Making in California" appeared in four installments in the *Overland Monthly,* beginning in the December 1871 issue and continuing in January, February, and May of 1872.[48] It was an absorbing discourse, by turns erudite and learned, but mostly practical. It began with a short history of the beginnings of vine planting and winemaking in California (which depended in part on the recollections of Arpad's father-in-law, General Vallejo). It touched on early commercial grape growing and winemaking in California (here Arpad included several references to his father Agoston), discussed grape varieties, described favorable techniques for cultivation of vineyards, delineated good cellar practices, and explored the business of making wine at a profit.

Arpad expressed some definite, if controversial, opinions in the articles. He thought, for example, that the choice of grape varieties was even more important in producing good wines than the locations in which the grapes were planted, though he acknowledged that soil and climate were contributing factors to excellence. He deplored the practice of unscrupulous merchants in the Eastern states of putting up spurious wines (composed sometimes only of apple cider with the addition of alum, cream of tartar, sulphuric acid, or sugar, water, and alcohol) and calling them "California wines," thereby damaging the reputations of all genuine wines produced in the Golden State. He called for changes in the federal tax laws governing wines and brandies, arguing that those laws were not only unfair to producers but deleterious to the economic welfare of the country. He praised vine grafting as a means whereby vine growers could change the varieties in their vineyards, getting rid of old and unfavorable varieties like the Mission and introducing superior European varieties (among the latter, he mentioned Riesling, White Frontignan, "Pineau," Traminer, Black Malvoisie, and Zinfandel by name).[49]

Echoing his own father's call for planting vineyards on hillsides, where the vines could not be artificially irrigated but had to depend on natural precipitation for their moisture, he called for more vineyard cultivation on mountain slopes, where grains could not be grown. "Millions of acres that are now covered with *chaparral* and *manzanita*-bushes will become utilized," he said; "for just those spots where these bushes grow, if there is any soil at all, are the very finest for vineyards."[50] He praised winemaking as an honorable and productive occupation, one which could provide a secure financial future for a man and his family. But he cautioned that it should not be regarded as a quick or easy road to riches:

> People must not go into the business of grape-raising, as many have done, with the view of making immense fortunes. This is not a gambling, but a legitimate pursuit, and only gives a percentage in the shape of income upon the investment. Nor must those about to engage in it demand or expect too much income from their vines. Many people have engaged, and are still engaging, in the business, who, with the possession of fifteen or twenty acres, expect to live in the style of bankers; and, if the income from their small vineyards does not suffice, they become disgusted, and condemn the pursuit. This class should not own vineyards, but engage, with the same capital, in the banking business, and learn from that what a legitimate income is.[51]

He lauded the California wine community for its spirit of enterprise and cooperation and attributed rapid improvements in winemaking techniques to the state's "isolated position, where necessity truly becomes the mother of invention." But he also praised "the unselfish manner in which our wine-makers meet each other, neighbor striving to help neighbor, and imparting freely all personal experiences," adding: "This open and generous interchange of acquired knowledge is a feature, not only with our wine-makers, but is perceived in every industrial enterprise of our State."[52]

Curiously, he concluded his discussion of California winemaking without any extended reference to "champagne," or the sparkling wine techniques he had developed at I. Landsberger & Co. But perhaps he did not need to do so, for he had expounded on those subjects at length in other venues, both orally and in writing. In his discussion of early California winemaking, however, he did pay tribute to the California padres, likening them to the Old World monks who had done so much to perfect the celebrated wines of Johannisberg, Hochheim, Clos de Vouegot, Chateau Yquem, Margaux, "and many others." "To them are we even indebted for the bright, sparkling, and ever-lively champagne, that warms without intoxication, and makes languid conversation bubble with the spirit of wit, like its own vivacious self. And what the monks did for the Old World, that did the Fathers for California. They planted the first vine, and they made our first wine."[53]

If Arpad seemed happy in 1871—pleased with his accomplishments at Landsberger & Co. and his literary recognition in the *Overland Monthly*—he was also aware that happiness is not a permanent condition, and that good fortune is often leavened with sadness or tragedy. His father's last months in Sonoma could hardly be characterized as happy. The debts that Agoston accumulated during his feverish expansion of Buena Vista, combined with obligations incurred in other personal enterprises, had weighed heavily on him, forcing him at last to declare bankruptcy.[54] Hoping to recoup his fortunes, he had left San Francisco in February 1868 for Nicaragua, where he formed a partnership with a man named Theodore Wassmer and began to develop a sugar plantation near the town of Corinto.

With his eldest son Gaza working with him (Gaza had returned from his Confederate imprisonment and been mustered out of the Union army at the end of 1866), Agoston hoped to produce rum that would find a good market in California and give him the financial means to return to winemaking in the Golden State. Arpad's seventy-nine-year-old grandfather, Charles, had followed Agoston to Central America, but after a few months boarded a ship for a return voyage to San Francisco, complaining that the tropical climate did not agree with him.[55] The climate did not agree with Eleonora either (or at least the diseases that thrived in that climate), for in July of 1868 she fell victim to a deadly attack of yellow fever and died.[56] Agoston returned to California to attend to some business interests in San Francisco and Sonoma before heading south once again to his Nicaraguan plantation. There, on August 6, 1869, he attempted to cross a river that ran through the plantation, fell from a projecting tree limb, and disappeared in the swirling waters below. The river was known to be infested with alligators, for a cow had been dragged into the waters by one of the reptiles a few days before. A search was mounted for the missing man, but it turned up nothing.[57]

News of Agoston's disappearance and presumed death made its way back to California, where it became Arpad's duty, as the principal spokesman for the Haraszthy family, to explain the circumstances of the strange occurrence. Arpad repeated reports he had heard about the alligators, which quickly gained a gruesome currency.[58] Whether Arpad was convinced by them, however, is uncertain. A few years later, recalling his father's tragic death, he speculated that Agoston may only have drowned, and not been eaten by alligators, or swept down the river and into the nearby ocean, where he could have been devoured by the man-eating sharks that infested those waters.

Whether Agoston was the victim of drowning, of predatory alligators, or of sharks, or might even have been captured and killed by the

Nicaraguan rebels who at the time of his disappearance were ranging through the countryside in an effort to topple the Nicaraguan government, his body was never found. In any case, his death was a tragedy, for he was only fifty-six years old and seemingly in good health when he disappeared. The tragedy was felt most personally by the children—Gaza remained in Nicaragua but the others were in California—and the grandchildren who mourned his passing. Strangely, Agoston's father, Charles, met his death only sixteen days after Agoston's, though neither man was aware of the other's passing. Charles was aboard the bark *Mary Belle Roberts* en route from Corinto to San Francisco when he died of dropsy and was buried at sea.[59] There was a quality of unreality to all of these events. Truly, it might be said, the last days of Agoston Haraszthy were stranger than fiction—as much of his life had been.

Acting again as spokesman for the Haraszthy family, Arpad penned an obituary of his father that was published in the *Alta*. In it, he called Agoston "one of the pioneers of California." He briefly sketched his early life in Hungary and Wisconsin, reviewed his enterprising career in San Diego in the early 1850s, and recalled the highlights of his life as a vine grower and wine maker. He recalled his father's famous trip to Europe in 1861 to gather choice European vine cuttings for the vineyards of California, and the book he published in 1862 detailing the experiences of that trip. He reviewed Agoston's accomplishments in Sonoma, his founding of the great Buena Vista vineyard, and his last (and ultimately tragic) adventure in Nicaragua. Arpad wrote:

> Colonel Haraszthy was a man whose whole aim was to introduce new elements of wealth, to search out new fields of industry, and thus to lead the way to a wider field of material progress in whatever country he lived. He was a man of good and generous impulses. He was hospitable and liberal almost to a fault. His hand was ever ready to help those who stood in need. He was full of ambition, but only in the line of being useful to his fellows. Those who knew him intimately loved and admired him, and all acknowledged a charm in his presence which they felt, but could not explain.[60]

It was the kind of praise that would have excited sympathy in a memorial service, uttered over the dead man's body (if the body had ever been found); a fond son's expression of love and respect for his father, and grief at his loss, and it is unlikely that anybody objected to its tone. Nor is it likely that another statement in Arpad's obituary of his father excited any greater objections. "He may with propriety be called the Father of Viniculture in California," Arpad wrote. To support the latter assertion, Arpad reviewed his father's many contributions to the development of California's wine industry in the 1850s and 1860s. But it is doubtful that many readers of the *Alta* felt he had to review them, for there were plenty of men in California in 1869 who had personal knowledge of Agoston Haraszthy's accomplishments as a vine grower and winemaker, and who were willing to concede Arpad's statements about his father's importance in the early history of wine in California.

Arpad's characterization of Agoston Haraszthy as "the father" of California viniculture was generally accepted—though the phrase was varied slightly to read "the Father of California Viticulture," or the "Father of Commercial Winemaking in California." It was repeated in newspapers across the state and the nation, even printed in the *New York Times*.[61] Men who knew Agoston Haraszthy personally respected it. Historians and wine writers endorsed it.[62]

A little more than a century after Agoston died, however, Arpad's assertion was challenged by two historians who argued that Agoston did not deserve the honor his son had accorded him. He was not, the historians pointed out, the "first commercial winemaker" in the state, and so he could not have been "the father" of the state's wine industry.[63] (Of course, Arpad had never claimed that Agoston was the first commercial winemaker in the state. He had acknowledged that others, notably Charles Kohler, had actually preceded his father in that endeavor by a year or two, and he had always honored the mission padres as the real pioneers of California winemaking.) But the dissenting historians took their argument a step further: They impugned Arpad's motives in conferring the "title" on his father. They said that he was trying to build up his own wine business by claiming an honor for his father that his father never deserved—that he was, in effect, falsifying the historical record for personal economic gain.[64] By the time the historians' arguments were made, Arpad himself was long dead, and he could not answer them. If he had still been living, however, he almost certainly would have done so. He was intelligent, articulate, and well-informed. But he was also forceful and never reluctant to stand up for the truth as he knew it.

CHAPTER THREE

ECLIPSE EXTRA DRY

Arpad produced wines under a variety of names in his early years with Landsberger. His still wines were denominated Sonoma White, Sonoma Red, Sonoma Port, California Vermouth, and, in the case of one of his favorite varietals, Riesling. His sparkling wines were Sparkling Sonoma, Sparkling California, Sparkling Muscatel, Sparkling Moselle, and Private Cuvée (the last a blend of grapes that, in the French tradition, was deemed proprietary).[1] The most famous wine he ever produced, however, was given a more distinctive name—a brand designation that came to be synonymous with his continuing efforts to produce a California sparkling wine that would put cheap American imitations of Champagne to shame and compete on a favorable basis with famous French imports. It was Eclipse Extra Dry—a name that, in time, came to be nearly interchangeable with the name of Arpad Haraszthy himself.

In France in the eighteenth and most of the nineteenth centuries, Champagne was sweet (or at least semisweet), for sweetness appealed to the tastes of most European consumers.[2] Further, it was generally easier to produce a sweet rather than a dry wine, for sweetness would help to mask any defects in the wine. The sweetness in French Champagne resulted from the sugary syrup (dosage) that was added to the bottles after they were disgorged. In the Champagne district, the syrup was typically composed of wine mixed with rock candy and some Cognac for flavoring. Towards the middle of the nineteenth century, however, more Champagne was sold in England, where preferences ran to dryer beverages. Sweet wines like Port and Madeira were favorite after-dinner indulgences among the English, but dryer wines were preferred before and during meals. French producers began to market Champagnes that appealed to the English taste and to the preferences of American consumers, which inclined to the English model.[3]

A more or less standardized system of designation developed to tell consumers how sweet a given bottle of Champagne might be: it was labeled *doux* if it was sweet; *sec* if it was somewhat dryer but not totally lacking in sweetness; *demi sec* if it was semi-sweet; and *extra sec* if it was dry. *Brut* (literally "brute" or "crude," but roughly equivalent to "natural") came to mean a Champagne that was almost totally dry—that is, a wine that had no (or very little) sugar in the dosage.

Arpad's Eclipse Extra Dry was an attempt to appeal to popular tastes by producing a sparkling wine that was not as sweet as the older, more traditional liquids. Exactly how much sugar Eclipse contained after the dosage is impossible to determine. Although it was probably still somewhat sweet by later tastes, it appealed to those who liked to drink sparkling wines during meals, or at special events such as weddings, christenings, and anniversaries.

We can only speculate as to the origin of the name Eclipse. Madie Brown Emparan, who included a biography of Jovita in her compendious study of *The Vallejos of California*, thought that the name was taken from a popular brand of cigars.[4] But Ruth Teiser and Catherine Harroun believed that it derived from the celebrated eighteenth-century English racehorse, Eclipse.[5] The latter seems more likely, because sparkling wine had already developed a close association with professional horse racing. In his nineteenth-century history of Champagne, Henry Vizetelly observed that, in England, Champagne was drunk when a favorite horse won a race, to "celebrate his triumph," and when the favorite lost, "to drown our sorrows." Bets were often paid in Champagne, and important races were named for the wine (there were Champagne Stakes in both England and the United States).[6] The famous horse named Eclipse was an undefeated British Thoroughbred born on April 1, 1764, and named for the solar eclipse of that date. Before his death in 1789, he sired more than three hundred winning racehorses. By some estimates, 95 percent of modern Thoroughbreds are descendants of Eclipse.[7]

Eclipse Extra Dry was first offered to the market in 1875, probably in time for the grand opening of the Palace Hotel in San Francisco in October of that year.[8] The Palace was the largest hotel in the United States when it was built (possibly the largest in the world) and easily the most luxurious.[9] Arpad's Eclipse Extra Dry was an authentically native San Francisco sparkling wine and an appropriate offering to this authentically native monument to San Francisco's new wealth and prestige. With his introduction of Eclipse, Arpad was looking beyond San Francisco, too, hoping to make a dent in Eastern and Middle Western markets for California wine.

In December 1875, the *Alta* reported that "Messrs. I. Landsberger & Co., who have done so much to raise the reputation of California for fine wines, both at home and abroad," were planning to make a large display of their wines at the Centennial Exhibition scheduled to open in Philadelphia the following summer. "They will there present their new brand of extra dry champagne ('Eclipse'), which solves all doubts about the ability of our wine-growers to compete with the French article—it is one of the best brands to be found in the market. One of their firm will be present to explain the merits of these California productions and draw the attention of the representatives from every quarter of the globe to the extraordinary capabilities of our State for producing fine wines. In this display the new 'Eclipse' brand will occupy the post of honor."[10] Arpad was, of course, the logical member of the firm to go to Philadelphia with the new exhibit, for he was the sparkling winemaker and the most articulate spokesman for Landsberger wines.

Landsberger wines were displayed in the cathedral-like Agricultural Hall at the Philadelphia Exhibition in the summer of 1876, along with those of such other California producers as Kohler & Frohling of San Francisco, Matthew Keller of Los Angeles, and Henry M. Naglee of San Jose.[11] Wines came from Ohio, Missouri, and New York, as well as California, and included "champagne, still and sparkling wines, port and claret."[12] One description of the Philadelphia Exhibition gave good marks to the American wines and said they were "acquiring a footing equal to the best foreign wines."[13] Sonoma's Buena Vista Vinicultural Society, still the largest winemaking establishment in the United States, won medals for its red, white, and sparkling wines.[14] The *Alta* reported that the awards to BVVS at the Centennial Exhibition confirmed "what has already been well known in our State: that the Buena Vista Vinicultural Society produces both still and sparkling wines of the finest quality."[15] But the same newspaper grumbled that more recognition was not given to other California producers. "It has been said that the Commissioners were prejudiced against California wines," the *Alta* said, "but their excessive ignorance is sufficient to explain all their blunders. They have given prizes to some good wines among the many—by accident."[16] Eclipse made a good impression at Philadelphia, although it did not initially receive a medal. It was only after the exposition had terminated that word was received back in San Francisco that the Centennial Commissioners had given Landsberger & Co. awards for its sparkling wines and its brandy.[17] Beyond Philadelphia, Landsberger wines were entered in 1876 in an exhibit mounted by the American Institute in New York, and there Eclipse won a silver medal.[18]

Arpad attended the events in both Philadelphia and New York. When he returned to San Francisco in September, the *Alta* congratulated him for having "done good service in the interests of the winegrowers of California."[19] He may also have done some good work for Eclipse, for he had introduced it to Eastern markets and spread its praise among European wine merchants, who were on the lookout for good wines in the United States. And at least partly as a result of his salesmanship, Eclipse soon won some prestigious awards around the country and in foreign countries, taking medals in Australia, Chile, and Belgium as well as closer to home in San Francisco, Los Angeles, Portland (Oregon), and Austin (Texas).[20] At the American Institute Wine Fair held in New York in 1877, Eclipse won a "medal of superiority," the highest medal the Institute had ever given for a beverage to that date.[21]

Awards were not the only (or even the best) measure of a wine's quality, but they were well-calculated to catch the public's attention, and Arpad assiduously sought to accumulate more.

As Arpad's efforts with Landsberger & Co. attracted more attention, San Francisco investors took an interest in the business, and several purchased shares in the partnership. A local businessman named Albert C. Heineken joined the firm sometime in the early 1870s.[22] He sold his interest to Edward Vollmer in 1874, and by 1876 Vollmer was joined by Simon Epstein and Louis Gross.[23] None of these men had any winemaking background—Arpad was still the winemaker and cellar master of the company—but they were ambitious businessmen who brought new capital into the firm. Before joining Arpad and Landsberger, Vollmer, Epstein, and Gross had been associated in various businesses in San Francisco and Nevada, where they operated stores and manufactured at least two lines of bitters.[24]

Bitters were popular items during most of the nineteenth century. Tinctures of alcohol mixed with exotic combinations of barks, roots, and herbs, they were widely used not only for flavoring mixed drinks but also for their supposed medicinal properties. Landsberger patented the brand name "Wild Blackberry Bitters" in 1872,[25] and an 1876 advertisement in the San Francisco-based *Wine Dealers' Gazette* proclaimed that the firm was selling "The Celebrated Wild Blackberry Bitters."[26] By 1876, Landsberger was also the proprietor of the very popular IXL Bitters, sometimes called "Dr. Henley's Celebrated Wild Grape Root IXL Bitters."[27] This had been invented in Oregon by a Dr. William Henley, who associated Louis Gross in his business.[28] As early as 1869, Vollmer, Gross, and Simon Epstein's son, Henry Epstein, were manufacturing IXL Bitters on Front Street in San Francisco.[29] By 1871 William Henley was a partner in their business (called H. Epstein & Co.), and by 1873 Vollmer, Gross, and IXL had all become part of I. Landsberger & Co.[30]

Beyond their vinous origins (bitters were typically wine-based liquids), it is difficult to determine how much Arpad had to do with "Wild Blackberry Bitters" or "Dr. Henley's IXL Bitters." He may have made the base wines for these products. Perhaps he supervised the mixing of the base wines and the herbal flavorings. Beyond that, however, Arpad continued to devote most of his time and attention to making the wines, still and sparkling, that were the backbone of I. Landsberger's business. In the San Francisco cellars where most of his work was done, he exhibited an air of authority. When visitors arrived, he welcomed them, escorted them through the maze of cellars, and expounded at length on the subject that never seemed to tire him—the manufacture in California of sparkling wine.

Late in the year of the Centennial Exhibition, one of Arpad's most interesting visitors made his way to the Landsberger cellars. He was Benjamin Cummings Truman, a Rhode Island–born journalist who had written scores of stories about Civil War battles for the *New York Times* before being elected major of a Union army regiment in Tennessee. After the war, he became a confidential secretary to President Andrew Johnson, traveled in Europe, and then came to California as Johnson's special agent for the U.S. Post Office. Major Truman (he was to bear the military title with aplomb for the rest of his life) was introduced to the good life of fine food and wine in Paris in 1866, and he never forgot what he learned there. He was a discerning critic who combined good taste with a flair for colorful expression, and soon after his first visit to California he became a "booster" of the Golden State. He lived first in San Francisco, but eventually settled in Los Angeles, where at one time he owned and edited the *Los Angeles Star,* the southern city's oldest newspaper.[31] All the while, he continued to write special reports for the *New York Times.*

Truman had been in Philadelphia during the centennial and found some of the California wines there "atrocious," but he knew they were not representative of the Golden State's best viticultural efforts. In his travels through California, he had found some very bad wines but also some very good ones. The most notable good wines were, in his estimation, those produced at Mission San Jose by a man named Palmer, and the sparkling wine made in San Francisco by Arpad Haraszthy.[32]

Arriving at the Landsberger cellars late in 1876, Truman was greeted by both Arpad and Isidor Landsberger, who were already hosting a room full of visitors. The major quickly sensed that the other visitors regarded him as an intruder, for they had read some of his newspaper stories and did not think they were sufficiently complimentary about California. They thought that every journalist who came to California was "in duty bound" to attract emigration and capital to the state by praising it. When Truman asked them "Why?" they immediately rejoined: "What do you come to California for, then?" Landsberger began to open some bottles of sparkling wine and asked for Truman's opinions about them. His comment that one bottle had "an after-taste that was bitter and earthy" provoked derisive laughter from the other visitors, who were convinced that he didn't know anything at all about wines, still or sparkling. Truman was angry. "Fortunately," he later wrote in the *Times,* "the great Haraszthy came to my relief, and stated that I was unquestionably right; that Landsberger had opened a bottle of wine which had only been 'disgorged' three days previously, and that the flavor of the syrup had not yet assimilated itself with the wine." Arpad thought that the journalist "evidently possessed a very discriminating palate," and he was "very glad indeed" to have his opinion.[33]

Truman had just tasted the Landsberger Private Cuvée. He was now asked to taste another bottle of sparkling wine. "It was faultless," he said. "This, the Eclipse, was good in flavor, exceedingly full-bodied, very sparkling, very dry, and had no after-taste whatever. Moreover there was not the same excess of carbonic acid [carbon dioxide] which had characterized the first." Truman was asked to taste other wines. As he did so, more men began to arrive on the scene, "until the room was full, and so were the visitors."

The major was taken through the cellars and shown the process of sparkling wine manufacture. "I saw that the wines mingled to form the champagne were not poor wines," he wrote, "but the best and richest in the land. I saw, moreover, that the saccharine matter was so abundant that it was unnecessary to charge the bottles with carbonic acid [carbon dioxide], for they were already self-charged. I saw that they were so full-bodied that it was unnecessary to load them with Cognac, as is done with French champagnes. I saw, too, that there were not little additions of essences, for the natural flavor was so delicious that it required no artificial touching up or heightening." In some bottles of Eclipse, however, he noticed a "bitter, earthy aftertaste" that he attributed to the syrup added to the bottles after they were disgorged. Instead of barley sugar or rock candy, as used by the French, Arpad's syrup was made from Honolulu molasses. Truman thought it took some time for this syrup to be thoroughly absorbed in the wine. But the demand for Landsberger sparkling wine was so "enormous" that most of it was sold out before it was a week old. "This being the case," Truman said, "I would take the liberty of advising the use of barley sugar, after all." Truman offered this observation as a helpful comment, not a criticism of the methods by which the Landsberger sparkling wines were made. "On general principles," he said, "there can be no question of the soundness of Haraszthy's views. But considering that the wine has no chance of absorbing the syrup before it is drank, I think that he is doing an injustice to himself as a producer and to the extraordinary merits of the wine. For it must be remembered that, considered as a natural wine, this champagne of California far exceeds the French, which is artificial to a very high degree."[34]

If Truman's comments about Arpad were flattering, they were typical of the coverage the young sparkling winemaker was getting in most newspapers. Like his father before him, Arpad had a knack for cultivating journalists, ingratiating himself with the corps of reporters who served as intermediaries between him and the general public.

Not long after Truman visited the Landsberger cellars, a writer for the *San Francisco Bulletin* made a visit to the same premises, and the comments that he published in his newspaper were, if anything, even more favorable to Arpad than Truman's. "The Haraszthy family hold a conspicuous place in the history of California wine-making," the *Bulletin* writer stated. "The elder Haraszthy (now deceased) was associated with some of the earliest efforts of wine-making on a systematic basis. . . . And the list of vines which he brought back with him to California embraces four hundred and ninety-two names, and includes about three hundred varieties. . . . The sons of the late Mr. Haraszthy have followed in his footsteps in the matter of devotion to the culture of the vine. Arpad Haraszthy is a member of the wine-manufacturing firm of Landsberger & Co. of this city. There is probably no man in California at present who is better informed on the subjects of vine-culture and wine-manufacture than he."[35] The *Bulletin* writer sought Arpad's views on the grape varieties then being grown in California. Arpad answered that foreign varieties of grapes were universally preferred by the vineyardists of the Sonoma Valley. "In addition to Malvoisie, the Zinfandel and the Riesling, the Chasselas, the Gutedel and the White Frontignan are being extensively cultivated there."[36]

California winemakers had recently gone through a difficult period. Demand for wines had fallen sharply and prices had plummeted, reducing revenues and sending many vine growers and winemakers into financial distress. The crisis in the wine industry paralleled a similar decline in economic activity all over the country, as business slowed almost to a trickle. Financial institutions, too, were badly hurt. In San Francisco, the powerful Bank of California had been forced to suspend payment of specie and shut its doors in 1875. It was a severe economic recession—possibly even a depression—one of several such events the United States had experienced in its early years and would continue to experience thereafter. Critics said that California winegrowers had planted too many vines—that California's vineyards had expanded at an unsustainable pace and that financial ruin was the inevitable consequence. Arpad was sensitive to issues of supply and demand among wine producers, but he maintained a generally optimistic, or at least hopeful, view of the future. He told the *Bulletin* correspondent that winemaking was "being concentrated in the hands of those who have the capital to invest in such an enterprise, and who have the skill to carry it out intelligently and successfully." He thought that this would bring about a general improvement in the quality of wines and remove the prejudice that had so long prevented California winemakers from finding markets in Eastern states. This new development, coupled with "further experience" in vineyard practices and winemaking techniques would, he said, "bring forth new and precious improvements."[37]

As much as he enjoyed his work in the Landsberger cellars, Arpad was also active outside his workplace. He seems to have been a natural "joiner," eager to congregate with other men who sought fellowship and good cheer. He realized, of course, that cultivating social contacts was good business and would help spread the word of his sparkling wines to the city and the world. Like his father, Arpad was a Mason and took an active role in the affairs of San Francisco's Excelsior Lodge, of which he became Master in the early 1870s; and when he retired from that office his lodge brothers presented him with "a rich and elegant service set of silver" as evidence of their esteem.[38] He was one of the first members of the Bohemian Club, a fraternity of writers, artists, and like-minded men who sought refuge from the din of the city in an environment that exalted the arts and literature. The Bohemians' first clubroom was in rented quarters over a storefront on Sacramento Street near Kearny, but as their membership grew they built an imposing brick edifice that took on the atmosphere of an upper-class cathedral of privilege and prestige. They also acquired a large tract of country property in Sonoma County, where they retreated for regular "High Jinks" among soaring redwoods. At the Bohemian Club's first election of officers in 1872, Arpad was elected treasurer; at its second, he became the vice president.[39]

The Bohemian Club's constitution proclaimed its objects as "the promotion of social and intellectual intercourse between journalists and other writers, artists, actors and musicians, professional or amateur, and such others not included in this list as may by reason of knowledge and appreciation of polite literature, science and the fine arts, be deemed worthy of membership."[40] Arpad became friendly with many interesting and some important people through his Bohemian Club membership. Notable names among the early members included Ambrose Bierce, the acerbic San Francisco journalist, short story writer, and compiler of the famous *Devil's Dictionary*; Daniel O'Connell, feature writer on the San Francisco *Bulletin*, who attained a measure of fame as a gourmet, bon vivant, and poet; Virgil Williams and William Keith, master painters of California landscapes; Samuel Marsden Brookes, foremost painter of still life subjects in nineteenth-century California; James D. Phelan, mayor of San Francisco and United States senator, who devoted much of his personal fortune to artistic philanthropies; Edward Bosqui, French-Canadian printer who helped to establish San Francisco's reputation as one of the centers of fine typography in the United States; and Charles A. Wetmore, a traveling journalist for the *Alta California* who was soon to become a major force in the California wine industry.[41] Robert Louis Stevenson, the Scottish writer who came to California in 1879 to seek the hand in marriage of Mrs. Fanny Van de Grift Osbourne of Oakland, was a frequent visitor to the Bohemian Club during his sojourn in San Francisco, and he remembered the friendship he made with Arpad years after he became the internationally celebrated author of *Treasure Island* and *Doctor Jekyll and Mr. Hyde*.[42] Edward Bosqui left some recollections of the early days of the Bohemian Club, writing: "Arpad Haraszthy, D. P. Belknap and Alexander G. Hawes were among the most efficient and constant in their earliest efforts in laying the foundation of the Club's success. The Bohemians themselves, by their splendid efforts at the monthly 'high jinks,' soon made those entertainments memorable; so much so, indeed, that an invited guest seldom failed to esteem it a privilege to be elected to membership."[43]

Samuel Marsden Brookes featured bottles of Eclipse in some of his most striking still-life arrangements, depicting them alongside the fruits, flowers, and waterfowl that typically starred in his paintings. Brookes's canvases reflected a realistic attention to detail that delighted connoisseurs of fine art in and out of San Francisco.[44] Daniel O'Connell's writings included kind words for Arpad's wines. In his volume titled *The Inner Man,* O'Connell described the wide popularity of Eclipse and noted that it was "highly esteemed in Europe," where the demand for it "is ever increasing."[45] O'Connell had reason to compliment Arpad's sparkling wines, for Arpad had himself helped O'Connell gather much of the material for *The Inner Man*, which was an appreciative history of dining and drinking in San Francisco.[46]

Ambrose Bierce was less charitable in his comments on Arpad's wine than O'Connell, but predictably so, for "Bitter" Bierce was well-known for aiming his acid pen at all manner of San Franciscans, from the wealthy and powerful to the lowly and ignominious. He was a master satirist who excited admiration in some of his readers (he was admittedly a good short story writer) and contempt in others. An oft-repeated Bierce story tells of a newspaper column in which he wrote: "The wine of Arpad Haraszthy has a bouquet all its own. It tickles and titillates the palate. It gurgles as it slips down the alimentary canal. It warms the cockles of the heart, and it burns the sensitive lining of the stomach."[47]

According to the story, Arpad was outraged by these words and instructed his attorney to demand a retraction, which Bierce obligingly provided in his next column: "The wine of Arpad Haraszthy does not have a bouquet all its own. It does not tickle and titillate the palate. It does not gurgle as it slips down the alimentary canal. It does not warm the cockles of the heart, and it does not burn the sensitive lining of the stomach."[48] Of course, Bierce's "retraction" provoked laughter in readers, for it was wickedly witty. But whether the story was strictly factual remains to be proven, for the quick "retraction" was really all that lent any interest to the original statement. Nobody with any sense (including Bierce) really believed that Arpad's wine "burned the sensitive lining of the stomach," and the original statement would have lacked its punch without the pithy "retraction." The earliest source for the Bierce story seems to be a pamphlet published in 1958 by Edmond D. Coblentz, an editor for William Randolph Hearst's *San Francisco Examiner*, the newspaper Bierce was supposed to have been writing for when he aimed his barb at Arpad; and Coblentz received the story, not from actual *Examiner* files, but from Garret McEnerney, attorney for the newspaper.[49] True or not, the story is entertaining enough to justify its frequent reprinting.

George Tisdale Bromley was a little-known San Franciscan who held a contract for sweeping the city's streets when he encountered Arpad Haraszthy. As he wrote years later, Bromley felt "a strong desire" to become a Bohemian Club member but was sure he didn't have sufficient qualifications:

> One very fine morning, as I was going my rounds to satisfy myself that the street cleaning of the previous night had been faithfully performed, I met Mr. Arpad Haraszthy, the wine merchant, and after the usual, familiar greeting said he:
>
> "How would you like to join the Bohemian Club?"
>
> I, somewhat surprised at such a question coming from him, said:
>
> "Why do you ask?"
>
> "Well," said he, "I should be pleased to present your application if agreeable to you."
>
> "Are you a member?" I asked.
>
> He said he was.
>
> "Then," said I, "there is hope for me."
>
> I gave him my application, and in due time received notice of my having been elected to membership, and this was an event that created a new epoch in my life's career. In those early days of the club's career, could those genial gentlemen, its founders, have had the most remote idea of what the future had in store for it, of the position it would occupy among the clubs of the age, I am afraid they would have felt too proud to speak to one another.[50]

Bromley became one of the Bohemian Club's most beloved members—known fondly as "Uncle George"—and a prominent businessman and public official who, from 1884 to 1887, served as the United States Consul in China. From 1888 to 1889, he was president of the Club.[51] During Bromley's years of membership, the Bohemian Club became a bastion of influence and prestige, boasting U.S. presidents, cabinet members, ambassadors, and prominent industrialists, as well as noted artists and writers, among its members. Arpad retained his Bohemian Club membership to the end of his life.[52]

Not surprisingly, Arpad also took an active interest in trade associations that concerned themselves with vine growing and winemaking. He was a member of the California Vine-Growers' and Wine and Brandy Manufacturers' Association, a statewide group that reorganized itself as the State Vinicultural Society (also called the California State

Vinicultural Association) in the 1870s.[53] He was a director of the state society for several years and, beginning in 1878, its president. Although it was a private association, the State Vinicultural Society obtained a state subsidy of two thousand dollars a year to help it with its work.[54] Arpad was a man of strong opinions, and he did not hesitate to use his office as president of the society to express them, often ruffling the feathers of wine men who disagreed. Despite their disagreement, however, his winemaking colleagues respected the experience that lay behind his views. While Arpad was a director of the State Vinicultural Society, he used his influence to initiate a notable printing project that excited strong comments both within and without the society.

It was a persistent complaint of California winemakers that consumers outside the state had little respect for California wines, dismissing them as the primitive products of a half-civilized community only barely removed from savagery.[55] Arpad shared the conviction of other California winemakers—a conviction that was the centerpiece of his own father's viticultural gospel a generation earlier—that California was uniquely suited to become a great wine-growing region; that its climate and soil were more favorable to vineyard cultivation than any other part of the United States—more favorable, even, than those of many of the most admired wine-growing nations of Europe. Like his father, he sought to elevate the reputation of California wines by improving vineyard practices and winemaking techniques and thus producing better wines, but also by championing California wines through print media. Grape varieties that produced outstanding wines in France, Spain, Germany, Italy, and Hungary, often grew more robustly and displayed more beautiful clusters of hanging fruit in California than in their Old World homes. To demonstrate this fact in graphic terms, the State Vinicultural Society commissioned the production of a folio of life-size, color images of different grape varieties grown in California.

The project started about 1875 when Hannah Millard, a New York–born watercolor artist who taught drawing in San Jose, was asked to go into the California vineyards and paint grape clusters and leaves from life. Her work was slow and painstaking, for she had to wait until the vintage season to find ripe clusters of berries hanging beneath canopies of late-summer leaves, and then travel from vineyard to vineyard to locate appropriate examples of different varieties.[56] When Miss Millard completed her paintings, she turned them over to William Harring, an engraver known for his ability to make brilliant color lithographs. Harring's images were called oleographs, and the process by which they were made was called oleography (in later years this process would be better known as chromolithography). Harring carefully etched copies of Miss Millard's paintings onto flat stones—one stone for each of the colors represented in the paintings—after which the etched images were covered with richly tinted inks and pressed onto fine paper. To produce multiple copies of each variety it was necessary to print thousands of images of each painting. When the oleographs were done, they were turned over to Arpad's Bohemian Club friend Edward Bosqui, who gathered them into folios with finely printed text that described each vine and conveyed useful information about the wines it yielded. Miss Millard was paid for her work with Vinicultural Society funds,[57] but Bosqui was so enthused with the project that he financed the printing costs out of his own pocket. Some of the folios were sold individually; some were framed and hung on gallery walls, where their beauty dazzled wine lovers; while others were gathered into a large folio book (with pages measuring approximately fourteen by eighteen inches) titled *Grapes and Grape Vines of California*. The title page of the book, which was printed in late 1877, revealed that the whole project was published under the auspices of the California State Vinicultural Association (as noted earlier, the alternative name of the California State Vinicultural Society).[58]

Ten varieties of grapes were included in the volume: the Mission, the Johannisberg Riesling (spelled "Riessling" in the book), the Rose Chasselas, the White Muscat of Alexandria, the Black Hamburg, the Flame Tokay, the Zinfandel, the Sultana, the Catawba, and the Emperor. The Mission, of course, was the old stand-by of the mission padres, a serviceable but undistinguished grape that had fallen into disfavor among discerning California winemakers. The Catawba was an import from the eastern United States that had at one time been extensively planted in Ohio, where it formed the basis for a Champagne-like wine called Sparkling Catawba. Zinfandel was by 1877 the most extensively planted vine in California for winemaking, a vigorous variety with what the accompanying text called "fine and excellent qualities, which are rarely found in connection with so great productiveness."[59] The author of the text that accompanied the illustrations was not identified. Perhaps it was Charles Wetmore, a gifted writer with a knack for describing grapes; or it may even have been Arpad Haraszthy, acting in his capacity as a director of the sponsoring vinicultural society. If Arpad himself did not write the text, however, he certainly conveyed some of the information it contained to the author, for whoever wrote about the Zinfandel closely followed Arpad's own recollected scenario of how the grape came to California—a scenario that in years to come would excite controversy.[60]

Grapes and Grape Vines of California was a work of inspired art as well as a valuable viticultural treatise. A hundred years after its first publication, it was reissued in two facsimile editions that, while not quite duplicating the original, nonetheless captured some of the qualities that made it so noteworthy in 1877.[61] In a note printed with one of the latter-day facsimiles, the veteran wine journalist Leon D. Adams said that *Grapes and Grape Vines of California* was "the first ampelography (scientific description of grapevines) published in North America, and a valuable contemporary description of many aspects of California viniculture as it existed more than a century ago."[62] And California historian Kevin Starr called it "an undisputed masterpiece."[63] Anyone who has been privileged to turn the pages of one of the original 1877 volumes (now painfully rare) will attest to the beauty of this long-ago contribution to the linked arts of color lithography, typography, and fine winemaking.[64]

Arpad's connection with *Grapes and Grape Vines of California* reflected his personal interest in books and literature. He was a good writer himself, with a healthy list of publications to his credit, and an avid reader. In 1878, San Francisco's Bancroft Company, a pioneer of the city's book-publishing industry, issued an interesting volume about libraries in California. Written by one of the city's pioneer women journalists, Flora Haines Apponyi, *The Libraries of California* assayed private and public collections of books through the state and described some of the most noteworthy. Mrs. Apponyi thought Arpad's collection of more than six hundred volumes was small, but she noted that he "has made it a principle never to buy a book that he could obtain in a public library." Thus his private collection was composed "almost exclusively of rare and out of the way books, with some fine illustrated works and rare works of French authors." At the time Mrs. Apponyi called on Arpad, his books were temporarily in storage, and she could not examine them. Had they been available, however, she thought "they would have afforded some interesting bibliographical notes."[65]

Perhaps Arpad was moving from one home to another at the time that Mrs. Apponyi came to examine his private library. He did move frequently in his early years in San Francisco, going from one house to another, and occasionally taking up residence in hotels. Between 1869 and 1871, he made his home in the Orleans Hotel, and in 1879 in the luxurious Palace Hotel. At other times, he had homes on Brannan and Jackson Streets, Filbert and Pine. The frequency with which he changed addresses suggests that he was a restless man, at least in his home life, and also hints at some of the unhappiness he suffered at home.

Jovita Vallejo Haraszthy was considered the beauty of the Vallejo clan, a large family noted for comely lasses and handsome boys, and Arpad was considered fortunate when he made his match with her in 1863.[66] But Jovita seems to have been unhappy much of the time. She gave birth to a daughter in 1864 and a son in 1867, but for years after the birth of her son her marriage to Arpad was childless. In 1876, there was so much unhappiness in the Haraszthy house in San Francisco that word of it reached General Vallejo in Sonoma, and he came down to the city to counsel with the couple. Arpad seemed anxious to mend his relations with Jovita. He apologized for his "mistakes" and begged Jovita to join him in an effort to "wring from the future many happy days—more than we ever had in the past." But Jovita was stubborn. When she threatened to sue for a legal separation, Arpad asked General Vallejo to "manage" the case, confident that his father-in-law would guard Jovita's "honor" and protect the interests of the Haraszthy family. (Divorce was then considered a terrible scandal, particularly among practicing Catholics like the Vallejos and the Haraszthys.) General Vallejo joined his children, Jovita's brothers and sisters, in urging her to accept Arpad's peace overtures. She eventually agreed to do so, but only grudgingly. Sometime after she and Arpad reconciled, Jovita announced that she was expecting another child. This child, a girl named Jovita, arrived early in 1878, but died shortly after her birth. Jovita was still in bed, convalescing, when, on May 5, 1878, she was seized with a heart attack. The terror-stricken Arpad put a mirror in front of her lips to see if there was any evidence of life. There was none. Jovita Vallejo Haraszthy was thirty-four years old at the time of her death.[67]

The tragedy of Jovita's early death was compounded after her passing by the refusal of San Francisco's Archbishop Joseph S. Alemany to permit her funeral to proceed from St. Mary's Cathedral. General Vallejo was outraged. He wrote to the archbishop and to his vicar-general, asking for explanations, but none was forthcoming. Meanwhile, Jovita's body rested in a temporary vault. After months had passed by, Vallejo learned that the archbishop had been told that Arpad and Jovita were not properly married in a Catholic ceremony. The certificate was produced showing that they had indeed been married by Father Peter Deyaert in the Vallejo home in Sonoma. The archbishop had also heard whispers that Jovita had not performed her Easter duty before her death. Vallejo protested Alemany's "rude and tactless treatment" of him and his family. "God is everywhere," he wrote his son Platon Vallejo, "—in church and out of it. In any case I am greatly aggrieved." When Alemany at last was satisfied that all was right with the Church, he permitted Jovita's funeral to proceed. But it took place, not in the cathedral, but in the chapel of the Catholic cemetery on Lone Mountain, west of San Francisco, with the Rev. Peter J. Kaiser of Mission San Jose, one of Arpad's friends, presiding. The ceremony was held on July 15, 1879, a year and two months after the unhappy Jovita Haraszthy's tragic death.[68]

Arpad was thirty-eight years old when Jovita died. His daughter Agostine was fourteen and his son Carlos ten. After fifteen years of unhappy marriage, he now set out on his own to manage his family and his business. He was the president of the California State Vinicultural Society and a partner in I. Landsberger & Co., winemakers. He was perhaps the most respected winemaker in California, and his views were often sought. He traveled widely over the state, inspecting vineyards, counseling with viticulturists, expressing opinions on issues facing the wine industry. He opposed efforts to reduce tariffs on wine imported into the United States from France, arguing that the government should protect domestic winemakers from foreign competition. He was concerned about a new and potentially devastating vine pest—the phylloxera—that had been discovered in some of California's valleys and threatened serious damage to California vineyards. And his own business seemed to be on the verge of a major reorganization, one that would take it—and his own career—in new directions. The issues that he and his fellow winemakers faced were many and pressing, and they demanded responses. His responses would sometimes be vigorous, sometimes thoughtful, but always definite. And, as he was to demonstrate more than once, they would sometimes be controversial.

Arpad Haraszthy, about 1873. Cabinet card. Bradley & Rulofson, S.F., c. 1873. Charles B. Turrill Collection, The Society of California Pioneers.

Arpad Haraszthy (center) with William H. Whitely and Col. E. McArthur, two of his friends in the "Economical Club," about 1880. Courtesy of Dean Walters.

Arpad Haraszthy, 1880s.
Brian McGinty collection.

Arpad Haraszthy, 1880s.
Brian McGinty collection.

Agoston Haraszthy (1812–1869). Often called "The Father of California Viticulture," Arpad Haraszthy's father, Agoston, was one of the most important pioneers in the history of California wine. He began the production of sparkling wine at his Buena Vista vineyards in Sonoma, sent his son to study Champagne making in France, and installed him as cellar master at Buena Vista upon his return from France in 1862. Agoston died in Nicaragua in 1869. Brian McGinty collection.

Mariano Guadalupe Vallejo (1807–1890). The leading Spanish-Californian of his time, Arpad Haraszthy's father-in-law was also a pioneering vine grower and winemaker. His vineyards in Sonoma were planted in the 1830s and 1840s, produced prize-winning wines in the 1850s and 1860s, and were destroyed by the phylloxera in the 1870s. The Bancroft Library, University of California, Berkeley.

Attila Haraszthy (1835–1888). Arpad Haraszthy's older brother was a pioneering Sonoma Valley vine grower and winemaker who supplied grapes and still wines for the Haraszthy sparkling wine cellars in San Francisco. Brian McGinty collection.

xxxii SAN FRANCISCO DIRECTORY.

E. RAAS, San Francisco.

E. WEILL, Paris.

WEILL & RAAS,

IMPORTERS OF

Beavers, Cloths, Cassimeres,

VESTINGS, ITALIAN CLOTHS, BILLIARD CLOTHS,

Tailors' Trimmings, etc.

616 SACRAMENTO STREET, SAN FRANCISCO,

1 Boulevard Magenta, Paris.

ORDERS FOR EUROPEAN GOODS PROMPTLY AND CAREFULLY FILLED.

I. LANDSBERGER & CO.

423, 425 AND 429 JACKSON STREET,

DEPOT OF SONOMA WINES AND BRANDIES.

MANUFACTORY OF SPARKLING WINE.

Five Premiums Received for the Best

WHITE, RED, PORT & ANGELICA WINES

AND BRANDY,

BY THE STATE AGRICULTURAL SOCIETY OF 1867.

GOLD MEDAL AWARDED FOR THE BEST SPARKLING WINE,

BY THE BOARD OF AGRICULTURE, JUNE 24th, 1868.

Extract of Report of Assembly Committee on the Culture of the Grape Vine of the State of California.

"Your Committee carefully tested some of Mr. LANDSBERGER'S SPARKLING WINE, made from California Wine, of the vintage of 1867, and we pronounce it a superior article of good and pure Wine."

In 1869, I. Landsberger & Co. advertised medal-winning still and sparkling wines and brandy, all produced by Arpad Haraszthy on Jackson Street in San Francisco. *San Francisco Directory*, 1869.

The houses and cellars of the Orleans Hills Vineyard. With his partner Henry Epstein, Arpad Haraszthy developed this property in Yolo County to supply grapes and wines for the Haraszthy sparkling wine cellars in San Francisco. Advertising brochure for Arpad Haraszthy & Co., "Eclipse Champagne." Special Collections Research Center, California State University, Fresno.

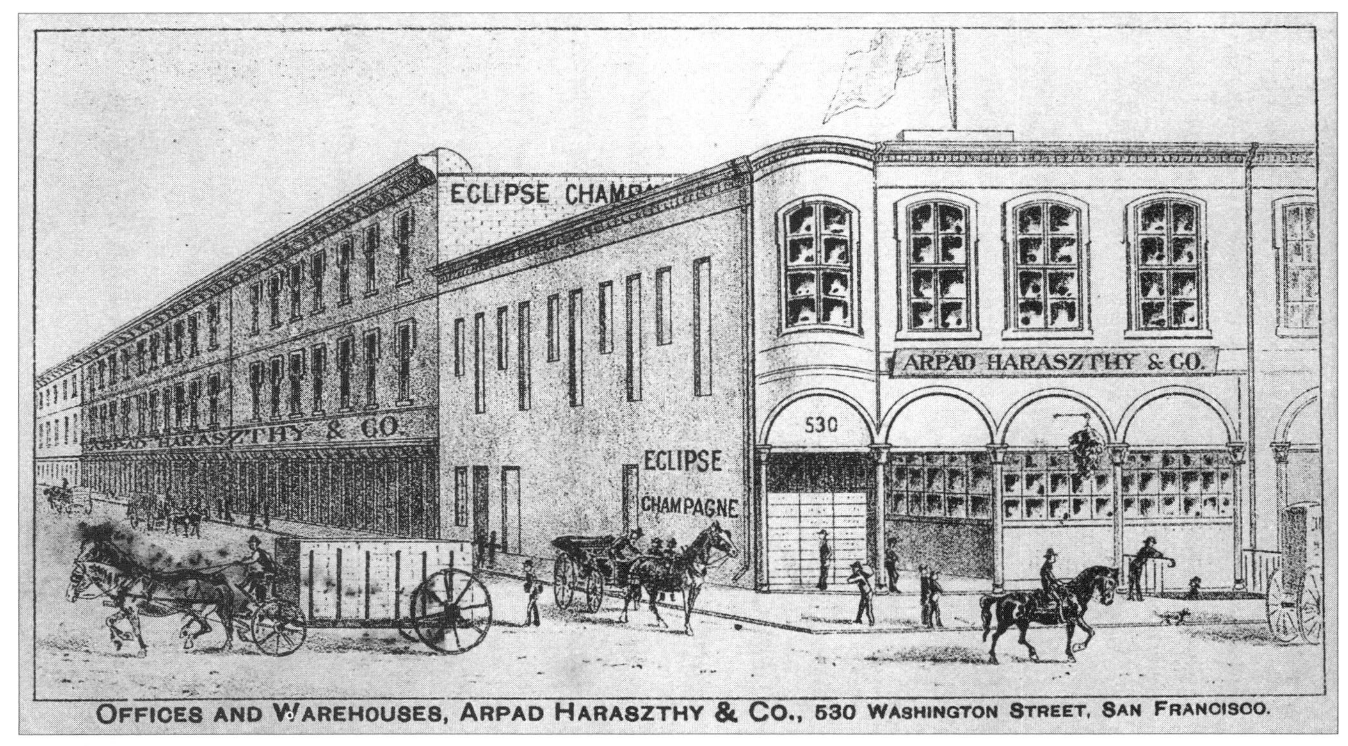

Offices and warehouses of Arpad Haraszthy & Co., 530 Washington Street, San Francisco. Advertising brochure for Arpad Haraszthy & Co., "Eclipse Champagne." Special Collections Research Center, California State University, Fresno.

WINE VAULT, ARPAD HARASZTHY & CO.

Wine vault, Arpad Haraszthy & Co., San Francisco. Advertising brochure for Arpad Haraszthy & Co., "Eclipse Champagne." Special Collections Research Center, California State University, Fresno.

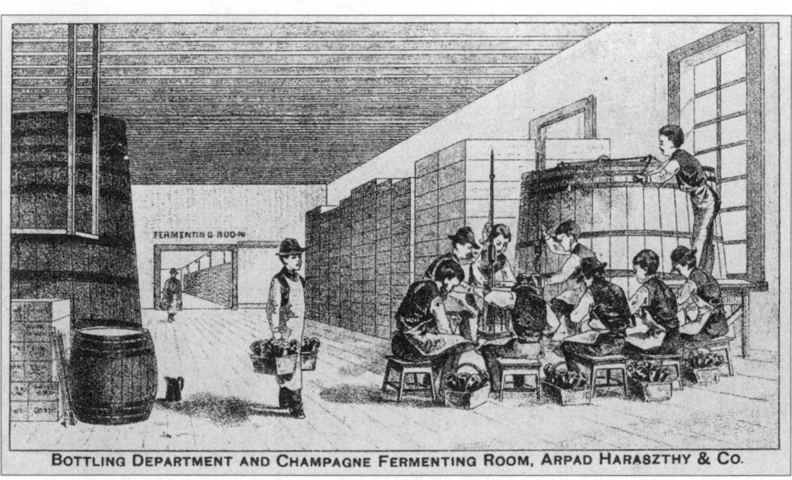
BOTTLING DEPARTMENT AND CHAMPAGNE FERMENTING ROOM, ARPAD HARASZTHY & CO.

Bottling Department and Champagne Fermenting Room, Arpad Haraszthy & Co., San Francisco. Advertising brochure for Arpad Haraszthy & Co., "Eclipse Champagne." Special Collections Research Center, California State University, Fresno.

Champagne cellars and racks, Arpad Haraszthy & Co., San Francisco. Advertising brochure for Arpad Haraszthy & Co., "Eclipse Champagne." Special Collections Research Center, California State University, Fresno.

Disgorging Department, Champagne cellars, Arpad Haraszthy & Co., San Francisco. Advertising brochure for Arpad Haraszthy & Co., "Eclipse Champagne." Special Collections Research Center, California State University, Fresno.

Cellar worker disgorging bottles of Arpad Haraszthy's sparkling wine in San Francisco. Note the wire mask that protects the worker's face from flying glass caused by the explosion of some of the bottles. From *Mexico, California and Arizona* by William Henry Bishop (1888).

ARPAD HARASZTHY & CO.

530 Washington St. **San Francisco, Cal.**

——PRODUCERS OF THE——

Eclipse Champagne & Fine Table Wines

FROM THEIR OWN VINEYARDS.

PARK & TILFORD, Agents, ... 917 Broadway, New York.
F. P. DILLEY & CO., Agents, ... 25 North 10th St., Philadelphia.
C. JEVNE & CO., Agents, ... 110 Madison St., Chicago.
C. JEVNE & CO., Agents, ... St. Paul, Minnesota.

PRODUCED BY FERMENTATION IN THE BOTTLE.

THE ECLIPSE CHAMPAGNE

I produced by fermentation in the bottle, of over two years' duration, and derives its recognized high grade qualities from an experienced blending together of the finest and most delicate wines made in California. Unlike imported Champagnes, it has neither Brandy nor Spirits of any kind added to it. All its qualities are derived from the **Pure Juice** of the grape alone. While it has no superior, and but few equals, **It is the Purest Champagne in the World!**

OUR ORLEANS VINEYARD

Situated in the foothills of Yolo County, consists of 360 acres, planted with 45 varieties of the choicest wines from Champagne, Burgundy, Bordeaux and Rhine Wine Districts. Among its finest productions are Clarets of the Bordeaux type, Burgundy, Orleans Riesling, Hock Wines, and White Wines of the Sauterne type. All of these are guaranteed absolutely pure and bottle ripe.

Deliveries of the above Wines will be made to any part of the U. S. or Europe.

Advertisement for Arpad Haraszthy & Co., with description of "The Eclipse Champagne" and "Our Orleans Vineyard." From Souvenir Program of National Educational Association Reception Concert, San Francisco, July 17, 1888. Brian McGinty collection.

Advertising card for Arpad Haraszthy & Co., Fine Table Wines and Eclipse Champagne. Brian McGinty collection.

Artist's rendering of a bottle of Eclipse Extra Dry and a bottle of Haraszthy Zinfandel, about 1889. Brian McGinty collection.

Not accountable for Leakage Damage or Loss by Transportation. All claims for disagreement with Invoice must be made within Five days after receipt of Goods.

SAN FRANCISCO, May 25 1889

Messrs Re[illegible] Bros
Nevada City

TO — DR.

ESTABLISHED 1863

ARPAD HARASZTHY & CO.

ARPAD HARASZTHY — HENRY EPSTEIN

Producers of Champagne by the only Natural Process; that of Fermentation in the Bottle.

DEALERS IN ALL KINDS OF

CALIFORNIA WINES, BRANDIES AND CHAMPAGNE.

PROPRIETORS OF THE I X L BITTERS.

530 WASHINGTON ST.

TERMS ____ P.O.BOX 1685

5 Imperial Pint 9.00 $45.—

ARPAD HARASZTHY. — HENRY EPSTEIN.

OFFICE OF

ESTABLISHED 1864

ARPAD HARASZTHY & CO.

P. O. BOX 1685. — PRODUCERS OF & DEALERS IN — Proprietors of the ORLEANS VINEYARD.

CALIFORNIA WINES, BRANDIES, CHAMPAGNES, Etc.

San Francisco, Aug 27 1889

Messrs. Rector Brs
Nevada City

Your valued favor of the ____
covering your check for $ 45 ##
is to hand and same duly credited to your account in settlement of Invoice rendered
May 25/89
for which accept our thanks.

Soliciting a continuance of your esteemed patronage, we remain

Yours to command,

Arpad Haraszthy & Co

Invoice and receipt of Arpad Haraszthy & Co., 1889. Special Collections Research Center, California State University, Fresno.

Cover of advertising brochure for Big Tree Exhibit at World's Columbian Exhibition, Chicago, 1893. Brian McGinty collection.

The Big Tree Wine Exhibit at the World's Columbian Exhibition, Chicago, 1893, was mounted in a replica of the base of a giant redwood tree that stood forty feet high and measured twenty-eight feet in diameter. The surface of the tree was covered with strips of redwood bark brought from Mendocino County. Brian McGinty collection.

The hollow base of the Big Tree Joint Wine Exhibit in Chicago was large enough to accommodate displays of Haraszthy wines and those of three of his friendly competitors. Brian McGinty collection.

Views of the Orleans Vineyards of Arpad Haraszthy & Co. near Esperanza (later Esparto) in Yolo County, California. Special Collections Research Center, California State University, Fresno.

Advertisement for Haraszthy Champagne: Brut, Carte Blanche, and Eclipse. Faust Souvenir Program, Tivoli Opera House, San Francisco, California Admission Day, September 9, 1895. Brian McGinty collection.

Now empty, this is one of the last surviving bottles of Arpad Haraszthy's sparkling wine. Dating from the late 1890s, it is preserved in the museum at Lachryma Montis, the Sonoma home of Arpad's father-in-law, General M. G. Vallejo. Photograph by Brian McGinty.

CHAPTER FOUR

ARPAD HARASZTHY & CO.

A little more than a dozen years after it opened its doors in San Francisco, the firm of I. Landsberger & Co. terminated its business and a new firm called Arpad Haraszthy & Co. emerged in its place. Arpad later remembered that the change occurred in 1879 when his partnership with Landsberger was dissolved and its goodwill was sold to a new firm formed by him and Henry Epstein.[1] A legal notice published in the *Alta California* shows that the actual date of the change was July 1, 1880. On that date, Landsberger withdrew from the business and Epstein joined Arpad to form Arpad Haraszthy & Co., "for the purpose of carrying on the Champagne, Wine and Bitter Business, at the old place, 10 and 12 Jones Alley."[2] No other written records of the transaction have survived, and Arpad left no explanation of the reasons for the change. We know only that Landsberger was willing to withdraw from the business he and Arpad had built into the first successful sparkling wine house in San Francisco—in fact, in all of California—and that Epstein was willing to take his place. But Landsberger was not yet ready to retire from business, for after his name came off the sparkling wine cellars he moved to other offices in San Francisco, where he operated a wine brokerage business for many years.[3] Perhaps Epstein made an offer to buy Landsberger's interest that was simply too good to refuse; perhaps Landsberger had grown tired of the sparkling wine business, which was beset from its inception with fierce competition from French Champagne makers and subject to the unpredictable ups and downs of the business cycle. Perhaps some friction between Arpad and Landsberger had prompted their separation (although no evidence of this has survived). All we know for sure is that Landsberger made his exit and Epstein his entrance, and Arpad became the senior partner in the firm that in the years to come was to make his name inseparable from California sparkling wine, and most particularly from Eclipse.

Henry Epstein was a man of affairs before he joined Arpad Haraszthy & Co. in San Francisco. Born in Bohemia about 1838, he had come with his parents to New York while still a boy, then crossed the continent to Nevada, where his family operated a store in the town of Genoa, overlooking the Carson Valley. He farmed some nearby land and in 1864, at the age of twenty-six, was elected to the first Nevada State Legislature as an assemblyman from Douglas County.[4] By 1869, he was in business with Louis Gross and Edward Vollmer in Belmont, a booming silver mining town in Nevada's Nye County.[5] In the same year, he and William Henley were manufacturing "Dr. Henley's Celebrated Wild Grape Root IXL Bitters" on Front Street in San Francisco.[6] Epstein lived in San Francisco with his father Simon Epstein, who was a partner in I. Landsberger & Co., while he pursued his own business interests scattered across California and Nevada.[7] By 1875, Epstein and Gross were conducting a commission merchant business on Front Street under the name of H. Epstein & Co.[8] At the same time, Epstein and H. H. Noble operated a stockbrokerage office on nearby California Street under the name of H. H. Noble & Co.[9] By 1879, Epstein was listed in the San Francisco Directory as a "capitalist," signifying that he was a man of some wealth with an appetite for acquiring new business interests.[10] If Arpad sought a business partner with financial means and know-how, one who might help him expand his sparkling wine business in San Francisco, Henry Epstein would seem to have been a good choice.

Before the new firm was organized, the Landsberger cellars had expanded from their original location on Jackson Street along Jones Alley almost to Washington Street. With Epstein as his partner, Arpad was able to take over a two-story brick building at the northeast corner of Jones Alley and Washington and occupy cellar space in the basement of two adjoining buildings.[11] The company's street address was now 530 Washington, but it occupied nearly the entire block bounded by Montgomery, Jackson, Sansome, and Washington Streets.[12]

Epstein's money and business acumen helped Arpad improve his winemaking facilities. They added a bottling plant on Washington Street, a cooperage on the east side of Montgomery, and a maze of cellars beneath the buildings. An artesian well was sunk in one of the cellars, and a steam engine and boiler installed nearby. Water from the well supplied the boiler and the engine, which in turn powered a stirring and pumping apparatus, and an elevator. A tunnel extended under Jones Alley, connecting the main cellars with five new vaults below the cooperage. Sixty vats rested on the first floor of the building, each containing between one and two thousand gallons of still wines (generically designated as Hocks and Burgundies and Clarets) and even some brandies. Nearby were thirty larger tanks containing as many as three thousand gallons of wine each. On average, six hundred thousand bottles of sparkling wine were stored in various stages of aging. Between seventy and eighty men (mostly Chinese) were employed year around. The brick walls that encircled the premises ensured an even temperature throughout the complex. When a reporter from one of the San Francisco newspapers visited the establishment, he was told that the thermometer did not vary more than ten or twelve degrees all year long. "No ice is required in the summer," the reporter noted, "nor fires in winter. The cellars may truly be termed an underground world."[13]

Another asset that Epstein brought to the new company was the Orleans Vineyard northwest of Sacramento. This stood on a tract of several hundred acres of rolling foothills at the western edge of the Sacramento Valley, where the broad valley floor runs up into the hills that form the eastern boundary of the Napa Valley. The property was in Yolo County, about fifteen miles west of the county seat of Woodland and thirty miles from the state capital at Sacramento. It was also three miles south of Cache Creek, a forty-mile-long stream that begins at the southern end of Clear Lake, flows through the Capay Valley (also called Cache Creek Canyon), and then loses itself on the Sacramento Valley floor. The vineyard was planted in the late 1850s and early 1860s by a German-born hotel proprietor and part-time winemaker in Sacramento named Jacob Knauth. Knauth had come to California from the Rhineland, where his father made wine near the celebrated vineyard of Schloss Johannisberg, and he was, as he said, "born and bred to the [wine] business." In 1853, he imported grape cuttings from Germany, which he planted in Sacramento near Sutter's Fort. The wine he made from these grapes was good enough that, in 1860, it won a diploma from the California State Agricultural Society for the best sample of wine from foreign grapes.[14] In the meantime, Knauth began to explore the country around Sacramento for a vineyard site like those he had known near Johannisberg. In 1858 he settled on a tract of land in the foothills of Yolo County and began to move his vines there from Sacramento.[15] Another Sacramento-based German named Carl Strobel found a neighboring plot of land and also began a vineyard. Knauth planted sixty different varieties of vines on his new property, carefully examining their growth and sampling their grapes to determine which were best suited to the location. Eventually he settled on two varieties, the Orleans (also called Orleaner, Gros Riesling, or Orleans Riesling) and the Johannisberg Riesling (often called White Riesling or just Riesling). In 1869, he and Strobel combined their vineyards to form a joint stock company they called the Orleans Hill Vinicultural Association (OHVA), in honor of the knob-like hills that graced the property and the Orleans vines that climbed their sides.[16]

The Orleans grape was a highly valued white wine variety in the middle of the nineteenth century, and widely planted in the Rhineland. It was particularly favored around Rudesheim, where its wines were nearly as celebrated as those of the world-famous Johannisberg Riesling.[17] When rooted in suitable soil, the Orleans was a vigorous vine with medium-sized clusters and slightly oval berries.[18] Although generally a better bearer than the Johannisberg grape, it was finicky about the ground in which it was planted. Knauth made his first Orleans plantings on low land at the base of the hills, where the soil was stiff and clayey, but the vines did not do well there. When he moved them higher up the slopes, where the soil was loose and chalky, they seemed to do better.[19] Observing that the Orleans grapes matured later than those of the Johannisberg Riesling, Knauth planted Orleans on the southern sides of the hills, where they were more exposed to the sun, and reserved the cooler, northern slopes to the Johannisberg grape.[20] Both varieties seemed to benefit from the arrangement. After the grapes were picked, Knauth transported them by wagon to Woodland, where he loaded them on trains for the trip to Sacramento. There he used a cellar owned by a man named Henry Gerke to make them into wines.

The OHVA had eight hundred and sixty acres of land in 1870, with ninety thousand grapevines that produced eighty thousand gallons of wine a year.[21] In addition to their Orleans and Johannisberg Riesling plantings, Knauth and Strobel planted an undetermined number of Zinfandels on the Orleans Hill property.[22] As was usual during the era, the wines made from these grapes were mainly sold in bulk, although some found their way into bottles. Hard times soon fell on the OHVA, however, and its property was sold at a foreclosure sale in 1876. A man named John Carroll acquired the vineyards, held them for five years, and in 1881 sold the property to Henry Epstein for a reported twenty-eight thousand dollars. The following year, Epstein transferred his interest in the property to himself and Arpad Haraszthy & Co., and Arpad and Epstein changed the name of the vineyard from Orleans Hill to Orleans Vineyard.[23]

By the time Arpad and Epstein acquired their Yolo County property, one of the most devastating pests known to the winemaking world had made its appearance in California vineyards, but its importance had initially been minimized, almost ignored. The phylloxera is a tiny, louse-like insect belonging to the aphid family that fastens itself on the roots of grapevines, where it sucks out the sap and forms disfiguring galls, eventually killing the plants. It was first encountered in France in the 1860s, where it spread quickly through the vineyards, mangling roots, yellowing leaves, and deforming grape clusters. French vineyardists were appalled by its devastation. Their California counterparts were at first smugly self-complacent, half-believing and half-hoping that the French misfortune would open up new markets for California wine. But their hopes began to unravel after the phylloxera was discovered in the Sonoma Valley in the 1870s and, from there, began to spread through neighboring valleys. French scientists took the lead in determining that the phylloxera had originated in the United States east of the Rocky Mountains, where the native vines (*Vitis labrusca, Vitis riparia,* and *Vitis rupestris,* among others) had developed a degree of resistance to its attacks. European vines (*Vitis vinifera*) had no such resistance and quickly fell to its onslaughts. There was an international trade in grapevines during the middle of the nineteenth century, with some native American vines going to Europe, and some to California, and many European vines going to America, thus providing opportunities for the almost invisible insect to travel with them, eventually infesting vineyards on both continents.

Since all of the vines imported into California from Europe (including the old Mission grape) were of the *Vitis vinifera* species, the phylloxera presented an ominous menace. As more and more information about it became public, California vineyardists began to reflect on problems they had earlier encountered in their vineyards—vines that seemed sickly, leaves and roots that shriveled, grape berries that failed to set. In Sonoma, Agoston Haraszthy's successors had condemned him for planting his vines too closely, convinced that the sickly vines they encountered at Buena Vista were due to his poor vineyard practices. But phylloxera was eventually found on the roots of the vines at Buena Vista, and the blame was fastened on the insect (Agoston, of course, had no knowledge of the pest, which was not discovered until after he left California).[24]

Sometime during the 1870s, Jacob Knauth became aware that the phylloxera, or something like it, had become a problem in the Orleans vineyard. When he initially attributed the problem to the soils in which the vines grew, he was partly correct—phylloxera does thrive in heavy, clayey soils but finds it hard to spread through light, friable ground. "I dug up several plants," he wrote in 1880, "and examined their roots with a powerful glass, finding many of the roots formed into something like knots, and giving conclusive proof that something had been doing damage. I also found several small insects, familiar to me, but not being in the habit of looking for lice, I did not find the phylloxera, or, if I did, I failed to recognize them."[25] If Henry Epstein was aware of the phylloxera at Orleans when he acquired the vineyard in 1881, he must have been confident that it could be controlled through good vineyard practices, and Arpad must have shared that confidence when Epstein transferred the property to Arpad Haraszthy & Co.[26]

Arpad was initially attracted to the Orleans property because of its large plantings of Orleans and Zinfandel vines. He had made a trip to the Cache Creek area in 1877 and on his return to San Francisco told a reporter for the *Bulletin* that he was impressed by the many foreign vines he found there. The Orleans Vineyard was "devoted almost exclusively to the Orleans and Zinfandel vines," he said, and the wines made from its grapes were "the best imitation of Rhenish wines" he had ever tasted. He praised the Orleans grape, noting that it had a "superior reputation" in Germany and that its "fruit is sweet, matures early, and ripens uniformly." He was aware, of course, that the soil and climate of the Sacramento Valley differed from those of Germany. In the summertime, the temperatures around the Orleans property can be very hot, but the air cools at night, permitting the grapes to cool. Rainfall averages nearly eighteen inches per year. In the winter the thermometer dips into the low thirties, but frost is not common.[27] There is much more rainfall along the Rhine, and the summer temperatures are cooler in the daytime, but there is a greater danger of frost in the winter. Arpad minimized the differences between the two locations. "A great many viniculturists maintain that climate and soil change the characteristics of the wine produced from the grape," the *Bulletin* reporter noted. "Mr. Haraszthy's experience teaches him the contrary. Notwithstanding the difference between the soil into which these foreign vines have been transplanted and the soil of their nativity, he recognized all the characteristics of the Riesling, the White Zinfandel and the Traminer in the wines of the various vineyards in the Sacramento Valley. He maintains that a difference in climate and soil may modify, but it does not destroy the peculiar qualities characterizing any particular foreign variety of grape."[28]

Arpad was also impressed by the fact that the Orleans vineyard had never been irrigated. As early as 1872, an article in the *Sacramento Daily Union* had reported that the vines at Orleans were "all on the hills and receive no irrigation."[29] Like his father before him, Arpad had long championed vineyards planted on hillsides and mountain slopes, where rain and dew were the only sources of moisture.[30] A few years after he acquired the Orleans property, he told a convention of wine-growers in Fresno: "I am interested in a vineyard in Yolo County, and last year there the thermometer stood at 120 degrees Fahrenheit in the shade; some of the vines are now twenty-eight years old. We have now dug down in some places and found it to be about sixty feet to water. We never had a drop of water on that vineyard except by our regular rainfall and the vines are quite thrifty." He acknowledged that his Orleans vines didn't bear as prolifically as those in Fresno (where the vineyards were irrigated), "but good wine is made from them."[31]

Whatever their reasons for acquiring the Orleans property, Arpad and Henry Epstein were anxious to develop it. Soon after they took over the property, they cleared off the old, shriveled vines at the base of the hills, treated the higher slopes with bluestone and a compost manure, and began to plant new grapes. In their first year, they set out forty acres of Johannisberg Riesling, Zinfandel, Feher Szagos, and Early Madeleine. The following year they added sixty acres of Folle Blanche, Burger, West's White Prolific (also known as French Colombard), and a grape called Black Burgundy.[32]

For the first four years, grapes from Orleans were hauled into Sacramento, where they were made into wine, then transferred to puncheons and transported by rail to the Haraszthy cellars in San Francisco. In 1885, Arpad and Epstein erected a winery on the Orleans property. It was a four-story building that measured 68 by 120 feet, with concrete foundations sunk in a hillside and frame walls above them. The cellars were entirely underground, while three tiers of fermenting and storage rooms rose above them. The winery had a storage capacity of two hundred thousand gallons.[33] Although temperatures outside were often high, the thermometer inside the building varied no more than three degrees from the mean of 55° F. Not far from the winery was a cookhouse, equipped with a large bell for summoning workers to meals, a bunkhouse, and a cottage for the superintendent, a German named Charles Silberstein. East of the winery was a distillery with a capacity for distilling up to five hundred gallons of brandy a day. On a knoll overlooking the winery was a bungalow called "Arpad's Cottage," which the sparkling wine master occupied on his frequent visits to Orleans. The roads that led into and crossed the property were lined with olive, fig, orange, and lemon trees, giving the place the appearance of a great garden.[34]

Twenty to thirty men were employed year around in the vineyards, press house, and cellars at Orleans, and about double that number in the autumn, when the grapes were picked and crushed. Many of the workers were Indians from nearby Lake County. Counting the workers at Orleans and those in San Francisco, Arpad Haraszthy & Co. provided steady employment for about a hundred men.[35]

The distance from Orleans to San Francisco was about seventy-five miles—not too far to bring all of the wines from the vineyard into the San Francisco cellars. The first three miles of the journey, from the vineyard to the railway station in the village of Esperanza, were made in specially built wagons drawn by six-horse teams.[36] From Esperanza (the name was changed in 1890 to Esparto), the puncheons rode the rails to Oakland, then crossed San Francisco Bay by ferry to Washington Street. After Orleans was acquired, Arpad continued to purchase grapes and wine from other growers, but in smaller quantities, for the Yolo County property supplied much of his needs.

Arpad Haraszthy & Co. produced a broad line of still wines, both dry and sweet. In an illustrated advertising brochure prepared in 1882 or 1883, the firm stated that it carried "a full stock of choice old table wines," consisting of Mission and Zinfandel Clarets, Hocks, Riesling, Gutedel, and Chasselas Burgundies, as well as Ports, Sherries (both dry and sweet), Muscats, Angelicas, and "pure grape" brandies. Some of the wines may have been purchased from other winemakers for resale through Arpad's San Francisco cellars. Many, however, were made in the Orleans Vineyard facilities. Haraszthy & Co. also sold altar wines made from grapes grown in the diocesan vineyards of the archbishop of San Francisco. Arpad's brochure included an artist's depiction of the main wine vault in the San Francisco cellars, with large casks labeled Zinfandel, Riesling, Gutedel, Hock, Claret, and Port.[37] Sparkling wines were sold under three brand names: Grand Prix, Sillery Mousseux, and Extra Dry Eclipse,[38] although Eclipse was the mainstay of the sparkling wine line. "The 'Eclipse Champagne' is produced by the blending, in proper proportions, of the wines pressed from six different varieties of imported grapes," his brochure stated, "grown in carefully selected localities in California, and is the only true Champagne as yet produced in this country. . . . The Eclipse will not only be found in every city in the Union, but has also found a market in the Republic of Mexico and on the Continent of Europe, where it is much appreciated by connoisseurs for its purity, lightness of alcoholic strength and exquisite flavor."[39]

Arpad's most critical duty as sparkling wine master of Arpad Haraszthy & Co. was to taste the still wines brought into his cellars, evaluate their flavors and bouquet, measure their sugars and acids, and determine which should be blended together to form cuvées for the firm's sparkling wines. His cuvées changed each year according to the properties of the wine he had to work with and the results he sought to achieve. Some were from the current year, others from previous years' vintages. In 1883, for example, his cuvée was made in four 12,000-gallon vats, each of which contained 6,000 gallons of the White Zinfandel of 1882, 2,100 gallons of the Orleans Riesling of 1882, 1,000 gallons of the Chasselas of 1882, and 1,000 gallons of Burger.[40] (White Zinfandel, of course, is not a white grape, but a white—or slightly pinkish—wine made by fermenting red Zinfandel grapes "off their skins".) In 1884, five vats were used, each containing 4,000 gallons of the White Zinfandel of 1882, 2,000 gallons of the White Zinfandel of 1883, 1,000 gallons of the Burger of 1883, 2,400 gallons of the Orleans Riesling, 2,300 gallons of the Chasselas of 1884, and 300 gallons of Feher Szagos. In 1885, the number of vats increased to six, and the blend for each was 5,000 gallons of the White Zinfandel of 1883, 2,000 gallons of the White Burger of 1884, 1,600 gallons of the White Colombard of 1885, 1,400 gallons of the White Malvoisie of 1884, 500 gallons of the White Verdal of 1884, 500 gallons of the Gray Riesling of 1884, 400 gallons of the Franken Riesling of 1884, and 100 gallons of Folle Blanche.[41] When all the cuvées had been completed, the more routine work of bottling, riddling, disgorging, dosing, aging, labeling, and wrapping followed.

When a reporter for the *San Francisco Merchant* visited Arpad's cellars in 1888, he noted not only the meticulous blending of the still wines but also that all of the sparkling wine was made by the traditional process of fermentation in the bottle. Such was not the case with all of the Haraszthy competitors. "There are bogus champagnes as well as bogus pianos," the *Merchant* reporter noted. "In San Francisco, for instance, are several concerns who pretend to manufacture champagne by pumping gas, generated from vitriol and marble dust, into inferior still wines, and palming the poison off to the unsuspecting many as natural[-]made California sparkling wine." Arpad's firm, the *Merchant* told its readers, was "the only house in the State which was ever able in all these years to turn upon the market continuously first-class champagne, produced only by the natural process, that of fermentation in the bottle. . . . Mr. Haraszthy's ambition being to make wine that is absolutely pure. That he has succeeded is shown by the rapid increase in the sale of his champagne, which aggregated 9,000 cases in 1880 against 14,000 cases in 1886."[42]

Arpad's early experiments with sparkling wine, both in Sonoma and San Francisco, had shown him that it was not easy to produce good sparkling wine on a consistent basis, but he persisted in his efforts to do so, and as the 1870s merged into the 1880s, it seemed that he had been successful—at least to a point. The sales of Arpad Haraszthy & Co. were growing, but so were the expenses, and at the end of each year he could never be sure that the company's books would show a profit. He shared the entrepreneurial spirit of his father; but, like his father, he also believed that it was essential for winemakers to cooperate. It was all very well for a single winemaker to excel his competitors and reap the rewards of larger profits and more recognition, but a single winemaker could do even better if he joined with his colleagues in fighting common foes. Wherever he went, Agoston had taken the lead in organizing trade associations and societies and, when he thought it necessary, calling on the government for help. He was the president of the California State Agricultural Society in the early 1860s and, in that position, had petitioned the state government to assist winemakers.[43] The state legislature's 1861 decision to appoint him as a commissioner to go to Europe and report on "the ways and means best adapted to promote the improvement and growth of the grape vine in California" represented the state's first formal effort to promote the development of a wine industry in California.[44] In the 1870s and 1880s, Arpad fell heir to his father's mantle of industry leadership. From 1878 to 1886, he was president of the California State Vinicultural Society and one of the most vocal advocates of a second state program to promote the growth of grapes and the manufacture of wine in California.[45]

Another strong advocate of a state program was Charles A. Wetmore, who had known Arpad since 1872, when both men became members of the Bohemian Club. Thirty-three years old in 1880, Wetmore was a brilliant young man with an already-varied background as a journalist, real estate investor, lawyer, and wine broker. A graduate of the College of California in Oakland, he had lobbied the state legislature in his senior year for the establishment of the University of California, which in 1869 became the successor to the Oakland school. He had spent a year or so in Peru and, on his return to California, became a reporter for the *Alta California*. Arpad recognized Wetmore's talents and encouraged his interest in vineyards and wine. With Arpad's blessing, Wetmore went to the Paris Exposition of 1878 as the official representative of the State Vinicultural Society.[46] While there, he wrote a series of more than thirty articles on wine, which many thought owed their inspiration to the similar articles Arpad had written for the *California Farmer* in the early 1860s. Wetmore's articles helped convince the general public that California's wine industry was important to the state's economic health. Back in California, he helped Arpad lobby the legislature for a program of state support for vine growing and winemaking.

By the beginning of 1880, the state government seemed ready to extend the help that Arpad and Wetmore were asking for. The State Assembly's Committee on the Culture and Improvement of the Grapevine was chaired by the Honorable James Adams of Sonoma, who convened a meeting on January 30 in the Golden Eagle Hotel in Sacramento. Two witnesses were summoned to give testimony on the needs of the wine industry. Arpad was the first and most outspoken. He delivered a statement and answered questions from committee members. He explained the problems presented by the phylloxera (or as much of them as he then understood), expressed his strong opposition to a proposed treaty with France that would eliminate tariffs on the import of French wines, and extolled the virtues of hillside vineyards ("the best wines," he said, could be produced "on the sides of the mountains where goats would starve"). He suggested the need for state-supported experimental stations, at which vines could be planted and tested, and urged a state-supported program of publications and lectures that would disseminate information about good vineyard practices and winemaking techniques. He thought that a modest state appropriation would enable the Vinicultural Society to rent an office, employ a secretary, and print reports, but argued that the important work of conducting soil analyses should be carried out by a "state institution." "You have a State Institution," he told the committee, "and at a very small cost added to their present facilities, they could take and carry on these analyses, without doubt giving the most true and complete knowledge as to the adaptability of certain grapes to certain soils—that is, at the State University."[47]

The second witness summoned by the committee was Professor Eugene Hilgard of the "state university" that Arpad referred to, the University of California in Berkeley. Born in Germany but raised in Illinois, Hilgard had since 1875 been professor of agriculture at the university, where his primary interest in soil sciences gradually gave way to close study of the problems of growing vines and making wines. He took a keen interest in the phylloxera, although his early suggestions for its eradication were impractical.[48] He agreed with Arpad about the value of hillside plantings and experimental stations, but believed that the university needed its own wine cellar in Berkeley, so experiments could be carried out on fermentation techniques.[49] Both Arpad and Hilgard said that modest state appropriations—about six thousand dollars a year for the first two years—would be adequate for their needs.[50]

On April 15, 1880, the California Legislature passed an "Act for the promotion of the viticultural industries of the State." It created a new entity called the Board of State Viticultural Commissioners, whose members were to be appointed by the governor. The state was divided into seven viticultural districts, each of which was to be represented by its own commissioner. Two commissioners were to be appointed from the state at large. The commissioners were to be "specially qualified by practical experience and study in connection with the industries dependent upon the culture of the grapevine in this State." They were to meet semiannually "to consult and to adopt such measures as may best promote the progress of the viticultural industries of the State." They were also to appoint competent and qualified persons to deliver lectures on viticultural topics and to "devote especial attention to the phylloxera and other diseases of the vine." The Board of Regents of the university was required to provide special instruction "in the arts and sciences pertaining to viticulture, the theory and practice of fermentation, distillation, and rectification," all under the direction of the professor of agriculture. It was also authorized to accept donations of lands suitable for experimental vineyards and stations. To support all of this work, the legislature appropriated seven thousand dollars to cover the first fourteen months of work, with four thousand going to the state board and three thousand to the university.[51]

On April 19, Governor George C. Perkins appointed the nine commissioners called for by the legislature. Isaac De Turk of Santa Rosa was named commissioner for the Sonoma District, Charles Krug of St. Helena for the Napa District, Leonard J. Rose of San Gabriel for the

Los Angeles District, R. B. Blowers of Woodland for the Sacramento District, George West of Stockton for the San Joaquin District, and George C. Blanchard of Placerville for the El Dorado District. The two at large commissioners were J. de Barth Shorb of San Gabriel and Charles Wetmore of San Francisco. Arpad was the commissioner for the San Francisco district. All of the commissioners were dedicated wine men, most with extensive experience in cultivating vineyards and making wine. They held their first meeting in Charles Wetmore's office in San Francisco on May 24 and 25 and elected their officers. Arpad was chosen as president, Krug as treasurer, and Wetmore as vice president. Their secretary was John Bleasdale.[52]

The state board began its work by establishing a Committee on Phylloxera, Vine Pests and Diseases of the Vine. The commissioners traveled to Sonoma, where they personally inspected infested vineyards, then returned to San Francisco to engage Frederick W. Morse, an assistant to Professor Hilgard, as a vineyard inspector. Wetmore himself engaged in intensive study of the phylloxera and how it was being dealt with in France, and prepared publications on the subject. He thought that quarantines would help to prevent the pest's spread from one district to another, but this proved to be unenforceable. Eventually, both he and Hilgard came to the conclusion that grafting fine European grapevines (of the *Vitis vinifera*) onto phylloxera-resistant native American rootstocks was the best solution to the problem. The question was which native rootstocks were the best for this purpose. For a while, they thought that *Vitis californica* was the best choice, mainly because it was native to California, grew all over the state, and was easy to obtain.[53]

In 1881, the legislature increased the duties of the state board, constituting it as a Board of Health and requiring it to determine the utility of known and new remedies against diseases of grapevines and vine pests. It also created the office of chief executive viticultural officer, with powers, subject to the board's approval, to prevent the spread of vine diseases and pests by banning imports of vines into the state and restricting the movement of cuttings or vineyard debris from one part of the state to another. The chief executive viticultural officer was required to visit the different viticultural districts and prepare documents for publication "relating to any and all branches of viticultural industry, including treatises for the instruction of the public."[54] Charles Wetmore was appointed as the first chief executive viticultural officer. He was a good candidate for this position, for he was both scholarly and energetic, and he immediately began an ambitious program of publications on such topics as the chemical treatment of vine pests, the adulteration of wines, and the ampelography of grapevines in Europe and the United States.[55] With a salary of one hundred dollars per month, Wetmore was the only officer of the state board to receive compensation. Arpad and the other commissioners all served without salaries. The legislature increased its appropriations for the work of the state board (including that of the chief executive viticultural officer) to ten thousand dollars for each of the fiscal years of 1881 and 1882.[56]

Arpad seemed to take as much interest in his duties as president of the state board as in his sparkling wine work in San Francisco, or the supervision of his vineyards in Yolo County. He traveled through the state meeting with vine growers, inspecting vineyards, giving speeches, and offering advice and encouragement. He joined enthusiastically in the board's program of holding viticultural conventions in different parts of the state. Vine growers and winemakers gathered for these meetings, exchanged views, listened to speeches, and engaged in discussions. They brought samples of the grapes from their vineyards—wine grapes, table grapes, and raisins—and bottles of their wines for their colleagues to taste. They showed new equipment they were using in their vineyards and wine cellars and discussed new techniques for crushing grapes, grafting vines, and tilling the soil. The convention proceedings were published in the *San Francisco Merchant,* a bi-weekly journal of viticultural news and opinion that was available to readers throughout the state. A few years later, Arpad said that he knew of "nothing so conducive towards the rapid improvement in quality of our viticultural productions as the holding of such Conventions."[57]

Shortly after the California Board of State Viticultural Commissioners was organized, its members recognized the need for a library of books about wine and vineyard culture. They referred the matter to one of their committees and began buying works printed in English on vine growing, diseases of the vine, winemaking, and fermentation. When they felt they had exhausted the supply of English books on those subjects, they acquired French works, then German, Italian, and Spanish. By 1888, Arpad was able to report that the state board's library contained 421 volumes and was "without doubt the most complete viticultural library in America." He said it was a collection that California "may well be proud of" and furnished a catalog of its contents to the governor.[58]

Arpad continued to serve as president of the California State Vinicultural Society while he served as president of the State Board of Viticultural Commissioners. Wetmore was the chief executive viticultural officer of the state board during much of the same period. Both were commissioners, although in 1885 they traded the positions they held on the board, Arpad taking Wetmore's post as commissioner for the state at large and Wetmore assuming Arpad's position as commissioner for the San Francisco district. There had been some criticism that, because Arpad did not own a vineyard in the San Francisco district (the Orleans Vineyard was in the Sacramento district) he could not properly represent its interests. Wetmore had by this time purchased property in Alameda County's Livermore Valley and established a vineyard and winery he called Cresta Blanca. Alameda County was in the San Francisco District, so Wetmore could plausibly claim to represent the winemakers of that district. In and around San Jose, however, vineyardists had little in common with either San Francisco or Livermore, and they grumbled about the change. The *San Jose Herald* argued that the Haraszthy-Wetmore switch meant "nothing" and "was not intended to mean anything." "The only idea for the change was to apparently take away one ground of complaint on the part of the viticulturists of this district—that their representative had no direct interests in the district. Now it may be said that Mr. Wetmore has a vineyard in the district and that Mr. Haraszthy has not, but so far as representing the wishes and needs of the viticulturists of this county,

Mr. Haraszthy was to be preferred to Mr. Wetmore. Indeed, there was nothing to be said against Mr. Haraszthy, except that his interests were naturally with his property in Yolo county, and not here. Otherwise, he has always acted, so far as we know, as an honorable and high-minded gentleman."[59]

Arpad's position as president of the state board raised his professional profile and presented him with new business opportunities. In 1883, he became involved in two enterprises that held the promise of extending his viticultural activities into Southern California. The first came about in the summer of 1883 when Frank Kimball, a large land developer in San Diego County, made a public offer to give a thousand acres of land on the coast north of San Diego to anyone who would plant at least five hundred of those acres with grapevines. Kimball's land was part of a Mexican grant called Rancho Encinitas located on the California Southern Railroad line about twenty-five miles north of San Diego. On August 28 of that year, Kimball informed the *San Diego Union* that Arpad had accepted his offer, and the *Union* editorialized that Arpad's "almost world-wide reputation" as a winemaker was "a sufficient guarantee that in from three to five years we shall have in San Diego county, perhaps the largest winery on the Pacific Coast, and that means the largest in the world."[60] Just four months later, newspapers in San Francisco, Sacramento, and San Diego reported that Arpad was one of the investors in a company organized to hold and manage a large tract of land in the El Cajon Valley about fifteen miles east of San Diego.[61] Arpad had reportedly tasted some Zinfandel claret made from a vineyard in El Cajon owned by a Captain M. Sherman and liked it so much that he wanted to become personally involved in the development of vineyards in El Cajon.[62] In addition to Arpad, investors in the El Cajon Land Company included Charles Wetmore, George West, Joseph Jarvis, and George A. Cowles. Wetmore and West were colleagues of Arpad on the state board and important wine men in their own right, while Jarvis and Cowles were Southern California landowners. At a February 1884, meeting of the directors held in San Diego, Arpad was elected president of the El Cajon Land Company.[63] It seems likely, however, that the other directors were the principal investors. Wetmore had been active as a land developer in and around San Diego before embarking on his career as a viticulturist and certainly would have had some strong ideas as to how the El Cajon property should be developed. But the Encinitas and El Cajon projects did not materialize as Arpad, Wetmore, and the other investors hoped they would. As the late 1880s approached, it became clear to vineyardists all over California that there had been massive overplanting of wine vineyards. The Encinitas project was abandoned, and the El Cajon Valley Land Company was sold to other investors. The El Cajon Valley was developed in the late 1880s and early 1890s as a major raisin-growing center,[64] but it never became the winegrowing Eden that Arpad, Wetmore, West, Jarvis, and Cowles had hoped it might. Arpad must have been disappointed, but not excessively so, for he still had lots of work to do in his sparkling wine cellars in San Francisco, in his Orleans Vineyard in Yolo County, and in his position as president of the state board.

In 1885, the legislature again added to the duties of the California Board of State Viticultural Commissioners, requiring it to provide practical instruction regarding viticulture and winemaking and to distribute information concerning "the rational uses and dangers of abuses of fermented and alcoholic drinks." The chief executive viticultural officer was required to deliver lectures to students at the University of California (but only "on demand of the Board of Regents") and to forward annual statements of "merchantable products of viticulture" produced in California to the State Department in Washington, D.C., with the request that they be forwarded to consular offices throughout the world.[65] The 1885 enactment showed that the lawmakers still sought to support the commercially important state wine industry but that they were also sensitive to the growing temperance movement, which deplored the consumption of alcoholic beverages and sought to restrict (and ultimately prohibit) their use.

Arpad and the state commissioners were dogged advocates of pure wine legislation, seeking to prohibit the production of spurious and adulterated wines, both on the state and the federal levels. Their efforts fell on deaf ears in Washington, but they met with some success in Sacramento in 1887, when the legislature passed "An Act to prohibit the sophistication and adulteration of wine, and to prevent fraud in the manufacture and sale thereof." The law defined pure wine as "the juice of grapes fermented, preserved, or fortified for use as a beverage, or as a medicine," and provided that "pure champagne, or sparkling wine," had to contain "carbonic acid gas [carbon dioxide] or effervescence produced only by natural fermentation." It prohibited the use of materials "intended as substitutes for grapes" and coloring matters "which are not the pure product of grapes during fermentation." Aniline dyes, salicylic acid, glycerin, alum, and other chemicals "recognized as deleterious to the health of consumers, or as injurious to the reputation of wine as pure" were banned, as were water and "weak" wine when used for the purpose of "stretching." Distilled spirits could be added to wine, but only for the purpose of preservation and not for dilution. The law provided that wine containers should have labels prepared by the state controller attesting that they contained "pure California wine."[66] The 1887 law represented a breakthrough in pure wine legislation, but it met with strong opposition from wine merchants, who decried it as unenforceable. On petition of one of the leading merchants of San Francisco, the California State Supreme Court upheld the constitutionality of the law but invalidated the labeling requirement, saying that it was permissive and not mandatory.[67] The ruling effectively crippled the law, for without a mandate requiring that labels be affixed to containers there was no practical way to enforce the law. Recognizing defeat, the state board directed further efforts to secure pure wine legislation to Washington rather than Sacramento.

The National Grape Growers Association was one of the agencies that California winemakers hoped would advance their interests in the federal capital. Wetmore became the president of this organization. Arpad supported its efforts, but only indirectly. In the spring of 1886, Wetmore organized a National Grape Growers Convention in Washington, D.C. Delegates from Virginia, New York, New Jersey, North Carolina, Ohio, Missouri, Texas, and California met in the federal government's Agriculture Building for four days and held receptions in the Washington Masonic Hall. The highlight of the convention was an exhibit of wines, both still and sparkling, from participating states. The *San Francisco Merchant* reported that there were 107 wines from states east of the Rocky Mountains. The Board of State Viticultural Commissioners forwarded 152 California wines, while individual growers in California contributed another 110. "Only one Champagne from our coast was represented," the *Merchant* reported, "and surely with no discredit. People asked for Haraszthy's Eclipse over and over again at the reception after the stock had been exhausted."[68]

Back in San Francisco, Arpad continued to work long hours in his sparkling wine cellars, overseeing his cellar and office staffs, greeting the visitors who regularly came to sample his wines, selecting the base wines for his cuvées, and seeing to it that Eclipse and the other wines he produced were properly promoted. Benjamin Truman paid a visit to the San Francisco cellars not long after the Washington convention of the National Grape Growers. Reporting back to his *New York Times* readers, Truman noted that Arpad's cellars were a model of smooth and efficient organization. His cuvées were bottled and arranged in racks, and a square piece of wood was hung from each rack, marked with a serial number for identification. "580 E., July 29, 8,923," Truman explained, "means that the number of the *cuvée* is 580 E., that it was bottled on July 29, and that there were 8,923 bottles." Truman was informed that between 12 and 20 percent of the bottles in the current cuvée were expected to burst from the pressure inside them—it was one of the inevitable costs of business in a sparkling wine cellar. "After a lapse of from six weeks to three months," Truman wrote, "these bottles are taken from the second floor down into the cellars, where the temperature is much cooler and where there are on an average nearly 1,000,000 bottles in a state of 'cure.'" Truman had hoped to treat his *New York Times* readers to some of the "secrets of champagne making," but found he could not do so in the Haraszthy cellars, for Arpad had assured him: "We have no secrets: the cellars are always open during the daytime, and every portion of the establishment may be visited and operations explained."

Truman's latest visit to the Haraszthy cellars left him as favorably impressed as his first visit ten years earlier, and at the close of his *Times* article he quoted the sparkling wine master: "There is no reason to doubt that in the course of time our wines will not only be known as purer and better than anything imported, but that they will become as famous and command as good prices as those of the most celebrated vineyards of Germany and France."[69]

Like his father before him, Arpad was an optimist. He believed that a great future lay in store for California wine. History would prove him right, of course—but only "in the course of time."

CHAPTER FIVE

THE ZINFANDEL CONNECTION

The story of Arpad Haraszthy would not be complete without some discussion of Zinfandel and the role that he played in its early history. The mysterious grapevine that produces California's most famous—and, some would argue, charismatic—wine arrived in California in the early years of the Gold Rush as a viticultural orphan, an acknowledged member of the *vinifera* family of fine European grapes but unclaimed by any Old World ancestors. Even the name was mysterious, for it was spelled in different ways: sometimes "Zinfindal," sometimes "Zinfardel," "Zinfendel," "Zenfendal," "Zinfenthal," "Zenfenthal," "Zeinfandall," or "Zinthindal"; and in at least one incarnation it bore the totally unrelated name of "Black St. Peters." In the course of a few years, however, it rose from viticultural obscurity to achieve a celebrity unlike that of any other California grape. It was mentioned occasionally in the wine literature of the 1850s, more often during the 1860s, and even more frequently during the 1870s and 1880s, when Arpad was making his career as a winemaker and sparkling wine manufacturer in San Francisco.

At least by the 1870s, Zinfandel had supplanted the Mission grape as the most widely planted wine grape in California, and during that decade and the next it was praised as a superior variety, suitable for the production of fine red table wines and, as Arpad himself proved, worthy of inclusion in sparkling wine cuvées. As praise for Zinfandel mounted, so did its connection with the Haraszthys, both Agoston and Arpad. It was generally accepted by California winemakers that Agoston Haraszthy had brought the vine to the state and that Arpad Haraszthy had publicized his father's connection with it. Zinfandel was Agoston Haraszthy's special gift to California winemaking, most winemakers believed, his viticultural legacy to the state.

If the real history of Zinfandel was as simple as the common discussions of the nineteenth century seemed to make it, it would hold little interest for modern historians. But history teaches us over and over again that truth is stranger than fiction. The facts lead us along unexpected paths, and the discoveries we make as we follow those paths are often surprising. It is no less so with Zinfandel than with any of a myriad of other fascinating stories in the history of California wine.

Zinfandel is a vine of medium vigor, with light-colored, purplish canes, leaves that vary in shape and appearance, and large (or from large to medium) round berries, ranging from dark purple to reddish black in color. Its clusters are compact, large to medium-large, with one or more side bunches that form shoulders. The skins are thin and crack easily. When picked early, the grapes are tart and produce a dry table wine that combines the flavors of strawberries, raspberries, and cherries with a violet-like fragrance. When picked late, the juice is sweeter and suitable to the production of dessert wines. When the grapes are fermented off their skins, they yield a juice that is pink or nearly white in color and can be used to produce a white or rosé wine. In Arpad's time, the pink or white juice was blended with other wines to form the base for sparkling wines.

Depending on when the grapes are harvested, what soil and climate the vines are grown in, how the juice is fermented, and how long the wine is aged, Zinfandel may produce a light table wine of little or no distinction, or a flavorful wine with a fruity bouquet, rich tannins, and at least a claim to be ranked with the best red wines of France. In the 1880s, the German-born vintner and vineyardist George Husmann, who achieved respect as a winemaker in both Missouri and

California, said that he had "yet to see the red wine of any variety" that he would prefer to the "best samples of Zinfandel" produced in California. "A Zinfandel claret from locations best adapted to it," Husmann said, "carefully made, is good enough for anyone."[1] Nearly a hundred years later, the wine journalist Leon D. Adams said that a well-made Zinfandel, aged in wood and in bottle for several years, could develop "a bouquet as fine as the noble Cabernet."[2] Arpad Haraszthy praised Zinfandel on numerous occasions. He planted Zinfandel vines; he made and sold Zinfandel wine; he incorporated Zinfandel into his sparkling wine blends; and he spoke and wrote frequently about the grape. He also made assertions about how the vine got to California that embroiled him in controversy.

Zinfandel achieved recognition in California in the 1870s and 1880s because it was so much better than the old Mission grape. From the time of the padres, the Mission had been used to produce virtually all of California's viticultural products: dry and sweet wines, the liqueur known as Angelica, and the potent brandy the Spanish and Mexican Californians called *aguardiente.* Mission grapes continued to dominate California's vineyards long after the United States took possession of California in 1847, if only because they were so readily available. When it was generally recognized that Zinfandel thrived in California's long, dry summers, that it adapted readily to the well-drained soil of California's hillsides, and that the wines it yielded were richer and more flavorful than the Mission wines, it was recognized as a good wine grape that was well suited to the needs of California's growing wine industry.

If Arpad Haraszthy's recollections are a good guide, his familiarity with Zinfandel dated back to the early 1850s, when he was living with his mother in New Jersey in close proximity to the Hungarian exile, General Lázár Mészáros. Arpad was then a student in New York, but his mother became a good friend of Mészáros during the time she was living in Plainfield, New Jersey, about twenty-five miles from New York and just two miles from Mészáros's home in the village of Scotch Plains, New Jersey. Mészáros was an avid horticulturist who had a nursery at his Scotch Plains home that included grapevines and fruit trees, and he maintained a lively correspondence with Arpad's father in far-off California. Arpad later recalled that his father received Zinfandel cuttings with the help of Mészáros and others.[3]

Arpad returned to California in 1857 for two months, at a time when his father was transferring cuttings from the grapevines he had planted at Crystal Springs south of San Francisco to his new vineyard property in Sonoma. (Vines, of course, can be moved from place to place through cuttings, rooted or unrooted.) Arpad arrived just in time to help his brothers and his father with the move. He later recalled that Zinfandel was among the vines that his father moved from Crystal Springs to Sonoma.[4]

In the late summer of 1862, Arpad returned permanently to California from his studies in the Champagne country of France, at which time his father installed him as cellar master of his Buena Vista estate in Sonoma. Arpad recalled that one of his first tasks at Buena Vista was to make two casks of claret wine using Zinfandel grapes.[5]

Arpad began to achieve a viticultural identity separate from his father's in the mid-1860s, when he left Buena Vista and formed his partnership with Pietro Giovanari in Sonoma. In one season (probably 1864 or 1865), he and Giovanari made thirty thousand gallons of wine, using Mission grapes, Zinfandel, Black St. Peters (a grape that Arpad later identified as identical to Zinfandel), and a grape called Chagres Heneling.[6] In 1869, San Francisco's *Daily Alta* revealed that Zinfandel had become an important component of Arpad's sparkling wine cuvées when it quoted his statement that Zinfandel was the best grape for sparkling wine.[7] In Arpad's long essay on California winemaking published in the *Overland Monthly* in 1871 and 1872, he described Zinfandel as one of the "fine varieties of grapes" then grown in California.[8] And when, in 1877, he made a trip to the Cache Creek area of Yolo County (where he and Henry Epstein would later own and operate the Orleans Vineyard), the *San Francisco Bulletin* quoted his assertion that Zinfandel was "the best claret grape grown in California." The *Bulletin* also quoted his statement at that time that his father had imported Zinfandel "as early as 1852."[9] Arpad expanded on the latter statement when his friend Edward Bosqui published the lavishly illustrated *Grapes and Grape Vines of California,* also in 1877. In the "Zinfandel" article in that pioneer ampelography (if not written by Arpad himself, at least based on statements he made to the author), Arpad made his most definitive printed statement yet about how Zinfandel came to California. He said then that his father had imported the vine into California "between the years 1853 and 1854, . . . from Hungary, his native land, where he had known it to be held in great esteem as a wine grape," and that he had planted the vine "in his vineyard at Crystal Springs, San Mateo County, and afterwards in Sonoma."[10]

Arpad's assertions about his father's connections with Zinfandel were readily accepted by other prominent winemakers in California. Arpad was, after all, one of the most respected wine men in the state and, after 1880, president of the Board of State Viticultural Commissioners. Leonard J. Rose was the most prominent winemaker in Southern California at the time, the proprietor of the Sunny Slope Vineyard in the San Gabriel Valley and a member of the state board for the Los Angeles district. In a report to the California State Agricultural Society written in 1879, Rose asserted that Zinfandel was "introduced by the late Colonel Haraszthy from Hungary."[11] In 1880, Charles Wetmore published a scholarly report on the *Propagation of the Vine in California* in which he alluded in glowing terms to Agoston Haraszthy's contributions to the development of California wine. "Among his greatest successes," Wetmore said, "was the culture of the Zinfandel, a Hungarian grape heretofore little known in viniculture, but which is destined to lift California wine cellars into successful rivalry with the boasted cellars of Bordeaux."[12]

Not long after Rose and Wetmore published their comments, Arpad prepared a four-page, handwritten manuscript in which he elaborated on his father's connections with Zinfandel. This manuscript was completed no later than 1882, for the information it contains was set out virtually verbatim in John S. Hittell's *Commerce and Industries of the Pacific Coast,* published by Hubert Howe Bancroft in that year. In fact, the manuscript may well have been prepared for Hittell's and Bancroft's use. Bancroft was California's premier bookseller and publisher and was already establishing his reputation as the foremost historian of California and the western states. Hittell was an esteemed California journalist, a longtime writer for the *Alta California* and other publications, and a prolific producer of guidebooks and statistical studies that chronicled the progress of California agriculture and industry. Hittell had been personally acquainted with Agoston Haraszthy during his time in California; and he had some practical experience with California winemaking, for he was one of the group of fifty Germans who formed the famous Anaheim winemaking cooperative near Los Angeles in 1857.[13] In the manuscript, Arpad wrote that, after his father took possession of his property at Crystal Springs in 1853 he "laid out immediately an orchard, a very considerable patch of strawberries, and a large number of vines that were all imported by him from the East and from Europe through the late General L. Mésázros, former Minister of War of Hungary. These vines and trees, which were all in the ground before March 1854, were destined for nursery purposes, and yielded him considerable profit from their sale to all parts of the state. It was in this importation of vines that the first Zinfandel grape vine reached California, and ever after it was his pride to recommend its plantation as the best grape for red wine or claret." Hittell adopted Arpad's statements regarding Zinfandel and reprinted them in his book.[14]

Arpad's statements identifying Mészáros as the source of his father's Zinfandels were published about the time that Arpad and Henry Epstein were beginning the expansion of their newly acquired vineyards and cellars in Yolo County. The fact that the previous owners of the Orleans Vineyard had planted many Zinfandel vines on the property was, as previously noted, one of the factors that attracted Arpad to the Yolo County property, and the vines that he and Epstein added to the property in the early 1880s included many Zinfandels.[15] At the same time, Arpad Haraszthy & Co. was advertising Arpad's Zinfandel clarets for sale in San Francisco.[16] It was evident that Arpad was no mere theorist about Zinfandel, but a vine grower and winemaker who spoke from practical experience.

In 1885, however, a dissenting voice was heard. Robert A. Thompson was a Sonoma County newspaper editor and county clerk who was researching a history of the California wine industry (the history was never published).[17] He had exchanged some letters with William Boggs, a Napa Valley farmer who had lived in Sonoma more than twenty years earlier and was eager to share his recollections of the vineyards and grapes grown there in the 1850s and 1860s. Thompson's research had persuaded him that the correct spelling of Zinfandel was "Zinfindal," and he spelled it that way when he wrote a long letter on the vine to the editor of San Francisco's *Evening Bulletin* on April 23, 1885 (in fact, "Zinfandel" had been accepted as the standard spelling some years earlier). Thompson claimed that the purpose of his letter was to correct misapprehensions about how Zinfandel was introduced into California. Relying in part on Boggs's recollections and in part on published reports of the Massachusetts Horticultural Society from the late 1840s and early 1850s, Thompson announced his startling conclusion that Agoston Haraszthy was not the first man to import Zinfandel into California; that man was Frederick W. Macondray, a long-dead shipmaster and businessman who had come from his native Massachusetts to California in the early years of the Gold Rush. Thompson's assertion was made quite emphatically, although with a touch of embarrassment. "I would not deny Col. Haraszthy of a moiety of the credit due him as the first among the grape culturists and winemakers of this State," Thompson wrote in his *Bulletin* letter. "I would rather add to, than lessen the honor due him, but an investigation of the subject forces the conclusion that the glory of having introduced the grape into the State is not among the laurels he won in the field of grape culture." "To whom is the honor of its introduction due?" Thompson asked. "To an enterprising pioneer merchant of San Francisco, the late Captain F. W. Macondray, who raised the first Zinfindal vine grown in California, in a grapery at his residence on the corner of Stockton and Washington Streets, San Francisco."[18]

Since Macondray had died in 1863, Thompson had to rely on other sources for his research information. Macondray had never been a vineyardist or winemaker, so it was not easy to get information about him from winemakers living in California in 1885. He had, however, been a horticulturalist, and he had grown table grapes in hothouses in Boston, in San Francisco, and at his country home in San Mateo County (which by curious coincidence was only two or three miles away from Agoston Haraszthy's Crystal Springs vineyard). Published reports revealed that Macondray had been an active member of the Massachusetts Horticultural Society before he moved to California in 1849 and that he had been president of the California State Agricultural Society in 1854 (Agoston was president of the same society in 1862). Again delving into printed sources, Thompson learned that the "Zinfindal" had been known in Massachusetts, Connecticut, and even New York since the early 1830s, where it produced highly admired table grapes. In 1848 it was exhibited in Boston as part of a collection of about thirty table grapes that were later used to produce wine in California. This collection of grapes was stocked in hothouses and nurseries in New England and New York, where it was available for sale to the public. Thompson concluded from this evidence that Macondray "must have known" of Zinfandel in Boston, and he "must have" heard its merits discussed.[19]

All of this information was revealing, but it did not prove how the grape got to California. Had it come there from Boston, from Connecticut or New York, from somewhere in Europe? (It was clear to all that the vine couldn't have originated in New England, for it was a *vinifera* vine and belonged to the great European family of *viniferas*. It was definitely not a native American vine.) Beyond surmise, was there any evidence that Macondray had in fact brought it to California?

To explain how his "Zinfindal" got to California, Thompson relied on the recollections of William Boggs. Boggs was an interesting man, though never prominent in the California wine industry. He was one of the sons of Lilburn W. Boggs, who had been governor of Missouri from 1836 to 1840 and, in 1846, had led a wagon party over the plains to Sonoma, where he was warmly greeted by Arpad's future father-in-law, General Vallejo. It was a cold and dreary winter when the Boggs party reached Sonoma, and Vallejo generously gave them the use of his huge adobe ranch house at Petaluma, just over the mountain ridge west of Sonoma. When the weather cleared, the Boggs family decided to set down roots in Sonoma, where the former governor became the *alcalde* and William Boggs became a farmer and part-time viticulturist. When Agoston Haraszthy came to Sonoma in 1856, William Boggs was his neighbor and often accompanied him as he tramped over the hills and valley floor attempting to plot out the boundaries of his Buena Vista property. Boggs was also associated with Agoston in the Sonoma and Napa Horticultural Society, a joint stock company which Agoston organized in 1859 to establish a European-style botanic garden in Sonoma where seeds and plants could be gathered into a central location, planted, nurtured, observed, and then made available for sale to would-be growers. With characteristic energy, Agoston issued the initial call for the new society, and after it was organized, he became its president. General Vallejo was a vice president, and William Boggs was a member of the board of directors.[20] A botanic garden occupying ten acres of land on the banks of the Sonoma Creek was established, with Agoston serving as superintendent of the garden as well as president of the society.[21]

In his letter to Thompson, Boggs claimed that Agoston had agreed to buy a large supply of vine cuttings from a prominent Napa Valley farmer named J. W. Osborn, that Zinfandel was among them, and that the cuttings were brought to Agoston's botanic garden in Sonoma. Boggs said that he had personally transported Osborn's cuttings from Napa to Sonoma in two large wagons. Boggs claimed that nobody in Sonoma recognized the Zinfandel cuttings when he brought them to the botanic garden, but that General Vallejo's winemaker, a Frenchman named Victor Fauré, later recognized them as the Black St. Peters, a vine that grew in Vallejo's vineyards, and proclaimed them "the best claret wine grape he had seen." Boggs informed Thompson that Osborn had told him that he obtained the cuttings from Frederick Macondray. If Thompson was at all worried about the hearsay nature of Boggs's information (Macondray had spoken to Osborn who had spoken to Boggs who had written to Thompson), the letter he sent to the *Bulletin* in 1885 did not hint at it. His proof that Macondray had first brought Zinfandel to California was, he declared, "simple," and he took pleasure in doing Macondray "justice."[22]

There were, however, some problems with Thompson's assertions. First, Thompson argued that, since there was good evidence that Zinfandel was in California before Agoston made his famous vine-gathering trip to Europe in 1861 (the well-publicized trip during which he had gathered several hundred thousand European cuttings that he brought back to California in 1862), Agoston could not have been the first to bring the vine to California. "It is utterly irreconcilable to attribute the introduction of this valuable fruit to that importation," Thompson wrote.[23] Thompson thought that the Horticultural Society in Sonoma got their vine cuttings from J. W. Osborn in Napa in 1861, the year before Agoston's famous vine importation. Boggs was not clear on when the vines were obtained, stating on one occasion that he brought them back from Napa "about the year 1857 or 1858" and on another that he obtained them the year before Agoston's European trip (which would have been 1860).[24] But Boggs shared Thompson's conviction that, if Zinfandels were in California before Agoston's famous importation of 1862, Agoston could not have been the first importer. Both Thompson and Boggs were apparently unaware that Agoston had imported European vines to California years before 1862. Arpad, however, was not unaware of that fact.

Second, Boggs erroneously believed that there had been no European vines in the Sonoma Valley before he brought Osborn's cuttings there. Writing to Napa Valley's *St. Helena Star* on June 8, 1885, Boggs stated that "there were no foreign vines introduced into Sonoma" before Osborn's cuttings arrived there, "except one or two varieties of the table grape, Black Hamburg, and another grape that resembled the Zinfandel, called by General Vallejo's gardener, a well-known nurseryman by the name of Ryan—now deceased—Black St. Peter [*sic*], a few white Sweet Waters and the Catawba and Isabella." Boggs continued by stating that he was present when Agoston transferred his "fruit trees" from Crystal Springs to Sonoma and, contrary to Arpad's assertions, "there was no foreign vines [*sic*] shipped to Sonoma with these fruit trees."[25]

Contemporary written evidence proves Boggs wrong and Arpad right on this important point.

Agoston's own description of Buena Vista, published in the California State Agricultural Society's report for 1858, shows that he had 14,000 foreign vines in bearing that year and another 12,000 vines rooted in the nursery, and that these vines represented 165 different varieties.[26] A visiting committee of the State Agricultural Society inspected the vines and noted in the same report: "The Committee have seen the foreign varieties, being one and one-half years old. They were planted in February, one thousand eight hundred and fifty-seven—bearing splendid grapes from one pound up to thirty pounds to a single vine."[27] Advertisements that Agoston placed in agricultural journals at the end of 1858 reveal that he had a large number of European vines in Sonoma in 1858 and that he was offering them for sale. According to the advertisements, he had 30,000 cuttings (representing the same 165 varieties) and 2,000 rooted vines.[28]

Boggs's published letters included more misinformation about Zinfandel. Recalling that he had taken the cuttings obtained from Osborn to Victor Fauré, Boggs quoted Fauré as saying that the cuttings were of a "French grape, one of the best for red wine or claret."[29] If Fauré had in fact said that, he either misidentified the grape or was badly informed about its origins, for there has never been any credible information that Zinfandel (or even the grape called Black St. Peters, which was Zinfandel masquerading under a different name) was a French grape. Arpad, of course, had asserted that it was Hungarian. Boggs also claimed that, when Agoston first encountered Zinfandel grapes, he said "there was no grape grown in Hungary that was so sour as the Zinfandel or that contained so much tartaric acid as the Zinfandel." Agoston is supposed to have told Boggs that "Hungary was only celebrated for one special class of wine, notably the Tokay, which takes its name from the valley of the same name in that country."[30] Agoston, of course, knew full well that his native country produced fine wines of many different types, red and white, sweet and dry, table and dessert. Although Tokay is one of Hungary's most celebrated wines, it is far from the only one.

Shortly after Robert Thompson's letter appeared in the *Bulletin*, a vine grower in the Napa Valley who chose to identify himself only as "L. L. P." wrote his own letter to the San Francisco newspaper in which he set out some random observations about the history of wine in the Napa Valley. He recalled that Charles Krug had made "the first wine that we have any account of being made in Napa County" in 1859, after Krug came over to Napa from Sonoma, where he had been working in Agoston Haraszthy's vineyards. He recalled that Krug's first wine had been made with a cider press (the press was in fact borrowed from Agoston in Sonoma). L. L. P. also recalled that the first wine in Napa had been made from Mission grapes, and that credit for bringing the first foreign vines to California was generally given to Agoston Haraszthy. "But it does not belong to him," L. L. P. declared, "for as early as 1858 or 1859 a man by the name of Stock had a vineyard of foreign grapes at San Jose, the original cuttings for which were sent him by his father from Germany." Since 1858 or 1859 was earlier than 1862, the year of Agoston Haraszthy's most famous European vine importation, L. L. P. was sure that Agoston could not have been Zinfandel's first importer.[31]

Arpad chose to reply to Robert Thompson, William Boggs, and "L. L. P." by writing his own letter to the *Bulletin* on May 11, 1885. He called Thompson's reasoning "one-sided," said that Boggs's effort to credit Macondray with the honor of having introduced Zinfandel into California was "strained," and accused L. L. P. of having made "erroneous statements" about the first importations of foreign vines into California. He pointed out that his father had imported foreign grapes into California long before his famous importation of 1862, and that "he had cuttings of foreign grapevines in the ground . . . from five to six years before he left our State for Europe [in 1861]." Arpad cited the printed reports of the California State Agricultural Society that proved his allegations. "Your correspondent L. L. P. informs your readers," Arpad wrote the *Bulletin,* "that Col. Haraszthy's first importations of foreign grapes occurred in 1862, in which assertion he makes a most serious misstatement. Whereas in fact the importation of 1862 was my father's very *last effort* in that direction. His first importations went back into the early fifties."[32]

Arpad was clearly disturbed by Thompson's, Boggs's, and L. L. P.'s allegations, and he wanted to put them to rest. To that end, he included the following in his *Bulletin* letter:

> On behalf of the late Col. Haraszthy, my father, let me say, that up to within two weeks ago, though the members of his family, as well as hosts of his friends knew him to have imported vines from Europe and other countries in the early days of our State's existence, none of us or his friends claimed that he was the pioneer importer of such vines; within the last fifteen days, however, facts beyond dispute have come to my knowledge which by their positive dates and surrounding circumstances point Col. Haraszthy out as the *very first* importer of foreign grapevines into California since its American occupancy. I now claim for him whatever honor that fact may convey, and I also claim that he, too, first imported our present Zinfandel into California from Hungary.[33]

Arpad promised that within "a very short time" he would point out Robert Thompson's errors and refresh William Boggs's recollections about matters that Boggs had apparently forgotten. He said that he wrote, not to "rob anyone of the just merit of his achievements," but to preserve the reputation of a man "whose memory should at least not be maligned by those whom his public spirited labors have benefited."[34]

Boggs replied to Arpad in another letter dated May 26. He thought that Arpad's reply had been "over acusative [*sic*]" and that much of what he wrote stemmed from "his own vivid imagination." He admitted that Agoston may have had some foreign vines at Crystal Springs but insisted that Zinfandel was not among them, and he repeated (inconsistently) his assertion that the first foreign vines in Sonoma had been obtained from Osborn in Napa. Arpad's assertion that Zinfandel was a Hungarian grape was, he said, "mistaken," as he had it "from the very best authority" (Fauré) that the grape was French. "I desire to say further that much credit is due to Col. Haraszthy for the encouragement and promotion of the viticultural interest of this State, and I wish to accord to him all the honor due him that the interest he took at the commencement of making wine in Sonoma in early days amounted to enthusiasm, and too much praise cannot be accorded to him. I would be as far from detracting from his fame as a pioneer viticulturalist as Mr. Arpad Haraszthy himself would."[35]

The open dispute between Thompson, Boggs, and Arpad provoked additional comments about the origins of Zinfandel in California. In San Jose, an old viticulturist named Antoine Delmas now claimed that he had imported about a hundred foreign vines from Paris as early as 1852. Included with this importation, he said, was the Black St. Peters (which had since been proven to be identical to Zinfandel). Delmas said that he had exhibited Black St. Peters grapes at a fair in San Jose in 1854, and that he had sent cuttings to General Vallejo in Sonoma. Reporting Delmas's claim, the *San Jose Herald* said that, if these vines had not been imported into California earlier than 1852, "to Antoine Delmas of Santa Clara county belongs the honor of their introduction."[36]

At the time that the Zinfandel controversy erupted in the newspapers, Arpad was characteristically busy. In March of 1885, he and several San Francisco businessmen had visited the area around the Carquinez Strait northeast of San Francisco, seeking an appropriate location for a large warehouse and distribution center, where wines from all over Northern California could be stored pending their sale. The idea was to permit wines to be properly aged while their producers awaited favorable market conditions for their sale. Newspapers reported that the distribution center, if built, would cost in the neighborhood of two million dollars.[37] In the same month, Arpad conferred with some men in Santa Clara County about building a large wine cellar in the vicinity of Los Gatos.[38] A little later it was reported that he was planning to build one of the largest distilleries in the country and was purchasing large quantities of wine to supply it.[39]

At the end of May, he went to San Jose to participate in the viticultural convention of the San Francisco District. As was usual at such events, a host of subjects was discussed: fermentation techniques, the selection of proper varieties of grapes for different soils, the nomenclature of grapes, and the dangers that overproduction posed for the state's wine markets. Samples of wines were tasted and commented on. Arpad was asked about the Zinfandel controversy. He repeated his statement that his father had brought the Zinfandel to California from Hungary in 1852. He acknowledged that Zinfandel and Black St. Peters were the same variety. He said he had spoken to Frederick Macondray's gardener, and the gardener had said that Macondray never grew Zinfandel in his San Francisco grapery (Macondray's San Francisco grapery had been located just three and a half blocks from Arpad's sparkling wine cellars on Washington Street). Arpad said that Zinfandel was first in bearing in California at Crystal Springs in 1856, where his father had it, but it did not ripen there. His father had the grape as early as 1852, and it "probably came from a vineyard belonging to his mother in Hungary."[40]

He then left the subject of Zinfandel and spoke to the real subjects the winemakers had come to the convention to discuss. He spoke about the virtues of wine blending, which enabled vintners to combine different wines to bring out the best qualities of each, and he expressed his opinion that "the Burgundy grapes" (Pinot Noir and Chardonnay) were best suited to the area around San Jose.[41] The *San Jose Herald* reported that the afternoon session of the first day of the convention opened with "a good attendance." Charles Wetmore, commissioner of the Board of State Viticultural Commissioners for the San Francisco District, "made a speech devoted principally to praise of Mr. Haraszthy. . . . Mr. Haraszthy acknowledged the compliments paid by Mr. Wetmore and praised the latter in turn." The speeches over, the convention delegates returned to the business of discussing grapes and tasting wines.[42]

Arpad waited three years before again addressing the Zinfandel question, this time doing so in a multiauthor book titled *Sonoma County and Russian River Valley Illustrated,* published in San Francisco in 1888. He contributed a chapter on "Early Viticulture in Sonoma," in which he traced the history of winemaking in Sonoma County from the days when General Vallejo first came into the Sonoma Valley in the early 1830s. He set down many of his own recollections of early winemaking around the town of Sonoma, and constructed a list of more than fifty men who were involved in viticulture or winemaking there before 1863. His most interesting (and most pointed) remarks were devoted to Zinfandel. He repeated his earlier statements that when his father transported vines from Crystal Springs to Sonoma in 1857, Zinfandel was among them. He said that Agoston had imported Zinfandel from Hungary in February 1852. "This importation consisted of six varieties and were all rooted cuttings as shown by an original memoranda [*sic*] made on the 23rd of March, 1852, after they had been temporarily planted. With this lot of rooted cuttings there is also mentioned 150 plain cuttings, all of which were of Hungarian origin. These were permanently planted on the hillsides of Crystal Springs with other importations, but when the bearing age came, it was found that the grapes did not ripen on account of the fog, winds, and extreme cold. and though nearly thirty acres had been cleared and planted in 1855 the project was recognized as a failure and abandoned. It may have been that more than any other cause that turned Colonel Haraszthy's attention to the beautiful, mild, genial, weather-protected valley of Sonoma." Arpad described in detail his father's plantings of foreign grapes at Sonoma and referred to the printed reports that documented them. He also recited the names of many prominent men who had come to Sonoma to grow vines and make wines in Agoston's wake. "The tidal wave of inquiry swept over the quiet valley of Sonoma," Arpad wrote, "strangers came and went, and the express and U.S. Mail were laden with letters, papers, pamphlets, and cuttings and vines. . . . It was from here the Zinfandel was distributed to the four parts of the state prior to 1859, so likewise the Feher Szagos, the Black Prince, the Flame Tokay, the Black Morocco, the Muscat of Alexandria, the Emperor, the Seedless Sultana, the Chasselas, the Riesling, the Gutedel, the Traminer and numerous others."[43] The *Alta California* reviewed *Sonoma County and Russian River Valley Illustrated* on July 9, 1888, stating that its history was "full, complete and concise." The newspaper commented particularly on Arpad's "special historical article on early vine planting in Sonoma," noting that it included "a number of facts never before published, having been obtained from an old but recently discovered diary of his late father, Colonel Agoston Haraszthy."[44] Arpad's reference to the 23rd of March 1852, was clearly one of the "facts never before published" obtained from the diary.

With Arpad's words on "Early Viticulture in Sonoma," the Zinfandel question seemed to be closed—or nearly so.[45] For all that the available evidence shows, neither Robert Thompson nor William Boggs ever again addressed the California origins of the vine, at least not in public statements.[46] George Husmann spoke for many of his winemaking colleagues when, in the same year that Arpad published his "Early Viticulture in Sonoma," he published his own book on winemaking in California. Titled *Grape Culture and Wine-Making in California,* Husmann's volume was published in San Francisco to a good reception. Addressing many practical questions of interest to California winemakers, the Missouri-California wine veteran discussed Zinfandel. "The true origin and dissemination of this important variety is not yet clear," Husmann wrote. "It seems clear, however, that Col. Agoston Haraszthy brought it from Hungary, and that it was also received from some New York nurseries about the same time. . . . Be that as it may, it has proven of great value in developing the wine industry of the State, as it proved that a really good red wine, resembling choice claret, could be made in this State, a fact which was very much doubted before its introduction."[47] Discussing the important early pioneers of California winemaking, Husmann mentioned Charles Kohler, who had started his wine business in Los Angeles in 1855, as well as Jacob Gundlach, Emil Dresel, Charles Krug, and other pioneers of the Sonoma and Napa Valleys. "Nor should Col. Agoston Haraszthy and his son Arpad, be forgotten," Husmann wrote. "Col. Haraszthy imported perhaps the largest collection of foreign vines into the State at an early day, and the industry is greatly indebted to his efforts."[48]

The year after Husmann's book appeared, the San Francisco–based *Pacific Rural Press,* an influential journal of agricultural news and instruction, published an article titled "The Grape in California," in which it stated: "The viticultural industry in this State is largely indebted to Colonel Agoston Haraszthy, whose experience in the vineyards of the old country made him recognize in California a natural home for the vine. In 1851 he planted a vineyard at San Diego, and in 1853 another at Crystal Springs. He went to his native country, Hungary, for different varieties which he successfully cultivated. One of these was the Zinfandel from which claret bearing its name is manufactured." The journal acknowledged Agoston's efforts, "nobly aided by others in the industry," which resulted in the state commission that sent him to Europe in 1861 and resulted in his massive importation of European grapevines in 1862. "Those being choice selections from the most noted vineyards in the Old World," the *Rural Press* continued, "at one stride placed California on the high road to achieving a name for her wines, dried grapes and raisins second to no other country in the world."[49]

CHAPTER SIX

HIS CUP OF CONTENT

For more than a century, the question of Agoston Haraszthy's connections to Zinfandel seemed closed. In countless articles, chapters, and books, Agoston was credited as the man who first brought the grape to California. In the early 1970s, however, a wine writer named Charles L. Sullivan challenged the accepted version of the Zinfandel story. Sullivan was a history teacher who became interested in the history of California wine and read prodigiously on the subject, particularly in newspapers and journals of the nineteenth century. He had developed a special interest in Agoston Haraszthy and Zinfandel. When one of his winemaker friends asked him if there weren't "any historical mysteries about California wine" that needed solving, Sullivan replied: "Well, there is always Zinfandel. The Haraszthy story—I just don't buy it any more."[1] Encouraged to pursue "the Haraszthy story," Sullivan began to produce a series of articles—and eventually a full-length book—that fleshed out his theories about how Zinfandel came to California.

Sullivan had read the letters Robert Thompson and William Boggs wrote on the subject in 1885. His own research confirmed Thompson's assertion that Zinfandel had been grown in hothouses and nurseries in New England and New York in the 1830s and 1840s, and he used this information to formulate a theory under which Zinfandel could have been brought to California from New England or New York by any of various nurserymen or vineyardists in the 1850s.[2] Frederick Macondray, who Thompson had identified as the first Zinfandel importer, was high on Sullivan's list of the men who might have been the first to bring the vine to the state, but he was not the only one.[3] Sullivan even admitted the possibility that Agoston Haraszthy might have brought the grape to California from New England or New York, but he was hostile to Arpad's statements that his father had brought it from Hungary.[4] Arpad's claims about Zinfandel were, in Sullivan's judgment, "false."[5] Worse than that, Sullivan charged that they were made for pecuniary gain. He said that Arpad's business was in dire straits when he made those claims and that he made up the Zinfandel story to try to save it. Sullivan's construct seemed at first startling, then interesting—and eventually appealing. History loves to raise up heroes—but it also loves to knock them down. Agoston Haraszthy had become the hero of nineteenth-century California wine history. He had occupied his pedestal for a century, and it was now time to knock him down.

Sullivan argued that Arpad's story about Zinfandel was a "myth." It was "almost pure hokum," Sullivan said, no better than "historical nonsense."[6] Arpad "concocted" the story that his father brought the Zinfandel to California and promoted him as the father of the California wine industry "to keep his own business afloat."[7] Arpad was a "troubled man," Sullivan said. He suffered from "desperate personal problems," and his "family life was in shambles."[8] (The reference here was to the fact that Jovita had at one time asked Arpad for a legal separation. But Jovita had relented, accepted Arpad back, and given birth to a child before her own early, tragic death.)

Sullivan praised Thompson's letter about Macondray, saying that it "virtually demolished the Haraszthy claim."[9] He condemned Arpad's own statements about Zinfandel because they were made "fully thirty years after the fact" and were based on "questionable evidence."[10] He pointed out that Arpad had left California with his mother in 1852 and did not come back to live in the state until after his Champagne studies were completed in 1862, so he couldn't have had any personal knowledge of the vines his father imported in the 1850s.[11]

Sullivan's arguments were repeated frequently and with vehemence, and they gained some support, notably from Thomas Pinney, a professor of English in Southern California and the author of *A History of Wine in America: From the Beginnings to Prohibition*, published in 1989. Pinney adopted Sullivan's arguments almost entirely. He wrote that Agoston Haraszthy "was not the 'father' of California winegrowing; he was not the man who first brought superior varieties of grapes to California; and he was not the man who introduced the Zinfandel" into the state.[12]

There were some problems with Sullivan's arguments, however, and with Pinney's endorsement of them. They were based in part on solid historical research (Sullivan's investigations into the history of Zinfandel in New England and New York were extensive), but they suggested an eagerness to condemn Arpad and commend his detractors. It was apparent from the written statements of Robert Thompson and William Boggs that those men were unaware of Agoston Haraszthy's vine importations of the early 1850s, yet Sullivan (and Pinney) did not seem to be troubled by that fact. Both Thompson and Boggs argued that, since Zinfandel was in California before Agoston's well-publicized importation of 1862, he couldn't have introduced it into the state—it was there before 1862. But Arpad had never claimed that his father brought Zinfandel to California in 1862 (the grape's name does not appear in catalogs of the 1862 importation). In fact, he repeatedly asserted that his father made importations *before 1862*.[13] Boggs, surprisingly, argued that there were no, or practically no, foreign vines in the Sonoma Valley before he brought Osborn's cuttings there sometime some time before 1860. But printed reports of the California State Agricultural Society proved that Agoston had extensive stocks of foreign vines in Sonoma in 1858.[14] Boggs seemed to be confused, ignorant of some of the basic facts upon which his argument was based. Thompson shared his confusion, but Sullivan and Pinney seemed to attach no importance to this obvious weakness in their arguments.

Sullivan wrote that Arpad's assertions about how and when Zinfandel was brought to California were unsupported by any "shred of evidence."[15] But he failed to point out any evidence showing how or when Frederick Macondray (or any other California vineyardist or nurseryman of the 1850s) brought the vine to California. Yes, some horticulturists and vineyardists had the grape in California in the 1850s and 1860s, and there were men (like Thompson and Boggs) who in later years said that Macondray had it, too. Antoine Delmas claimed that he had the same grape (although his was called Black St. Peters). But there was no contemporary witness that Macondray or Delmas or anybody else had been the first to bring the grape into California. There was no firsthand testimony as to how these men got the grape, from whom, or when. If Arpad's statements about his father's importation of Zinfandel were suspect because they were made "fully thirty years after the fact," why weren't William Boggs's statements about how and when Zinfandel cuttings were brought to Sonoma suspect because they were made twenty-six years after the fact? And why wasn't Antoine Delmas's recollection that he had imported the Black St. Peters from France in 1852 suspect because it was asserted thirty-three years after the fact?

Much of Sullivan's argument depended on his contention that, because Arpad was out of California during the 1850s, he was not qualified to speak about the vines his father imported in that decade. But Arpad was in New Jersey in 1853 and 1854 when his father was in contact with Lázár Mészáros, and Arpad was in a good position to know what vines Mészáros was sending his father from New Jersey. Further, Arpad was actually present in California for two months in the spring of 1857 and in a good position to know what vines his father was then moving (or had just moved) from Crystal Springs to Sonoma.

The role that Lázár Mészáros played in this drama is curious. Like the Haraszthys, Mészáros was a Hungarian noble with an avid interest in agriculture and horticulture. He had made his career in Hungary as a professional soldier, advancing to the rank of brigadier general before he was called upon to serve as minister of war in the anti-Hapsburg government headed by Lajos Kossuth in 1848. When fighting erupted between the Austrians and the Hungarians, he took personal command of an army of Hungarian freedom fighters. But the Russian czar decided to aid the royal rulers of Hungary by sending in an army that crushed Mészáros's forces and sent him and other officers of the Kossuth government into exile.[16] Now a fugitive from his native land, Mészáros made his way through Europe, Turkey, the Isle of Jersey, and England, eventually coming to the United States. He was in New York City in September 1853, where he published an open letter in the *New York Times* proclaiming his intention of becoming an American citizen and expressing the hope that in his new home he could "regain with the spade and pruning knife" what he had "lost with arms."[17] Later in the same year, he moved about twenty-five miles west of New York to the village of Scotch Plains, New Jersey, where he settled on a farm.[18]

Mészáros probably knew the Haraszthys before he arrived in New Jersey, for he was born and grew up in the Bácska, the southern region of Hungary in which Agoston and Eleonora lived before they came to the United States. A letter he wrote from the Isle of Jersey in 1852 referred to Agoston as "the founder of Harasztopolis" (the town of Haraszthy in Wisconsin);[19] and, after he arrived in New Jersey, he wrote letters back home in which he referred to Eleonora as a "Dedinszky girl" from the Bácska and to Agoston as "Guszti" Haraszthy.[20] Mészáros and Agoston were nobles from the same Hungarian county, so they had very likely attended meetings of the county nobles together. And it is almost certain that Mészáros had read Agoston's Hungarian-language book about the United States, for nearly all Hungarian visitors to the United States in the late 1840s and early 1850s consulted that volume before embarking on their first visit to the "blessed country."

On his Scotch Plains farm, Mészáros assembled a nursery of fruit trees, shrubs, and grapevines with which he hoped to support himself. By the spring of 1854, he informed a friend back in Hungary that he had more than 150 different kinds of trees, more than 2,000 saplings, and 500 rooted vine cuttings.[21] Some of the vines may have been sent to him from nurseries in England, France, or even Hungary (although he was persona non grata with the government then in power in Hungary, he could still maintain a lively correspondence with friends and family in the old kingdom). Others were almost certainly obtained from nurseries in and around New York, in some of which there was a good supply of *vinifera* grapevines (including Zinfandel). One of the most notable nurseries in the vicinity of New York was the Linnaean Botanic Garden operated by the family of William Robert Prince in Flushing, Long Island, about ten miles east of New York City. With a very large collection of trees, shrubs, vines, and other botanic specimens, the Linnaean Botanic Garden was known for its extensive collections of grapevines, including a vine that William Robert Prince intriguingly identified as the "Black Zinfardel [*sic*] of *Hungary*."[22] This vine was possibly, but not certainly, the vine that later became famous in California as Zinfandel. Interestingly, after Mészáros left his New Jersey farm in 1855, he took up residence in Flushing, where he lived until he left for England in 1858.[23]

The proximity of Eleonora's Plainfield home to Mészáros's nursery at Scotch Plains, coupled with the memories that both shared of their homeland, made Mészáros and Eleonora Haraszthy good friends. She was the first to console him when, in March 1854, a fire destroyed his home in Scotch Plains and he lost plants stored in his basement and dug into the nearby ground. But he quickly rebuilt his nursery and, by April of the same year, noted in a letter that he had six varieties of pears, forty of apples, twelve of peaches, and twenty-four different varieties of grapes.[24] On July 4, 1854, Eleonora was one of the guests when Mészáros gave a party in Scotch Plains for his sister, who was returning to Europe after a short visit in New Jersey.[25] All the while, Agoston and Mészáros exchanged letters and vine shipments. After Mészáros moved to Long Island, Agoston invited him to join him in California, but the general could not make the long trip on his own and Agoston was unable to pay his way.[26] And so the two Hungarians had to content themselves with a friendship maintained only by mail. Arpad, now in his mid-teens, was an intelligent young man with more than a passing interest in horticulture and viticulture. He was naturally interested in the correspondence between the exiled general and his father in far-off California, and he stored memories of what he heard and saw. In 1882, Arpad told John S. Hittell that his father had set out a large number of vines at Crystal Springs that were "obtained for him from the Eastern States and Europe through General L. Mészáros, one of his Hungarian compatriots."

Arpad said that Zinfandel was among these vines. Arpad did not specify when Mészáros obtained the vines for Agoston. He could have done this while he was in New Jersey, while he was living in Flushing in close proximity to Prince's Linnaean Botanic Garden, or even before he arrived in the United States. (Of course, the Hungarian general's interest in horticulture did not start in New Jersey—it went all the way back to his native land.) And Agoston could have received the vines at almost any time—when he was living in San Diego and cultivating a vineyard there; when he established his nursery in San Francisco in 1852; when he set out his large vineyards at Crystal Springs in 1853; or even after he moved his operations to Sonoma in 1856 and 1857. If Mészáros sent the vines to Agoston while he was in New Jersey or on Long Island, Arpad would have been nearby, ready to confer with Mészáros about what he was sending to Agoston. If Mészáros sent the vines before he came to the United States (perhaps while he was living on the Isle of Jersey in the English Channel), Arpad could have discussed the earlier shipments and learned from Mészáros what they were and when they were made.[27] In any case, Arpad was in a good position to know what vines Mészáros sent his father. And when he came back to California for two months in 1857, he was in a good position to see what vines his father had planted in his vineyards.

Sullivan's failure to deal with Lázár Mészáros or Arpad's 1857 return to California weakened his contention that Arpad had no basis for making statements about his father's vine importations of the 1850s. And Sullivan's contention that Arpad manufactured stories about his father's importation of Zinfandel to save his foundering wine business is unpersuasive. Arpad Haraszthy & Co. was not foundering in 1882, 1885, 1887, or 1888, when Arpad spoke out on the question. Thompson's and Boggs's public letters on the Zinfandel question came in 1885, at a time when Arpad and Henry Epstein were expanding their vineyards and cellars at Orleans Vineyard in Yolo County and Eclipse was the toast of San Francisco—and much of the rest of the country. And Sullivan's suggestion that Agoston's marital troubles made him lie about Zinfandel is gratuitous. There is no valid basis for ascribing Arpad's efforts to exalt his father's achievements and memory to venal motives or marital troubles. Filial affection was an ample motive for Arpad to do and say what he did about Zinfandel.

But this does not mean that all of Arpad's statements about Zinfandel were correct, or that he did not sometimes misremember facts, misidentify dates, or exaggerate some of his claims about his father's importations. He was, by nature, an emotional man, given to occasional bursts of anger. He was a proud man (perhaps excessively so)—proud of his own achievements as a California winemaker, proud of his record as the first successful manufacturer of sparkling wine in California, proud of his service as president of the California Board of State Viticultural Commissioners, and proud of his father's winemaking legacy. For more than thirty years, Arpad spoke and wrote about California wine, providing information that was thoughtful and practical. Some of his statements were imprecise, even muddled. Some were clearly wrong.

It is impossible to judge the accuracy of all of Arpad's statements about his father's importations of Zinfandel. His statements that Agoston brought Zinfandel to California along with other foreign vines before 1862 are entirely plausible. There is abundant evidence that Agoston brought foreign grapes to California in the 1850s, possibly even in the early 1850s, and that he experimented with different varieties, constantly seeking the best grapes for making good wine. There is also good evidence that he had foreign vines at Sonoma in 1858. Those vines must have been brought there from his Crystal Springs vineyards, as Arpad said they were, for they were in full bearing in 1858 and could not have been set out as cuttings only a year earlier. Arpad was in a good position to know what vines Lázár Mészáros had sent his father and what vines were growing at Crystal Springs, so his statements that there were Zinfandels at Crystal Springs as early as 1853 or 1854 are similarly plausible, even credible. Mészáros could at least have obtained Zinfandel cuttings from nurseries that kept them in stock in New York during the time he lived in New Jersey and on Long Island. For much of that time, he lived only a few miles from one of those nurseries, Prince's Linnaean Botanic Garden.

Arpad's assertions that his father received Zinfandel cuttings directly from Hungary are more problematic, but they should not be dismissed out of hand. Mészáros undoubtedly had horticultural contacts in Hungary, and he could have arranged for shipments of Zinfandel (and other vines) to have been made from Hungary to California during the time he lived in New Jersey, or even before. Arpad's statements that Zinfandel "probably" grew in one of his mother's vineyards in Hungary, and that his father had known it as a good grape for claret in Hungary, are more dubious. There is no evidence for this contention other than Arpad's own statements on the subject, and they are not very persuasive. Arpad was only two years old when he left Hungary, and he could not have had any personal recollection of the vines that grew in his parents' vineyards there. One of his parents could, of course, have told him that they knew (or even grew) Zinfandel in Hungary, but there is no evidence that either of them did so. This statement smacks of exaggeration and suggests that, when Arpad made these claims, he was engaging in speculation. In any case, these claims were not vital to the central point he was making—that his father brought Zinfandel to California in the 1850s.

Arpad's statements that his father had Zinfandel in California as early as 1852 were frequently repeated. Sullivan scoffed at them, pointing out that Agoston was a member of the California State Legislature in 1852 and thus in no position to import grapevines.[28] But the legislature of 1852 met in the city of Vallejo, only twenty-five miles north of San Francisco. Agoston was active during the legislative session, but not so active that he could not take time out for personal business. On March 25 and 27, 1852, in the midst of the legislative session, he purchased 210 acres of land in San Francisco, where he immediately began to develop a nursery and a horticultural garden in which he grew grapevines.[29]

In 1885, Arpad wrote that "facts beyond dispute" had just come to his knowledge proving that his father was "the *very first* importer of foreign grapevines into California since its American occupancy."[30] And in 1888, he referred to "an original memoranda [*sic*] made on the 23rd of March, 1852," showing that six rooted varieties of foreign grapes and

"150 plain cuttings," all of "Hungarian origin" were planted at his father's San Francisco property.[31] A set of ten leaves of handwritten notes taken from Agoston Haraszthy's account book is preserved in the Bancroft Library along with "The Haraszthy Family," a forty-eight page typescript dated July 1, 1886, that was either prepared by Arpad himself or with his help. These notes are not in Arpad Haraszthy's handwriting—someone else clearly made them. They are mostly a jumble of dates and dollar amounts, some referring to the year 1848 (when Agoston Haraszthy lived in Wisconsin), some to 1849, 1850, and 1851 (when he was in San Diego), others to 1852 and 1853 (when he was developing his San Francisco property), and yet others to 1853 and 1854 (when he was planting his vineyards at Crystal Springs). The notes were haphazardly set down, and not in any particular order. They are not in themselves very illuminating, but they strongly point toward the source of the "facts beyond dispute" and the "original memoranda" that Arpad referred to in the 1880s. That source was almost certainly a contemporary account, day book, or diary kept by Agoston Haraszthy showing his activities at various dates. The original book was very probably in Arpad's custody (or that of another member of his family) in the 1880s. It has since disappeared, as have the great bulk of Arpad's personal papers, many of which were destroyed in the great San Francisco fire of 1906. Only the ten pages of jumbled notes preserved in the Bancroft Library remain to hint at what the original book contained. But a more specific reference, recorded in print, still remains to be considered. It is a short article printed in the *Pacific Wine and Spirit Review* for January 5, 1892, under the heading of "Introduction of the Zinfandel." It reads:

> Recently while looking over the records and daybook of the late Colonel Haraszthy, with Mr. Arpad Haraszthy, the writer saw an entry which read: "March 23, 1852, to 5 choice European vines, $23." These were the original Zinfandels, and from them came all vines of that sort now in the State.[32]

This entry almost certainly referred to the same book that Arpad mentioned in the 1880s. Arpad must have had possession of the book when he spoke and wrote about "facts beyond dispute" and "original memoranda" and later showed it to the writer for the *Pacific Wine and Spirit Review.* It tends to corroborate some of what Arpad asserted, but it hardly constitutes the "facts beyond dispute" he said it did (the statement that "these were the original Zinfandels, and from them came all vines of that sort now in the State" was a later editorial comment and not part of the original entry). It shows at the least that Agoston had some European vines by the time he purchased his San Francisco property in early 1852. Some were rooted and some were not. But did they include Zinfandel? The entry does not tell us.

As part of his argument that Arpad's statements about Zinfandel were deliberately dishonest, Sullivan suggested that Arpad might have destroyed (or concealed) an 1864 issue of the *California Wine, Wool, and Stock Journal,* which contained an early article Arpad wrote on red wine grapes, fearing that his critics would discover that it did not mention Zinfandel. "It would have been embarrassing indeed," Sullivan wrote, "in the midst of a public fight over the Zinfandel's introduction, to have a famous son making claims that flew in the face of what he had written a quarter-century earlier."[33] Sullivan asserted that Arpad's early article on red wine grapes was "missing from both known collections of this rare periodical" (one is in the Bancroft Library and the other at the Boston Public Library). Sullivan wrote that it was "particularly curious that it should be missing from the Bancroft collection because it was made up of Arpad's personal copies."[34] But my own careful examination of the Bancroft Library's copies of the *California Wine, Wool, and Stock Journal* belies Sullivan's charge. First, the Bancroft Library collection does not appear to be made up of Arpad's "personal copies." If ownership of those copies can be determined, they probably belonged to General Vallejo, for some of the issues bear an inscription in Arpad's own handwriting to Vallejo. Once Arpad had presented these issues to his father-in-law, he no longer had custody of them and could not have destroyed or concealed one of them in the 1880s. One issue has the name "A. Haraszthy" written in pencil in the upper right-hand corner of the cover, but this is not in Arpad's very characteristic handwriting, nor does it appear to be in the handwriting of Agoston. It may have been written by Arpad's brother Attila, who was Vallejo's closest neighbor in Sonoma, as well as his son-in-law. If this issue belonged to Attila, Arpad again would not have had custody of it in the 1880s. Second, Arpad's article on red wine grapes is not missing from either the Bancroft or the Boston Library collection. It appears in the March 1864 issue, which is part of both collections.[35] Sullivan's suggestion that Arpad deliberately concealed or destroyed evidence that might contradict his claims about Zinfandel is unfounded.

But a close reading of the March 1864 article that Sullivan claims Arpad concealed may be more revealing. In that article, Arpad discussed six red grape varieties: Cabernet Sauvignon, Franc Pineau (now better known as Pinot Noir), Merlot, Malbeck (now spelled Malbec), Chiraz (Syrah), and Verdot (Petit Verdot). There is no mention of Zinfandel anywhere in the article. If, as Arpad claimed in the manuscript he prepared for the use of John S. Hittell and Hubert Howe Bancroft around 1882, his father recognized the virtues of Zinfandel as early as 1854 and "ever after it was his pride to recommend its plantation as the best grape for red wine or claret,"[36] why didn't Arpad mention the vine in his 1864 article? If his father was indeed recommending that other vine growers plant Zinfandel as early as 1854, why didn't Arpad praise the vine in 1864? Why didn't he tell his readers that Zinfandel was "the best grape for red wine or claret"? His failure to do so is striking.

There are possible explanations, of course. Perhaps Agoston did in fact recognize that Zinfandel was a superior wine grape, as Arpad asserted, but not until sometime after 1864. Perhaps he did in fact have Zinfandel vines at Crystal Springs in the early 1850s but did not recommend that other winegrowers plant them until a few years later. Arpad may have innocently misremembered the chronology of his father's involvement with the vine. He may have known that his father was a champion of Zinfandel but mistakenly dated his enthusiasm for it. Throughout his career as a California winemaker, Agoston was an outspoken champion of foreign grape varieties. He urged winegrowers to seek out the best varieties for winemaking and urged experimentation to determine which grapes were best suited to particular soils and climates, and it strains credulity to argue that others recognized the virtues of Zinfandel while he did not.[37] But Arpad's 1864 article is also susceptible to a more unfavorable explanation. Perhaps he did not mention Zinfandel in that article because his father was not then touting the virtues of the vine—or because his father did not even have it growing in his vineyards. The latter explanation seems implausible. Even accepting Robert Thompson's and William Boggs's questionable assertion that Agoston got his first Zinfandel vines from J. W. Osborn sometime before 1861 (Thompson and Boggs were unclear on the year), by 1864 he surely would have had some of the vines growing among the hundreds of acres of his Buena Vista vineyards in Sonoma. The most likely explanation seems to be that he had the vine by 1864 but wasn't recommending it to other vine growers, even at that late date.

An interesting footnote to the Zinfandel mystery centers on the European origins of the vine. Even if it is proven that the first Zinfandels brought to California came from hothouses or nurseries in New England or New York, the question remains: How did the vines get to New England and New York from their Old World home? Sullivan speculated on that question, backing up reasonable guesses with research into botanical collections and nurseries in central Europe in the middle of the nineteenth century. In the nineteenth century, and for most of the twentieth century, viticulturists and ampelographers searched in vain for any vine that resembled Zinfandel, or that bore its name, in any of the famous winemaking countries of Europe. For all that anybody could determine, Zinfandel was unique to California—it was "California's own vine." But everybody knew that it must have had a European home somewhere, for it was a *vinifera*. Arpad frequently asserted that Zinfandel was a Hungarian grape, and he occasionally said that his father had obtained it from Hungary. Others, such as William Boggs and Antoine Delmas, claimed that it was French, or came from France.

In the late twentieth century, a team of grape geneticists in California and Croatia, led by Professor Carole Meredith of the University of California, Davis, compared the DNA profiles of selected grapevines from southern Italy and the Dalmatian coast of Croatia with the DNA profile of the California Zinfandel and announced that they were genetically identical. The Italian match for Zinfandel was the Primitivo, which grew in the "heel" of southeastern Italy, and the Dalmatian match bore the tongue-twisting name of Crljenak Kaštelanski (which signified that it was a red grape from the Dalmatian town of Kaštela). These grapes were not particularly distinguished in either Italy or Croatia, and they did not produce famous wines. The Dalmatian grape grew in a small, almost vestigial stand among other grapes on a coastal island, and historical evidence suggested that the Italian grape may have been a fairly recent arrival in that country, possibly brought there in the eighteenth or nineteenth centuries from across the Adriatic Sea. Carole Meredith speculated that the Crljenak Kaštelanski may at one time have been widely distributed along the Dalmatian coast before it was attacked by the phylloxera, almost to the point of extinction.[38]

In the early 2000s, plant geneticists in Italy confirmed the discoveries of Professor Meredith and her associates, but also announced that they had found another grape that was genetically identical to Zinfandel. This was the Kratošija, an old grape variety that grew in many different forms in Montenegro, southeast of Dalmatia.[39] Historical documents, ampelographic literature, and botanical paintings suggested that vines genetically identical to Zinfandel had been present in and around the Dalmatian coast and the neighboring countries of Hungary, Montenegro, and Austria for centuries. In the middle of the nineteenth century (and for hundreds of years before that) Croatia had been a part of the Kingdom of Hungary, ruled by the Hapsburgs. After the formation of the Austro-Hungarian Empire in 1867, the part of the Dalmatian coast around the town of Kaštela was assigned to Austria, but it was still part of the Austro-Hungarian Empire. All of this suggested that the original homeland of the vine known in California as Zinfandel (and in Italy as Primitivo, in Croatia as Crljenak Kaštelanski, and in Montenegro as Kratošija) was somewhere in or around Croatia in regions controlled in the seventeenth, eighteenth, and nineteenth centuries by Hungary and the Hapsburgs. From this homeland, it was probably taken into the centers of Hungary and Austria, where botanical collections were kept, and from there it was brought to California, either indirectly through New England and New York, or directly to California. In California in the nineteenth century various winemakers had speculated that the vine was of French origin. Scientific discoveries of the twentieth and twenty-first centuries suggest that Arpad was closer to the mark when he said that it was Hungarian.

Even if Arpad's claim that his father was the first to introduce Zinfandel to California remains unproven, it tells us little about Arpad's assertion that Agoston deserved to be called the "father of California viticulture." It is undisputed that for more than a century, vine growers, winemakers, and writers about wines and vines accorded him that honor.[40] And during that same century, it was never suggested that any other man should be called the "father" of California winemaking, or that any other pioneer did more than Agoston Haraszthy to lay the foundations of the winemaking industry.[41] It was only after Sullivan and Pinney penned their histories that Agoston's recognition as the "father of California viticulture" was disputed. It is ironic that Sullivan should have led the effort to "demote" Agoston from his place of viticultural honor, for in the course of his researches Sullivan had himself reached very positive conclusions about Agoston Haraszthy. He had written that Agoston was "a very extraordinary historical character," and that he was "a real hero" who wanted a "proper history."[42] He had said that the Haraszthy name was "probably the most famous in the history of California wine, and rightly so,"[43] and that Agoston Haraszthy was "truly an important figure in the history of the American West."[44] Sullivan didn't believe that anyone had "contributed more" to the "growth and development" of the California wine industry. "He was a great publicist," Sullivan wrote. "He was the young industry's public conscience, promoting better wine through the use of better grapes and rational cellar practices. He advocated vineyard and cellar techniques in the 1860s that were considered prescient in the 1880s."[45] Yet Sullivan insisted that Agoston was not the "father of California viticulture" that generations had believed him to be and that it was "laughable" to assert that he was.[46]

I considered this question in my biography of Agoston Haraszthy. I reviewed Agoston's contributions to the early development of the California wine industry: the vineyards he planted and induced others to plant; the hillside tunnels he dug; the stone cellars he built at Sonoma, the first of their kind in California; the wines he made and taught others to make; the grape varieties he introduced; the speeches he made; and the articles and books that he wrote publicizing the promise of California wine to the state and the world. I concluded that, if Agoston Haraszthy was not the "father" of the California industry, there was no "father," for "no other man did as much to launch the industry in its pioneer days and induce others to help make it prosper and thrive."[47] I speculated that the problem might lie more in the word "father" than in Agoston Haraszthy's own achievements, for "father" does suggest a primacy in time, and there is no question that there were other California winemakers before Haraszthy—neither Agoston nor Arpad had ever denied that. I noted that the great wine and food writer James Beard had called Agoston "the great name in California wine history"[48] and suggested that Beard's phrase might be more appropriate than the old title of "father of California viticulture." Perhaps Beard got it right after all.

What did Arpad's contemporaries think about the "Zinfandel controversy"? What did his vine growing and winemaking colleagues think about the man who had, for nearly two decades, championed his father's reputation as the "father of California viticulture" and the man who introduced Zinfandel into California? Some sense of their feelings may be gained from political events that unfolded in the Board of State Viticultural Commissioners in the year 1888.

Arpad's term as commissioner for the state at large expired on April 19, 1888. Governor Washington Bartlett had died the previous September, and Lieutenant Governor Robert W. Waterman had become governor in his place. Waterman decided not to reappoint Arpad to a new term. His decision did not reflect on Arpad's performance in office, or on the performance of the four other commissioners he also declined to reappoint, but on political considerations extending beyond the state board. Waterman first named Morris M. Estee to succeed Arpad. Estee was a powerful Republican lawyer and part-time Napa Valley vine grower who was known as one of Waterman's strongest political supporters. But Estee was about to become chairman of the Republican National Convention, and he declined the appointment. Waterman then gave the position to John T. Doyle, another prominent lawyer and part-time winemaker. When Arpad learned that Waterman had decided not to reappoint him as commissioner, he tendered his resignation as president of the state board, to take effect on April 18. But his colleagues on the board refused to accept it.[49] They expressed confidence in his work as president, as did newspapers throughout the state. The *San Francisco Merchant* commented on his "capability," and on "the untiring energy which he has at all times displayed in the discharge of his official duties."[50] The *San Diego Union* said that the state had "gained much through his public services, and all will regret his resignation."[51] The *Alta* observed that if Arpad had been reappointed as a commissioner, he would have been reelected as president.[52] The *Merchant* reported that a delegation of men representing the state's wine and brandy producers were going to Sacramento to urge the governor to reconsider and reappoint Arpad.[53] But the governor declined to do so.

On his retirement from the state board, Arpad prepared a twenty-eight-page report on the board's work, filled with statistics on vine planting and wine production, and reviewing the board's considerable accomplishments during the eight years he had served as its president. The *Merchant* commended him for the time and effort he devoted to the report, saying that "his co-laborers in the California vineyards will hardly fail to appreciate this latest instance of Mr. Haraszthy's devotion to the interests of the industry, which he has at all times been so ready to further and perfect."[54]

Arpad was pleased when, on July 19, 1888, a new United States Navy cruiser, the U.S.S. *Charleston,* was christened with a bottle of Eclipse. The 3,730-ton ship was built by the Union Iron Works in San Francisco, headed by Arpad's Bohemian Club friend, Irving M. Scott. The *Charleston* was to have a distinguished life as a naval vessel in the

Pacific and Atlantic Oceans and play a prominent role in the occupation of the Philippine Islands during the Spanish-American War. In San Francisco, Arpad was delighted that a San Francisco ship should begin its life at sea with the blessing of a San Francisco–made sparkling wine. A note in the *Alta* recorded the christening and wished "all honor to the local pride of her builders."[55]

On August 2, 1888, vine growers and winemakers from throughout the state gathered at 8:00 P.M. in San Francisco's Pioneer Hall for a banquet honoring Arpad. The crowded hall was decorated with wreaths of wine leaves intermingled with ivy and large bunches of grapes that hung from the chandeliers. Music was furnished by San Francisco's German String Band. At one end of the hall was a large cartoon depicting a bottle of Eclipse mounted on a gun-carriage being fired off by what the *San Francisco Call* called "a very jolly looking monk." "It was intended," the *Call* told its readers, "to represent the fight made by Mr. Haraszthy and others in the cause of pure wines." The menu was described as "particularly choice and more than usually elaborate," with course after course of specially prepared foods washed down by the oldest and rarest vintages of California wines. There was a Riesling of 1877 with an "exquisite bouquet," a Sherry of 1884, "delicious in flavor," and a Zinfandel of 1883, "fine as the best Chateau Lafitte [*sic*]." This was all followed by samples of Arpad's favorite Eclipse which, the *Call* said, he "rarely lets out of his cellar." "The guests, all connoisseurs, tasted the vintages with the appreciation of their value. Flavors, compositions, and bouquets were discussed with interest. Wine-makers from the plains and those from the foothills compared brands and exchanged experiences." When all the wines and delicacies had been consumed, Charles Wetmore, the host of the evening, rose to address the throng. He said it was not necessary to make a speech introducing Arpad Haraszthy, who was "so well known to all present." He chose only to present the man "whose genius, understanding, industry and patriotic zeal have won for him a place in the hearts of the people."[56]

As cheers filled the hall, the banqueters rose to drink to Arpad's health in what the *Call* called "bumpers of his own champagne." There were rounds of toasts. Then Arpad rose to speak. "He said the honors that had been thrust upon him had not been sought. He had worked hard and earnestly at the cultivation of the vine and at his business of wine-making. He had not been selfish in keeping the knowledge he had gained to himself, but had willingly let others partake of it." As he concluded, he said that "his ambition was satisfied and his cup of content was full."[57]

The roster of men who attended the banquet in Arpad's honor was almost a Who's Who of the California wine industry, with an added delegation of prominent citizens from other walks of life. It included Charles Kohler, Charles Krug, Albert Lachman, Benjamin Dreyfus, Isidor Landsberger, Morris M. Estee, Frank Pixley, Federico Pohndorff, Henry Crabb, George West, Isaac De Turk, Andrew Hallidie, Charles Bundschu, Francis Korbel, Charles Wheeler, T. C. Van Ness, California Supreme Court Justice Thomas B. McFarland, and University of California President Horace Davis, as well as many others.[58]

The banqueters filed out of Pioneer Hall sometime after midnight.[59] Arpad went home to his house on Larkin Street, the taste of his Eclipse still fresh on his tongue and the words and cheers of his friends and colleagues still spinning fondly in his head. His cup of content was full.

CHAPTER SEVEN

THE LAST ECLIPSE

Eighteen eighty-eight was one of the busiest years of Arpad's life. It was the year in which he terminated his long service with the California Board of State Viticultural Commissioners and completed his final report to the governor, detailing the many accomplishments of the board during his tenure as its president. But personal affairs also occupied much of his time that year, as did his writing, and his growing concern for the economic health of the California wine industry—and that of his own sparkling wine business.

The year began on a sad note with news that Arpad's brother Attila had died at his home in Sonoma.[1] Like Arpad, Attila Haraszthy had spent all of his adult life as a vineyardist and winemaker, although he preferred to do so in the familiar surroundings of the Sonoma Valley while Arpad did it in the largest city on the Pacific Coast. Attila was just fifty-two years old when he died on February 2, 1888, leaving his widow Natalia and two sons and two daughters to mourn his passing. He had been one of the first winemakers in California to identify the phylloxera that was infesting the state's best vine-growing regions, reporting his discovery to the Sonoma Vinicultural Club as early as 1873. He dug up roots of his own vines and those of his father-in-law, General Vallejo, and was horrified to find that the life-sucking insects had infested them all.[2] It took years for plant scientists in France and

California to settle on the best means for combating the scourge, but while the search for remedies went on, vineyardists suffered. Attila was a respected member of the Sonoma community, a director and vice president of the Sonoma Valley Bank and president of the town's board of trustees (the equivalent of mayor).[3] But as the phylloxera proceeded through his vineyards, his finances worsened and, as early as 1880, his vineyards were reduced to a single vine that grew behind his house.[4] By the time of his death, his hundred-acre property adjoining General Vallejo's lay in ruins, and he was heavily in debt.[5] Attila was the second of Agoston Haraszthy's six children to die (Agoston's oldest son, Gaza, had died in Nicaragua in 1878, where he was serving as an officer of the Nicaraguan army).[6]

April brought happier news to the Haraszthys. On the eleventh of that month, Arpad's daughter Agostine was married to Lieutenant George D. Strickland of the U.S. Navy. The wedding day was also the bride's twenty-fourth birthday, a fact that might have sparked a great church wedding, but in deference to Attila's recent death the ceremony was a modest one that took place in Arpad's home on Larkin Street. The house was decorated with flowers brought from all over California, and an orchestra played for the assembled guests, as Father John Sullivan of Sonoma performed the ceremony in the presence of about seventy family members and friends. After the reception, the newlyweds left for the city of Vallejo, as Lieutenant Strickland was stationed at the nearby Mare Island Naval Shipyard.[7]

With Agostine's departure for Vallejo, Arpad's attention turned more to his twenty-one-year-old son, Carlos, who was now a student in Toland Medical College of the University of California.[8] Carlos's earlier schooling had been in Santa Clara and Berkeley. He was a handsome young man, tall, with dark hair and eyes and a trim moustache. He was popular with his associates, partly because of his dignified manner, partly because of his musical talent. He played the flute and the guitar and read music with ease. An article in the *Call* reported that his memory was "something wonderful."[9] Toland Medical College was located just a few blocks from Arpad's San Francisco house, so Carlos (who was sometimes called Carl or Charles) lived at home while he pursued his medical studies.[10]

Arpad continued to write. While he was still president of the state board, he completed the manuscript of one of his most popular essays, titled "How to Drink Wine." It was a long and erudite discussion of wine-drinking practices around the world that Arpad read to the assembled delegates of the state viticultural convention on March 10, 1888.[11] In it, he discussed traditional rules for the polite consumption of wine and offered practical advice derived from his years of experience, not only as a winemaker but also an enthusiastic consumer. He began by reviewing wine-drinking traditions in ancient India, Egypt, Greece, and Rome, then discussed proper glasses for the consumption of wines (they should be made of clear, unornamented crystal so the color and clarity of the wine can be appreciated). He offered commonsense advice for enjoying wine, but mixed it with some idiosyncratic opinions. He believed, for example, that wine should always be drunk at table and never between meals ("drinking between meals is a pernicious habit, amounting almost to second nature in our American population, and is injurious in every way").[12] He described the proper temperatures at which wines should be served (sparkling wine should be "as cold as it can be made without absolutely freezing," but never served with ice; red wines should be "moderately warm"; and white wines should be "comparatively cold or cool").[13] It was "absolutely barbarous," he said, to drink red wine from tumblers half-filled with ice, and people who added lumps of sugar to red wine "do not deserve the name of wine drinkers."[14] He included a lengthy discussion of sediment in wine, expressing the opinion that deposits should be found in all old wines, as proof that they had spent a long time in the bottle. "Wines improve more in bottles than any of us can justly estimate," he said.[15]

Arpad discussed the English fondness for "crusty" old Port Wine (Port with a film or "crust" of sediment on the inner face of the bottle)[16] and gave elaborate instructions for the proper decantation of old red wines. He remembered the first time he witnessed a formal decantation of an old Bordeaux wine. It was while he was traveling through France with his father, and they were guests in an elegant chateau near Bordeaux where the master of the household himself performed the decantation "ceremony." He was "a baron—a stately, elegant, dignified gentleman of the ancient regime," Arpad wrote; "the wines were Yquem of 1822 and Margaux of 1846, each of which were drawn into colorless cut crystal decanters of exquisite form. That was in the fall of 1861. I shall never forget it, nor the lessons learned. Memorable occasion! Elegant company, matchless wines, unrivaled dinner!"[17]

He spoke of the virtues of wine drinking but strongly counseled moderation in the use of wine. "Moderation varies with the capacities of different individuals," he said. "For one person a glass is quite sufficient, or even half that quantity; whereas for another a bottle is hardly sufficient. The determination of the quantities to be used without injury should be made by each person for himself, and once determined adhered to," adding: "Wine, if properly selected and used, is not merely a stimulant, but a food assistant, and I might say next door to a nutriment. It should be drank [*sic*] but never guzzled. It should please the eye, flatter the olfactories, give relish to the palate, quench the thirst, and respect your head. If it does not fill these conditions for you, you had better drink water."[18]

He believed that everyone had to judge for himself which wines he preferred to drink. "A wine expert can only pronounce upon the state or condition of a wine, and its relative quality compared to other wines," he said, "and if well versed in the art can measurably well detect its age, the grape from which it is produced, and the district from whence it came. He may even go so far as to select from a number of wines, that wine which might please the greatest number of consumers. More than this he cannot do, and therefore the best judge for you is your own palate, and your own digestive system."[19] As the producer of California's most famous sparkling wine, it was natural that Arpad should include some praise for his own product. "Champagne is *par excellence* the convivial wine," he wrote. "Its action is rapid—more rapid than any other wine—tending to elevate the mind and increase the flow of spirits and mirth. It is a wine which no other varieties have been able to supplant for banquets or social gatherings, and latterly it has been greatly used by physicians in various kinds of fevers, and during convalescence."[20]

"How to Drink Wine" was well received by winemakers and wine consumers alike. The full text was published in the official report of the Sixth Annual California State Viticultural Convention in 1888 and reprinted the following year in *Wines and Vines of California*, an influential book produced by a young San Francisco journalist named Frona Eunice Wait.[21]

Despite his retirement from the Board of State Viticultural Commissioners, Arpad's views on conditions in the wine industry were still sought out. In August of 1888, for example, the *Alta* asked him about rumors that a trust might be formed by wealthy San Francisco capitalists to control the wine market, keep prices down, and force small producers out of business. He thought the fear of such a combination was unwarranted, for there were no men in San Francisco with enough money "to control the market completely." Further, if any such combination were made, competition would eventually bring it down. "The price of wine, like every other commodity, is regulated by the law of supply and demand."[22]

Despite his confidence in the market's ability to maintain an equilibrium between producers and consumers, however, Arpad was more and more concerned about the rapid expansion of California's vineyards. When he left the state board, he estimated that there were one hundred fifty thousand acres of vines planted in California, and that all of them would be in full bearing within three years. The state's production of wine had risen from four million gallons in 1877 to more than fifteen million gallons in 1887. Of that quantity, however, only about six million gallons were consumed in California and the other western states, and about seven million were sent to the eastern states.[23] That clearly pointed to an excess production of about two million gallons per year. This fact, added to weakening financial conditions throughout the country, threatened economic hardships for vineyardists and winemakers alike. When a grape crop was harvested, it had to be sold on the fresh grape market or turned into wine. When wine was made, many vineyardists needed prompt payment for their products, for they could not afford to store and age their wines for several years. When new wines were sold at current prices, many winemakers found they could not even cover their costs of production. Arpad thought that one solution to the problem would be to turn much of the annual grape harvest into brandy, which was a more efficient store of value than wine. The brandy could be collected into large warehouses, stored and aged, and released on the market when prices rose to reasonable levels. With Isaac De Turk of Santa Rosa and George West of Stockton, two of the state's leading wine producers, he proposed the formation of a "Brandy Union" that would build a large central warehouse and distillery and contract with growers throughout the state to buy their wines and brandies at reasonable prices.[24] The idea had some appeal, but the necessity of raising the estimated one million dollars needed to finance it did not, and the proposal languished. Meanwhile, production increased. At Arpad's own Orleans Vineyard in Yolo County, 1889 saw a wine yield of about two hundred thousand gallons, a huge increase over 1888's eighty thousand gallons.[25] (Whether this was the result of new plantings or part of a natural fluctuation in the bearing of the vines is unclear—perhaps it was the result in part of both.)

As his production increased, Arpad sought to expand his markets in the eastern states and in foreign countries. He hired sales representatives in New York, Boston, and Chicago and sent cases of Eclipse by ship to Honolulu, Tahiti, Australia, Central America, and England.[26] Robert Louis Stevenson, with whom he had struck up a friendship in the Bohemian Club in 1880, was fond of Eclipse and ordered cases of it sent to his new South Seas home in Samoa.[27] When celebrities came to San Francisco, Arpad welcomed them to his Washington Street cellars. The steel barons Andrew Carnegie and Henry Clay Frick came in 1892 with Andrew Dickson White, the founding president of Cornell University, and the *Pacific Wine and Spirit Review* reported that Arpad Haraszthy & Co. "produced a very desirable impression" on them. Carnegie and Frick "liked their wines immensely" and ordered twenty-five cases of Eclipse, along with cases of Arpad's Chateau d'Orleans (a Bordeaux-style red wine) and Riesling. "These are a desirable class of people to initiate into the merits of California wine," the *Review* reminded its readers.[28]

Arpad was sensitive to critics who argued that his sparkling wines were not as good as those imported from France. French Champagne makers maintained a strong presence in the San Francisco market, despite the good reputation earned by his own Eclipse, and in New York, Boston, and Chicago the French products seemed to have an almost unbreakable hold on the popular taste. The fact was, of course, that French Champagne varied widely in quality, with some makers consistently producing crisp, delicately flavored wines and others as consistently selling wines that disappointed discriminating palates. But the aura that surrounded the French-made Champagne was so great that it was difficult for an American producer—particularly one like Arpad who insisted on producing all of his sparkling wine by the traditional méthode champenoise—to make substantial inroads in the markets.

In 1889, the newspapers published some disparaging statements about American sparkling wine that were attributed to Baron von Mumm, the German head of the French Champagne house of G. H. Mumm. Mumm charged that American "champagnes" (he was apparently willingly to use this word to describe the American products) did not have sufficient effervescence because American soils were not chalky, and American manufacturers had to resort to artificial carbonation to get their wines to sparkle. This was, of course, nonsense. At a meeting of the Grape Growers and Wine Makers' Association in San Francisco, Arpad produced an open letter in which he asked Baron Mumm a series of pointed questions:

> Do you not know that climate exercises greater influence on the character of wine, than soil itself?
>
> Do you not know that we have whole counties lying on carbonate of lime formations, covered with light clay, mingled with silica and oxide of iron, and that this character of soil is practically the same as that existing in the champagne district?

> Is it not a fact that while the champagne district produces a limited quantity of fine wine, that other parts produce large quantities of inferior, thin, acid, flavorless wine, and that you yourself have admitted that these all go into the blends of the various champagne firms?[29]

Charles Wetmore applauded Arpad's letter to Mumm, as did Isaac de Turk.[30] The *American Analyst,* a New York journal of viticultural news and opinion, joined Arpad in taking aim at Mumm, charging the European with "lying" about American champagnes and saying that "he knows perfectly well that there are several American champagnes which are made precisely as his wine is made, and in the case of one American brand, Arpad Haraszthy & Co.'s Eclipse, with better and more uniform results."[31]

Mumm's aspersions on American sparkling wines were not the only evidence that California wines were held in low esteem in some quarters. California producers were convinced that consumers and marketers in the East were prejudiced against domestic wines in general and California sparkling wines in particular, and that this prejudice was damaging their eastern sales. An incident that excited the San Francisco press in May 1891, served to enforce this conviction. President Benjamin Harrison had announced his intention of visiting California, presumably to gather support for his reelection bid in 1892. When Harrison reached San Francisco, a grand banquet was prepared for him at the Palace Hotel. The elegantly engraved menu was filled with choice dishes and delicacies, but when some local wine men got a preview of it they noticed that the wines to be served were all French. They were listed not only by type, but also by the names of their producers. The local men complained to the president's hosts. Harrison had come to California, they said, to taste its fruits and wines, and it was "an insult to the wine producers of California to exclude native wines from the banquet table." The hosts then hastily prepared a supplementary list, with a good selection of California wines, including Arpad's Eclipse.[32] But when Harrison sat down to the table, it was noticed that he drank only the French wines. The locals were again offended. "Had President Harrison shown the slightest tact," one of them said, "he could easily have averted the bitter feelings that were engendered, for he could have rejected any of the foreign wines and selected the native ones, thus smoothing our ruffled feelings by complimenting us upon their flavor and quality." Some of the locals said that they were so dismayed by the Harrison banquet that they would switch their allegiance from the president's Republican Party to the Democrats in the upcoming election. "We will give him a sample of our temper in the next presidential campaign," growled Eugene J. Cantin, one of Arpad's most vocal sales representatives.[33] It is impossible to determine if the offended California wine men swung the California election results from Benjamin Harrison to the Democratic candidate, Grover Cleveland, in 1892. But it is a fact that Cleveland carried the Golden State by only 147 popular votes that year, that he won eight of California's nine electoral votes, and that he went on to become president in 1893.[34] Perhaps the wine list at the Palace Hotel banquet in San Francisco in 1891 did have some effect on the ultimate outcome.[35]

San Francisco wine men detected another snub of California wines a few months after Harrison's Palace Hotel banquet. The Press Club of San Francisco hosted a banquet for visiting press delegates and made the same mistake that Harrrison's hosts had made: the list of wines they chose to serve to their guests contained not a single California product. The *Pacific Wine and Spirit Review* led a chorus of jeers, charging that the Press Club had up until then been considered "the last place on earth for an exhibition of snobbery. Its members are supposed to be, even if they are not, above any unreasoning prejudice against home products." "An end to this snobbery," the *Review* snarled. "The action of the Club was shameful—outrageous." Arpad detected an opportunity to turn the Press Club's slight into an advertising advantage and published an open invitation to the visiting delegates to visit his cellars on Washington Street. He took pleasure in personally requesting that they "witness the process of making the Eclipse, the only champagne on this coast produced by actual fermentation in bottle. Our cellars, eighteen in number, contain 500,000 gallons of various wines in cask, and 600,000 bottles of champagne in process of aging." The *Review* reported that his invitation had some results, and that he had "many visitors."[36]

If Mumm's opinion of American sparkling wine was negative, and Benjamin Harrison's interest in the products of California's vineyards was nonexistent, and the Press Club of San Francisco was oblivious to the virtues of the Haraszthy product, there were others who had a good opinion of California wine, and particularly of Arpad's Eclipse. In 1891, the *Pacific Wine and Spirit Review* published an excerpt from a letter written by a man in New York who was connected with one of the largest French Champagne houses. He in turn referred to the opinion of the cellar master of one of the French firms, who praised the American products. "There is one brand in particular," the New Yorker affirmed, "—the Eclipse of Arpad Haraszthy & Co.—which has made a reputation for itself, which can be found at every grocers and on every wine list of hotels throughout the country. . . . I credit the success of the wine referred to as mainly due to the fact, first, to their using real and natural wine as a basis. Secondly, that their preparation is after the French method. Thirdly, that it is put up in California known as the greatest wine-producing territory in this country."[37] After a shipment of Eclipse reached the East Coast, New York's prestigious *Bonfort's Wine and Spirit Circular* reported that it was "by far the best wine of the class that we have ever seen shipped from California. It is perfectly sound, of good body, well blended, admirable bouquet, fine, clean, of good flavor, and will hold its own in comparison with any American, German and many French sparkling wines." Then *Bonfort's* added: "Dear brethren of the press, in copying this, do not say that we have said that the Eclipse is as good as any champagne; it isn't, but it is a good wine that does credit to the grower, blender and handler, and it deserves praise and success."[38]

As the 1880s gave way to the 1890s, Arpad continued to enter his wines in competitions at fairs and expositions inside and outside California, and the list of his medals continued to grow. Eclipse Extra Dry and Eclipse Brut, together with Haraszthy Riesling, Gutedel, and Zinfandel were entered in the Exposition Universelle held in Paris in

1889, where the collection received a silver medal.[39] In the same month, Haraszthy sparkling wines, still wines, and brandies won a gold medal at San Francisco's Mechanics' Institute Fair.[40] In 1892, Arpad's claret was recognized at the Distillers' and Brewers Exposition in Dublin with a certificate of merit. His sparkling wine garnered a gold medal at the same exposition, with the comment that it was "peculiarly Californian and of a very agreeable type."[41] In 1893, Arpad received a gold medal at the Mechanics' Fair for the finest sparkling wine produced by fermentation in the bottle, and diplomas for the finest Zinfandel, the finest sweet red wine not classified as Port or Malaga, the finest Rhine wine, the finest sweet white wine, and the finest brandy under five years of age.[42] He won a bronze medal at Lyons in 1894 and another bronze at Bordeaux in 1895.[43]

Arpad was a regular participant in the annual Mechanics' Institute events, which helped him maintain his contacts with his San Francisco colleagues. The Mechanics' Pavilion, where the fairs were held, presented a convivial atmosphere, with San Franciscans dressed in their finest promenading among agricultural and industrial exhibits from all over Northern California. Arpad varied his Mechanics' Institute displays from year to year, seeking the most attractive ways to exhibit his wares. In 1895 he hit on the novel approach of moving a section of his own cellar into the pavilion, where he set up a rack showing the actual process of fermenting wine in bottles according to the méthode champenoise. "Mr. Haraszthy's exhibit is immediately next to the band stand in the center of the Pavilion," the *Pacific Wine and Spirit Review* reported, "and is in a splendid position for attracting the attention it deserves."[44]

The bandstand, and the musicians who occupied it, were highlights of the Mechanics' Fairs. Concerts were presented there, with works from the classical and light classical repertoire interspersed with popular dance tunes and songs. Some of the works were composed especially for the San Francisco audiences. In 1887 a concert polka by Frederick Austin entitled "Eclipse Champagne" was performed on the cornet by the composer, with the band accompanying.[45] In 1888, the band presented a galop by Hans Christian Lumbye titled "Eclipse Champagne."[46] Arpad enjoyed the Mechanics' Fair concerts. He was known as a music lover and a regular attendant at San Francisco operas. The city's Grand Opera House on Mission Street was the showcase for serious operatic works by Rossini, Verdi, and Wagner, while the Tivoli Opera House at the corner of Eddy and Mason specialized in operettas by Suppé, Offenbach, and Gilbert and Sullivan. In 1895, a souvenir program for the Tivoli included the full piano score of the "Haraszthy Champagne" Polka, a spirited work by a composer identified only as E. Piron.[47] Of course, the "Eclipse Champagne" polka and galop and the "Haraszthy Champagne" polka were advertising tools for Arpad's sparkling wines, but they were spirited works, as bubbly as the wines they celebrated, and audiences enjoyed them.

One of Arpad's favorite pastimes was riding through Golden Gate Park on weekends, admiring the broad sweep of lawn and trees and feeling the fresh ocean breeze as it blew against his face. He had a carriage that was pulled by an old trotter, but in 1891 he acquired a mate for the horse. It was a gelding, somewhat smaller than the trotter but, as the *Pacific Wine and Spirit Review* told its readers, "as consistent and willing a trotter as there is in the Park." Together, the two horses made a "splendid team." The *Review* commented that it would "take a team which can go away under three minutes to pass Mr. Haraszthy for a case of fizz."[48]

When he was not listening to popular tunes in the Mechanics' Pavilion, enjoying operas in the Grand Opera House or the Tivoli, or riding in his carriage through Golden Gate Park, Arpad continued to work long hours in his San Francisco cellars and at his vineyards in Yolo County.[49] He had a large complement of employees in both places whose livelihoods depended on his continuing success. There were family members, too, who looked to him for employment. His brother Bela worked for a while as a salesman for Arpad Haraszthy & Co.[50] Bela had been employed for eight years as superintendent of the Lake Wine and Vineyard Company in Pasadena,[51] and he knew enough about winemaking to be an effective salesman for Arpad's products. Bela represented Haraszthy wines before moving to Arizona in the early 1890s, where he settled in the town of Yuma, served as a county supervisor and school trustee, and devoted his time to his new passion of gold mining.[52] Arpad's brother-in-law Napoleon P. Vallejo, brother of his deceased wife Jovita, also worked as a sales representative for Eclipse,[53] and his young nephew Agoston F. Haraszthy, son of his deceased brother Attila, spent three years in the San Francisco cellars, first as a clerk and then as a foreman. For a part of his time in the San Francisco cellars, Agoston F. Haraszthy (who, like his grandfather Agoston, was affectionately known as "Guszti") lived in his Uncle Arpad's home on Leavenworth Street.[54] Arpad's son Carlos also spent some time in the Haraszthy cellars as a superintendent.[55] His medical education seems to have stalled sometime in the early 1890s—whether from lack of interest or inability to complete the necessary studies the record does not reveal.[56]

The importance of Arpad's family connections was vividly brought home to him when, in January 1890, he received news that his father-in-law had died in Sonoma. Eighty-three years old when he died on January 18 of that year, Mariano Guadalupe Vallejo (habitually called General Vallejo) had long been honored as one of California's most eminent pioneers, a living link between the old Spanish and Mexican regimes and the new American commonwealth. He also happened to be one of the pioneer viticulturists of California—his vineyards in Sonoma were planted in the 1830s and 1840s, produced prize-winning wines in the 1850s and 1860s, and were destroyed by the phylloxera in the 1870s. Arpad went up to Sonoma from San Francisco where, on January 21, 1890, he served as one of the pallbearers at Vallejo's funeral. His nephew "Guszti" Haraszthy (Vallejo's grandson) was also a pallbearer.[57]

Arpad entered his wines in the World's Columbian Exposition held at Chicago in 1893. The Chicago exposition was originally scheduled to open in 1892, the four hundredth anniversary of Columbus's discovery of America, but another year was needed to complete the two hundred buildings planned for the vast exposition site. Arpad helped California winemakers prepare for the Chicago event, offering advice on the best way to present the state's wines to the millions who were expected to attend.[58] California wines were displayed in the exposition's large, mission-style California Building and its even larger, Beaux Arts–style Horticultural Hall. A special display of Arpad's wines was mounted in the Horticultural Hall, in a replica of the base of a giant redwood tree that stood forty feet high and measured twenty-eight feet in diameter. The surface of the tree was covered with strips of redwood bark brought from Mendocino County, while the base was hollow and large enough to accommodate Arpad's display and those of his friendly competitors, C. Carpy & Co. of Napa, J. Gundlach & Co. of Sonoma and San Francisco, and the Napa Valley Wine Company. A winding staircase inside the tree led visitors to a gallery which commanded a fine view of the displays below.[59] Dubbed the "Big Tree Exhibit," the redwood exhibition space was described by the *Pacific Wine and Spirit Review* as "the most striking figure of the whole wine exhibit."[60] It reminded visitors that California was not only the leading wine-producing state in the United States; it was also home to the country's biggest and oldest trees. Before it closed in October 1893, the Chicago Exposition attracted an estimated twenty-seven million visitors, but so many wines were displayed (many from California, but many more from foreign countries) that the wine-judging process nearly broke down. Californians detected a prejudice against their state's wines and complained about it, and in the end, the judges resorted to the expedient of awarding bronze medals to all of the exhibitors. Arpad Haraszthy & Co. received medals for its "champagnes," claret, sauterne, and Chateau d'Orleans, and for its cabernelle (described as a "good mellow wine with delicate flavor). But the medals were all but lost among the scores of awards handed out to other exhibitors.[61] More revealing, perhaps, than the medals were the special comments made by Charles F. Oldham, a veteran wine merchant from London, who tasted the California wines and made specific comments on all of them. Oldham was generous in his praise of Arpad's sparkling wines, proclaiming the Eclipse Extra Dry "an excellent wine, of champagne character, very clean and free from acidity," and describing the Eclipse Brut as "a similar wine . . . but considerably drier." He thought the Haraszthy Carte Blanche was "a very agreeable, soft, smooth wine," and its Cabernet blend was a "good style of wine" with a "nice bouquet, in perfect condition." Arpad's Burgundy had "beautiful color" and "good bouquet," but "rather too much acid" for Oldham's taste.[62]

Arpad was even more involved in the viticultural programs of the California Midwinter International Exposition, which opened in San Francisco's Golden Gate Park in January 1894. Popularly known as the Midwinter Fair, the San Francisco event took its inspiration from the Chicago Exposition, although it was conceived on a smaller scale (its grounds covered only 184 acres compared to Chicago's 600) and its financing was more modest. The driving force behind the San Francisco exposition was M. H. de Young, editor and publisher of the *San Francisco Chronicle,* who had been California's commissioner to the Chicago Exposition and believed that his home city's industrial prowess deserved a similar showcase. California wines were exhibited in the Midwinter Fair's Palace of Viticulture, a smallish structure surmounted by two mission-style towers and a dome, with an entrance framed by the oval end of a large wine cask. Inside, a plaster sculpture of Mercury and Bacchus astride a globe surveyed wine casks from the cellars of Kohler and Frohling, Carpy, Gundlach, and others, and what the *Pacific Wine and Spirit Review* called "the great Rhine wine bottle of Arpad Haraszthy & Co."[63] A *weinstube* (a small German wine bar or tavern) next to the main building was furnished with tables and chairs so visitors could linger while they tasted their wines.

Arpad was chairman of the Midwinter Fair's Wine Awards Committee. In that capacity, he promulgated a detailed set of rules that governed the wine judges as they tasted and evaluated the more than two hundred wines entered in competition.[64] All wines had to be wrapped with paper before they were tasted, Arpad decreed, so their makers could not be identified, and the merits or faults of each wine had to be measured according to a point system.[65] He spoke at several of the Fair's events, making remarks that the *Review* called "witty, humorous and pointed,"[66] but his most ambitious speech was the "instructive address on Hungarian patriots" that he delivered on April 24, the Fair's Austro-Hungarian Day.[67] An estimated two million visitors attended the Midwinter Fair, although only sixty thousand passed through the Palace of Viticulture. The Fair was clearly no World's Columbian Exposition, although it probably helped to advertise California's wines.

Despite its good intentions, the Midwinter Fair came at an awkward time for California winemakers. Economic conditions in the wine industry had been weakening since the late 1880s, with vineyard production growing steadily while wine consumption fell. Prices for both grapes and wines declined into the early 1890s, making it more and more difficult for small and modest producers to cover their costs of production. The weakening grape and wine market paralleled the deteriorating condition of the overall economy, with prices falling throughout the state and the nation, and consumption dropping dramatically in almost all industries. Individuals attempted to redeem United States gold and silver certificates for bullion, but the federal treasury was unable to meet all of the demands. As 1893 opened, a series of economic crises sent shivers through the financial markets. The Philadelphia and Reading Railroad was forced into bankruptcy in February, initiating a panic in the stock exchanges. A wave of bank failures spread across the country, causing more than five hundred banks to suspend payments and close their doors. Before the year was out, four of the most powerful railroads in the country—the Philadelphia and Reading, the Northern Pacific, the Union Pacific, and the Atchison, Topeka and Santa Fe—were forced into bankruptcy or receivership.

By the time the Midwinter Fair opened there was widespread agreement that the country was in the midst of a depression—and that it was one of the most severe in its history. The *Pacific Wine and Spirit Review* was filled with gloomy assessments of the wine market, and even gloomier assessments of its future prospects. It was a time of "midnight gloom," many said, a "fearful depression" that was "thoroughly demoralizing everything" in the business. Some makers balked at selling their wines, vowing to hold onto them until prices rebounded. Others, unable to wait for better prices, had to dump their wines on the market, causing further price declines. Winemakers argued among themselves about what caused the crisis in the wine industry and what could be done to end it. Some attributed it to the overplanting and overproduction of the late 1880s. Others thought that the poor quality of much of the wine that was sent to market was responsible, arguing that if better wines were made Americans would buy them. Some thought that consumer ignorance about the quality of California wines was to blame, for most Americans clung to the notion that good wine was produced in France, Germany, or Italy but not in California. Yet others pointed out that, whatever its origin, wine was regarded by many consumers as a luxury, and luxuries could be dispensed with altogether when times were hard and money scarce.

It was in this atmosphere that proposals were made for an association of California's leading wine firms that would have the power to stabilize the California wine market, control the supply of wines, and prevent further erosion of wine prices. A young English-born accountant and entrepreneur named Percy T. Morgan made the proposals a reality by organizing leading San Francisco firms in the formation of a joint stock company called the California Wine Association. Incorporated on August 10, 1894, just a month after the Midwinter Fair closed its doors, the CWA was initially composed of seven existing wine firms: C. Carpy & Co., Kohler & Van Bergen, S. Lachman & Co., Napa Valley Wine Co., B. Dreyfus & Co., Kohler & Frohling , and Arpad Haraszthy & Co. Each company agreed to transfer its assets to the CWA in return for stock in the new corporation, with appraisers determining the value of the assets and the board of directors allocating the shares of stock. Eleven directors were chosen from among the member firms, with Charles Carpy of C. Carpy & Co. serving as president and Henry Epstein of Arpad Haraszthy & Co. as first vice president. The association established its headquarters in the huge Kohler & Frohling Building at Second and Market Streets and prepared handsome engraved stationery listing the names of its member firms, including that of Arpad Haraszthy & Co. Henry Epstein transferred legal title to the Orleans Vineyard (which he still held in his and his wife's names) to the CWA,[68] while appraisers set about the business of valuing the other assets of Arpad Haraszthy & Co. The CWA agreed to transfer thirteen hundred shares of stock valued at thirteen thousand dollars to Arpad Haraszthy & Co. and to pay Arpad personally five hundred dollars per month to manage the sparkling wine business for the association.[69]

By October, however, there were hints of a snag in the arrangements. The *Pacific Wine and Spirit Review* reported on October 5 that the wines of several of the member firms had been sent to the Kohler & Frohling cellars for storage and that the still wines of Arpad Haraszthy & Co. would probably be sent there too. But the Haraszthy sparkling wine would not be. The Eclipse cellars, the *Review* stated, would remain on Washington Street.[70] It appeared that there was a disagreement about the values to be assigned to the Haraszthy assets. The Orleans Vineyard property was valued at $11,000 (a figure that Epstein apparently agreed to) while the inventory of the Haraszthy cellars on Washington Street was valued at $142,247.78 (a figure Arpad did not agree to).[71] He made his disagreement known, and there were negotiations. In the end, the directors were not willing to meet his demands, and he asked to have the assets of the sparkling wine business returned to him. The directors agreed to do this, but only at a price. Arpad would have possession of the assets in the Haraszthy cellars, but legal title would remain with the CWA until he had paid it the sum of $41,646.55. He would receive no stock and no salary for running the business. He was permitted to sell existing cases of Haraszthy champagne, but he had to pay 75 percent of the sale proceeds to the association, and he was forbidden to sell more than one hundred cases at any one time. He would have three years to fully discharge his debt to the CWA.[72] On April 18, 1895, Arpad issued a public circular to the wine trade:

> From Arpad Haraszthy
>
> *To the Trade*: Please be advised that I have severed my connection with the California Wine Association and bought from it all the bottled Champagne Wine, stock and material previously the property of Arpad Haraszthy & Co. In future the champagne business will be conducted solely on my behalf and account, at 530 Washington street, where it has been located the past fifteen years.

> Recognizing the necessity of devoting my entire attention to the development and perfection of my Champagne brands, I will, in future, limit myself solely to their production and sale. A new brand with a new name will shortly be placed upon the market, whose delicate qualities promise it the brightest future and greatest popularity.
>
> Hoping to receive your early and numerous orders, I am respectfully yours,
>
> Arpad Haraszthy, *Wine Grower and Producer of Carte Blanche, Eclipse and Brut Champagnes.*
>
> Remember that all Champagne made or sold by me is the product of the noblest grapes grown in our Golden State, and its sparkle is produced only by natural fermentation of two years' duration in the bottle.[73]

The *Pacific Wine and Spirit Review* noted that Arpad had retained ownership of all of the trademarks and brands associated with his business, and that he also retained the right to make dry and sweet wines as a *vigneron* (winemaker) but that he would "not place them on the market." "It is his wish and desire to devote all his time and energy to perfecting the champagnes which have already made his name familiar throughout the United States and England." The *Review* said it was "sincerely glad that Mr. Haraszthy will hereafter give his entire time and attention to the production of champagnes. He understands the business to perfection, and he can be depended upon, unhampered by other interests, to raise the standard of his products to a very enviable position."[74] Arpad's public letter did not mention Henry Epstein, who remained with the CWA.

After thirty years in various partnerships, first with Pietro Giovanari in Sonoma, then with Isidor Landsberger in San Francisco, and finally with Epstein in San Francisco and Yolo County, Arpad now faced the business future alone, confronted with one of the most severe economic crises in American history, stripped of the vineyards that had supplied most of his vintages for the previous fifteen years, and saddled with a large debt which he had only three years to discharge. He should have been discouraged—and perhaps he was. In public, however, he put on a brave face, seeking to conduct himself with his usual aplomb and self-confidence. He entered his sparkling wines in competitions in San Francisco and at the California State Fair and came away with prizes. He continued to ship his sparkling wines to distant markets, notably to England, where consumers were developing a taste for Eclipse.[75] He entered his wines in an international exposition in Berlin and received medals.[76] When, in 1895, the California Legislature decided to abolish the Board of State Viticultural Commissioners (a move that he deplored), he joined with a group of his winemaking friends in an effort to establish a College of Practical Viticulture in San Francisco to carry on the work of the board.[77] The college would collect exhibits, conduct studies, publish papers, and maintain a staff of qualified men to respond to the challenges that confronted the wine industry.[78] Documents incorporating the new institution were duly filed, trustees selected, and officers chosen. Arpad was elected president of the board of trustees, while John Swett was chosen as vice president, and Charles Wetmore became the corresponding secretary.[79] But the new college never got up and running, and the idea was eventually shelved. By decision of the legislature, the University of California took over the duties formerly performed by the state board (and its estimable wine library, as well).[80] And it was just as well, for under the leadership of Professor Hilgard and the staff he gathered around him the university was demonstrating that it could discharge those duties very well.

On Saturday evening, May 2, 1896, Arpad was the principal speaker at a banquet in San Francisco's Saratoga Hall commemorating the millennium of the founding of Hungary, his native country. The *Pacific Wine and Spirit Review* reported that he was the "lion of the evening," and he was designated in the souvenir program as "*Tiszteletbeli Elnök*" Haraszthy Arpad (Honorary President Arpad Haraszthy). He delivered a long speech (in English) on the history of Hungary, from its founding in 896 A.D. to its amalgamation into the Austro-Hungarian Empire in 1867, and paying particular attention to the struggles of Lajos Kossuth and others for Hungarian independence. The banquet hall was decorated with a tableau representing the Magyar chieftain, Arpad, legendary founder of Hungary, while music was provided by Rosner's Hungarian Orchestra. Wines, both still and sparkling, came courtesy of Arpad Haraszthy. The *Review* reported that Arpad responded eloquently to a toast to "Our Adopted Country" and that the event was "one on which the already great fame of Haraszthy Champagne was enhanced and extended. At the conclusion of the celebration, Mr. Haraszthy was borne aloft by his enthusiastic countrymen, all of whom expressed their highest regard for him as a typical Hungarian in spite of his having adopted the nationality of America."[81]

Arpad continued to produce his sparkling wines, now advertising them as "The Haraszthy Champagnes" rather than the products of Arpad Haraszthy & Co. He boasted of their "European quality" and cited the many medals he had won as proof of the boast. The *Pacific Wine and Spirit Review* reported in 1897 that "Mr. Arpad Haraszthy is doing a steady business in the new brands of champagne which he is placing on the market. The old 'Eclipse' brand still remains in vogue, but the later lots of 'Haraszthy Sec' and 'Haraszthy Brut' are meeting with much appreciation from connoisseurs."[82] In February 1897 he presided at a meeting of about fifty wine men convened in San Francisco to oppose a proposed treaty with France under which import duties on French wines and Champagnes would be reduced.[83] The wine men of California were strict protectionists when it came to European imports.

But as California winemakers moved hesitantly into the late 1890s, it was obvious that they had to contend with problems other than French competition. The American economy was still staggering—if the depression begun in 1893 had proved anything, it was that it was persistent. More than six hundred banks scattered across the United States had failed, more than fifteen thousand businesses had been forced into bankruptcy, and one-third of all of the railroads in the nation had become insolvent. In California, wine businesses, including most of the wine estates in Sonoma and Napa counties, had been forced into liquidation. While Arpad sought to fend off competition from French Champagne makers, he also had to meet competition nearer at home. The old producers of artificially carbonated "champagnes" had managed to hang on (the firm called A. Finke's Widow, with San Francisco cellars close to Arpad's own cellars on Washington Street, was a persistent competitor in this line). But there were also new entrants in the field of bottle-fermented sparkling wine. From its cellars in northern Sonoma County, the Italian-Swiss Colony was advertising its "naturally fermented" Montecristo at "liberal discounts to the trade." Charles Wetmore, who had lost control of his highly esteemed Cresta Blanca vineyard in the Livermore Valley, had started a new business and was now making a specialty of "Sparkling Sauterne."[84] And in San Jose, a young Frenchman named Paul Masson, son-in-law of an old Santa Clara Valley wine pioneer named Charles Lefranc, was producing "premiere cuveés" of "Champagne," both "dry" and "special." Masson had taken the second place medal to Arpad's first place for his still and sparkling wines at the Midwinter Fair in 1894,[85] but he was an enterprising young man, and through Lefranc he claimed a venerable viticultural tradition. He was a force to contend with in the California sparkling wine business, if not now, at least in the future.

The pricing of Arpad's sparkling wines was always a tricky matter. He had to charge less for his Eclipse and other brands than his French competitors charged for theirs because the French products had a cachet that American products could not duplicate. The French products were also subject to higher taxes, which had to be passed along to consumers. But Arpad had to price his bottle-fermented wines above the cheap, imitation "Champagnes" produced with artificial carbonation because his costs of production were much higher. In a typical price list, he offered his Eclipse at $14.50 per case of twelve quart bottles and $17 per case of twenty-four pints. His artificially carbonated competitors offered their bottles as low as $7.00 per case of twelve and $8.00 per case of twenty-four. Among imported Champagnes, Pommery and Roederer brought $34.00 for a case of twelve and $36.00 for a case of twenty-four, while Moët et Chandon White Seal was priced at $32.00 and $34.00 and Moët et Chandon Brut Imperial at $37.00 and $39.00.[86] Arpad's sparkling wines thus occupied the sensitive middle ground between expensive French imports and cheap American imitations, offering him little room for price adjustments. To make matters worse, the prices declined precipitously as the 1890s drew to an end. In 1900, for example, a chain of grocery stores that maintained outlets in San Francisco, Oakland, Berkeley, Alameda, and San Jose offered Eclipse at $4.10 for a case of twelve bottles and just thirty-five cents for a pint.[87] And the Emporium, San Francisco's biggest department store, offered quarts of "Arpad Haraszthy's Natural fermented champagne" at sixty-nine cents per quart bottle.[88] These prices would hardly have covered Arpad's costs of production. It was a disaster.

Arpad's obligation to the California Wine Association came due in 1898. The available records do not show if he paid it, but the circumstantial evidence suggests that he did not—because he could not. The debt was a hard nut to crack, and economic conditions were working against him. As the year 1899 opened, familiar advertisements for Haraszthy sparkling wines disappeared from the *Pacific Wine and Spirit Review.* In their place was a modest notice from Leo Metzger & Co. informing the trade that it was a "depot for Haraszthy champagnes," along with the wines of other makers such as To Kalon Vineyard and the Pioneer Winery.[89] Metzger's store was located at 118 Battery Street. Arpad's old cellars on Washington Street were, so far as published references reveal, closed. The Haraszthy sparkling wines that Metzger and other stores were selling were almost certainly the vintages of previous years. No new wine was in the offing.

In March 1900, Arpad attended the annual dinner of the founders of the Bohemian Club. Twenty-two members were in attendance. Each Bohemian arose to give a little speech, then sat down to reminisce about the early days of the famous club, and to listen to a verse sent to the convocation by Bohemian Charles Warren Stoddard, who could not leave his home in Washington, D.C., to attend:

Happy the heart that in its youth
Was featured in a field so fair;
That lived and loved in very truth
Without one care.[90]

Two months later, in far-off Arizona, Arpad's brother Bela made preparations for a trip to Nome, Alaska. Great new gold fields had been discovered in the northern territory, and Bela, an avid miner, told the *Arizona Republican*, published in Phoenix, that he had located some valuable claims in the Nome district and that he was going back to work them "on an extensive scale." Bela left Yuma with a man named Tom Lewis and headed for San Francisco, where Arpad joined them. Together, the three men headed for Alaska. In October, Bela reported back to the *Republican* that he had a good claim in the north and that he expected "to take out a fortune."[91] Arpad returned to San Francisco in November. The newspapers reported that he "had located some very rich claims and had brought down heavily gold-laden nuggets." He was, the *San Francisco Bulletin* said, "confident that he was on the road to fortune and he was determined to return to Alaska in the spring and prosecute his discoveries."[92]

But Arpad was not feeling well when he reached San Francisco. He attributed his discomfort to severe indigestion and thought it was due to the bad food he had been forced to eat in Alaska. He made an appointment with Dr. Paolo De Vecchi[93] for an examination. On the evening of Thursday, November 15, he made a visit to some of his old friends, the Julius Von Schmidt family, who lived at 1612 Washington Street. He intended to dine with the Von Schmidts and go home early to rest. He made the little trip by foot and on the San Francisco cable cars. It was a stormy night, and when he bid the Von Schmidts good-bye he had to walk through a driving rain. He had only reached the corner of Hyde Street when, umbrella in hand, he crumpled to the ground. He was still breathing when passengers on the Hyde Street cable car saw him and summoned a horse-drawn ambulance to take him to the Receiving Hospital. When he arrived there, he had stopped breathing.

Arpad's daughter, Agostine, was summoned to the morgue. She was distraught, particularly because of the distressing circumstances under which her father had died. A while after she left, an elderly woman with snowy white hair arrived and asked for Agostine. When the deputies on duty told her that Arpad's daughter was no longer there, the woman said that she must see her, that it was "a case of life or death." If Agostine returned, the woman said, the deputies should tell her that "Columbia's mother" had asked for her. "Columbia's mother" and "Columbia"—who could that mysterious person be? When San Francisco newspapers reported Arpad's death the next day, they speculated that "Columbia" might be a young woman in whom Arpad had a romantic interest—that he might even have been engaged to her. They knew that he had been widowed years earlier, and they assumed that he retained a lively interest in the fair sex. A headline in the *Call* advised readers that "Romance Brightened Haraszthy's Old Age," and reported that his death had resulted in the "partial disclosure of a secret." When Mrs. Von Schmidt read the stories, she was horrified, and quickly explained to the newspapers that the woman called "Columbia" was her daughter. Columbia had worked for Arpad some years earlier as a stenographer, Mrs. Von Schmidt said, but ill health had forced her to seek other employment. Arpad had generously helped her in the effort, but Columbia had no romantic relationship with Arpad. It was with Arpad's son Carlos, to whom she had been engaged five years earlier. But Carlos had broken off the engagement and gone "off to France." Columbia herself told the reporters that she was never engaged to Arpad. There was "never such a thing between us," she said.[94] When Agostine spoke to the reporters, she confirmed that her father had not been engaged to Columbia Von Schmidt, or any other woman. "He was a widower and was not engaged," Agostine insisted. Then, betraying a suspicion that some effort to claim an interest in her father's estate might be afoot, Agostine added: "His estate is not so big that there need be any fear of efforts to prove claims to it by any but his recognized heirs."[95]

Arpad's funeral was conducted from St. Mary's Cathedral the following Sunday. A list of eminent San Franciscans was among the pallbearers reported in the *Bulletin*: Vanderlyn Stow, a regent of the University of California, a trustee of Stanford University, and president of the Bohemian Club; Irving M. Scott, the head of the Union Iron Works, San Francisco's most important industrial plant, and the builder of a host U.S. Navy ships; Bryan Clinch, an Irish-born writer, editor, and architect who had designed some of the largest Catholic churches in Northern California, including the cathedrals in Sacramento and San Jose; Edward Bosqui, the distinguished printer who had been a friend of Arpad throughout his Bohemian Club years and in 1877 published the classic folio *Grapes and Grape Vines of California*; and T. C. Van Ness, son of James Van Ness, the mayor for whom Van Ness Avenue was named, and one of the most eminent lawyers in the turn-of-the-century city.[96]

An autopsy revealed that Arpad had died of heart failure. He was sixty years old. His body was buried in San Francisco's Calvary Cemetery, where Jovita had been interred twenty-one years before.[97]

AFTERWORD

After Arpad died, the San Francisco newspapers reflected on his life and the unusual circumstances of his death. The *Bulletin* said his death came as a "shock," both to his family and to his many friends in and out of the city. He had long been "a prominent figure in viticultural circles," the *Bulletin* wrote, and at one time was "a very wealthy man." But his determination to make Eclipse a brand that would "oust from public favor the famous brands of Europe" had taken a heavy toll on his finances. "It was not for himself that he worked," the *Bulletin* said. "It was for his family, and the many and influential friends that hastened to the morgue this morning offering their services with heartfelt sorrow." His friends "testified to the fact that there are many of our most prominent people who held in love and respect the name of Arpad Haraszthy."[1]

The *Call* noted that, "on all matters connected with the growing of wine grapes and the making of wines Mr. Haraszthy was an expert and took pleasure in imparting to others the valuable results of his observations, reading and experience." He was "a generous soul," the *Call* reflected, "—too generous for his own good—a high liver and possessed of a keen sense of enjoyment of life's pleasures." "His generosity led him into acts of financial imprudence, and his eagerness to assist his friends with his signature made large inroads upon his income."[2]

The *Chronicle* noted only that Arpad's death had been "sudden" and that it had "caused much surprise" among his friends. He was a "well known winemaker," the *Chronicle* said, and "a citizen who has had much to do with the development of the viticultural interest" of California.[3] The *Examiner* noted that he was "a man of striking appearance and courteous bearing, with much of the old-time gallantry in his manner . . . a link between the old world and the new, a reminder of stormy revolutionary days and a somewhat pathetic figure in the bustle and energy of peaceful business life."[4]

In Sonoma County, the *Santa Rosa Republican* noted that Arpad's death had surprised his "many Sonoma county friends." He was, the *Republican* reminded its readers, "the well known winemaker" and "a son of the pioneer vineyardist of this portion of the state."[5]

The *Pacific Wine and Spirit Review* knew Arpad better than the daily newspapers. It remembered him as "dear old Arpad Haraszthy, nobleman by birth, and nature, and one of the pioneers and founders of the wine industry in California, which is now the source of millions of dollars annual revenue to the State." His "connection with the industry as the first to produce champagne by the French method in America, made him more widely known than any other wine man of California," the *Review* continued, adding that his pioneering work in the wine industry "would doubtless have brought him well merited success financially, had it not been for the many unforeseen and well-nigh insurmountable difficulties that lined his path." He had spent large sums of money "in discovering how to properly convert California wines into champagne," the *Review* said, "and had this been accomplished before his product was placed upon the market, his fortune would have been assured; but it was not; the opportunity passed by and he was too old and disheartened to take up the trying battle again. Hence his last resort—courting the Fickle Goddess within the Arctic Circle after he had reached the age of sixty."[6]

The *Review* might have noted the striking parallel between Agoston's effort to recoup his shattered fortunes in Nicaragua and Arpad's effort to do the same in Alaska. Both men had met with financial disaster in California and pursued the "Fickle Goddess" in a remote corner of the globe. And both had again met failure. For a last time, Arpad had shown that he was indeed the "Son of his Father."

The *Pacific Wine and Spirit Review* remembered Agoston and the European grapevines he had introduced into California—including "the 'Zinfandel' from his native Hungary," the grape which "more than any other . . . has determined the character of California wine and will doubtless always continue to do so." The *Review* referred to Agoston as "Count Haraszthy," as did the *Chronicle*, the *Call*, the *Bulletin*, and the *Santa Rosa Republican*. They recalled Agoston's thrilling exploits as a rebel against the autocratic rule of the Hapsburgs in Hungary. They spoke of the cruel and unjust death sentence that had forced him to flee his native land for the freedom of America. Of course, all of this was part of the "Haraszthy Legend" that Agoston had constructed in his early years in America and that his family had learned to repeat, almost by habit. In fact, Agoston had not come to America to escape political oppression but in search of economic opportunity. The Haraszthys (both Agoston and Arpad) were in fact Hungarian noblemen, though in Hungary they would have answered to the title of Spectabilis Dominus or Tekintetes Úr rather than "Count." But the legend seemed so much more appealing than the truth, both to the public and the family.[7]

But not all of what the newspapers wrote after Arpad died was family legend. Agoston Haraszthy had, in fact, been one of the most important pioneers of the early years of the California wine industry, as had Arpad. Arpad had labored valiantly to make the dream of a high quality California sparkling wine a reality. He had studied the art of making Champagne in France, and he had done more than any other man, before or since, to transport the méthode champenoise to California. The *Pacific Wine and Spirit Review* was mistaken when it declared that he was "the first to produce champagne by the French method in America." There had been others before him, but none of them had the success that he did, and none persisted so long and with such determination to perfect their art. He was the first to make bottle-fermented California sparkling wine on a sustained basis, and the first to prove to his state and the nation that naturally fermented sparkling wine could be made in California, from grapes grown in California, crushed, fermented, and bottled in California. For more than thirty years, he produced good (some said exceptionally good) sparkling wine in California, first in Sonoma and then in San Francisco. It was not an easy task. Popular tastes, natural hazards (the phylloxera notable among them), and, finally, the great economic depression of the 1890s, conspired against him. And, in the end, a sudden death deprived him of the opportunity to continue his efforts.

Arpad Haraszthy never compromised his viticultural ideals. He never resorted to artificial carbonation to make his wines sparkle. He never foisted onto an unsuspecting public wines that were other than what they purported to be. He did not misrepresent his Eclipse or any of the other sparkling wines he produced in California. They were products of California, made according to traditional French methods, and he never attempted to create the impression that they were French—although he argued again and again that they were *as good as the French.* Born in Hungary, trained in France, he was as fervent and loyal a champion of his adopted state as any winemaker who ever lived. He was a Californian. He made "California champagne," and he was proud of the fact.

But Arpad's legacy was not just the wines, still and sparkling, he made and sold, or the innovative cuvées he blended, or the medals his wines won at fairs and expositions all over the world, or the fame he brought to the name Eclipse. It consisted just as much of his years of work as a writer and speaker, and as a leader of other vine growers and winemakers. Arpad was one of the most literate men who ever devoted his career to the art and science of winemaking. He was a gifted writer, who imparted valuable information to his fellow vine growers and winemakers, and for nearly forty years he was generous in sharing his knowledge. He was an engaging storyteller, a man who ate well, drank well, and lived well. As president of the California State Vinicultural Society, and president for eight years of the Board of State Viticultural Commissioners, he led the California wine industry through difficult times of expansion and retrenchment. Arpad was a leader in the effort to enact pure wine legislation, and though he encountered difficulties when the California Supreme Court struck down the state law of 1887, he continued to champion the goal of pure wine, free from adulteration and contamination. When, in 1906, the United States Congress passed a national Pure Food and Drug Act, it applied to wine as well as other products intended for human consumption, vindicating the goals that Arpad and his fellow winemakers of the late nineteenth century had fought hard to achieve.[8]

If Arpad was admired for his own accomplishments as a winemaker, he was also admired for his devotion to his father. Agoston Haraszthy was an entrepreneurial whirlwind who pioneered scores of enterprises in Wisconsin, San Diego, San Francisco, Crystal Springs, Sonoma, and finally Nicaragua. As a winemaker, he blazed a trail that Arpad (and countless others) followed in the last half of the nineteenth century. Agoston provided much of the inspiration for Arpad's career, but he may also have led Arpad astray—at least in one important particular, and in a way he could never have anticipated. Arpad's stubborn insistence that his father brought Zinfandel to California—not only that his father brought the grape to the Golden State but that he was *the first man to do so*—may have been Arpad's Achilles Heel. In his own voluminous writings on grapes and wines, Agoston never mentioned Zinfandel. This is not surprising, for he never mentioned any particular grape variety—in fact, it was never his object to discuss particular grape varieties. He chose instead to argue that the best grape varieties known to the world of winemaking should be brought to the state, planted, cultivated, and made into wine, and that California winemakers should always and ever pursue excellence. In his own winemaking career, he practiced what he preached, bringing hundreds of grape varieties to California, planting them, cultivating them, and making them into wine. Arpad argued that Zinfandel was his father's favorite. It may have been, although there is no documentary evidence to support his claim. If Agoston had lived to hear the argument about Zinfandel's California origins, he may well have been surprised—perhaps even amused. His winemaking legacy never depended on a single grape, and it was wrong to assume that his reputation should stand or fall on the single issue of whether he was the first man to bring the celebrated vine to California. It is unlikely, however, that he would have been surprised by his son's vehemence in defending his memory. Arpad Haraszthy was, as Charles

Wetmore said, "the son of his father." Agoston knew that Arpad would defend his reputation, and he did just that—in the process, perhaps, damaging his own.

Arpad's reputation, and that of his Eclipse sparkling wine, survived his death, but only tenuously. Some bottles of Eclipse remained in wine cellars and vaults for years after he died. Some were placed on sale in San Francisco and other cities.[9] Most were destroyed in the great earthquake and fire that devastated San Francisco in 1906. Strangely, perhaps, Arpad's sparkling wine cellars on Washington Street survived the great disaster.[10] His offices at 530 Washington Street stood proud and firm into the twenty-first century, facing not the old Montgomery Block, but the soaring Transamerica Pyramid that replaced the historic building in the 1970s.

Arpad's old Orleans Vineyard in Yolo County had a much shorter life than his San Francisco cellars. After Henry Epstein transferred the property to the California Wine Association in 1894, the CWA continued to harvest the grapes, but the vines were sick and growing sicker. The phylloxera was at work. Epstein left the CWA after a few months to pursue other business enterprises. The CWA continued to acquire wine cellars, vineyards, and brand names, and soon became the largest and most powerful wine producer in the state—perhaps in the United States.[11] Its detractors called it the "wine trust," but it accomplished its stated purpose of bringing stability to the California wine industry, and it continued to dominate the California wine markets until the coming of prohibition in 1920. When Arpad left the CWA in 1895, he missed what was, in hindsight, his best opportunity to perpetuate his business legacy. Had he remained with the CWA, Arpad Haraszthy & Co. would have survived his death as one of the CWA's brands. Eclipse would very likely have survived, although not under his personal management. But Arpad's effort to continue the business on his own ended with his death in 1900. Two years after he died, the *Pacific Wine and Spirit Review* reported that Arpad's Yolo County vineyard had also died. "The Orleans Vineyard, in Yolo county," the *Review* wrote in 1902, "which was planted and made famous by the late Arpad Haraszthy, has been sold and will be converted into a wheat farm. Phylloxera did the business."[12]

Arpad's own family survived only a little longer than Eclipse and Orleans. Carlos Haraszthy abandoned his medical career in the early 1890s. By the time his father died in 1900, Carlos had moved to Tahiti, where he died on September 19, 1903.[13] He was thirty-six years old and still unmarried. Arpad's daughter Agostine left San Francisco sometime after her father's death. She was a widow (her husband George Strickland had died in 1896). In New York, Agostine pursued a career as a photographer. She was one of the pioneers of women's portrait photography, and her works were praised in photography magazines and displayed in prestigious exhibitions.[14] Agostine returned to San Francisco where she died on June 13, 1913.[15] She was forty-nine years old and still a widow. Neither Carlos Haraszthy nor Agostine Strickland left any heirs.

But Arpad Haraszthy's legacy had some durability. He was referred to often in the literature of California wine as a pioneer champagne maker. In 1973, his essay "How to Drink Wine" appeared again in a reprint of Frona Eunice Wait's *Wines and Vines of California,* this time with an introduction by Maynard A. Amerine, a distinguished professor of viticulture and enology at the University of California in Davis. In 1978, the Book Club of California reissued his *Overland Monthly* essays of 1871 and 1872 as a separate volume under the title *Wine-Making in California.* The book was beautifully printed and issued with a biographical introduction by wine historians Ruth Teiser and Catherine Harroun. And when, in the last years of the twentieth century, new occupants sought to refurbish Arpad's old sparkling wine cellars on Washington Street in San Francisco, they found corks in the basements. They were at first puzzled by their discovery, then astonished to learn that the corks were remnants of what had once been the largest and most famous sparkling-wine cellars in California.[16]

Beyond the publications, beyond the durable wine cellars on Washington Street, beyond the corks in the dark recesses of the century-old basements, Arpad Haraszthy's legacy had an even more lasting quality, for in the more than thirty years that he worked in San Francisco he proved to himself and the world that it was possible to make superior sparkling wine in California. He proved that his nineteenth century dream of a world-class California sparkling wine was not a fantasy, but an attainable goal. All winemakers rely in large measure for their success on the accomplishments of their predecessors. The dozens—even scores—of winemakers who produced superior sparkling wine in California in the twentieth and twenty-first centuries would, if they examined their history closely, find that they owe at least part of their success to efforts made by their predecessors in the nineteenth century.[17] If these modern-day producers stand tall today, it is in part because they stand on the shoulders of pioneers like Arpad Haraszthy.

NOTES

INTRODUCTION

1. In Hungarian, Haraszthy is pronounced HOAR-os-tee (in Hungarian, the first syllable of every word is always stressed). The anglicized pronunciation favored by Haraszthy's American descendants is HAIR-us-tee.

2. Agoston Haraszthy was generally referred to by such designations as the "Father of California Viticulture," "Father of California Wine," or "Father of Modern Winemaking in California" for more than a century after his death in 1869. After 1970, the designation was vigorously challenged by Charles Sullivan, Thomas Pinney, and other wine historians. For discussion, see Chapter 6.

3. Carosso, *California Wine Industry,* 71, says that Chinese laborers at Buena Vista in Sonoma cost the employer "no more than approximately a dollar a day each." Street, *Beasts of the Field,* 743n54, says that the Chinese at Buena Vista were paid eighteen to twenty dollars a month plus room and board, or one dollar a day if they provided their own room and board. Whites were paid thirty-five dollars a month plus fifteen dollars for room and board, or two dollars a day without room and board. The pay in San Francisco may have been a little more than in Sonoma, but not much.

4. Beginning at the turn of the twentieth century, sparkling wine designated as "champagne" was produced in South Africa, Australia, Russia, Canada, Germany, and Argentina, as well as the United States and France. At one time or another, South African, Australian, and Portuguese "champagnes" have been sold in the United States. Knoll, "Champagne," 309–10, 312.

5. This word is spelled with a capital "C" when referring to the Champagne region and to the sparkling wine made in that region by the méthode champenoise. It is spelled with a lower case "c" when used to describe sparkling wines made in other regions or countries.

6. Sparkling wine made outside the country was described as "champagne" in the United States about 1832. As early as 1839, American-made sparkling wine was designated as "champagne" on wine cards of hotels in New York and Philadelphia. Knoll, "Champagne," 310, 312.

7. Quoted in Davies, "Sparkling Wines," 264.

8. Simon, *Champagne,* 12.

9. 26 United States Code Sec. 5388 (use of semi-generic designations); Mendelson, *From Demon to Darling,* 155.

10. In 1866, Congress imposed a tax of six dollars per dozen bottles on "all wines, liquors, or compounds known or denominated as wine, made in imitation of sparkling wine or champagne, and put up in bottles in imitation of any imported wine, or with the pretence of being imported wine, or wine of foreign growth or manufacture." This tax was nearly confiscatory. Act of July 13, 1866, An Act to reduce Internal Taxation, etc., 14 Stats. 98. Sec. 36. In 1868, however, this tax was limited to "wines not made from grapes grown in the United States." Act of July 20, 1868, An Act imposing taxes on distilled spirits and tobacco, and for other purposes, Secs. 48, 105, 15 Stats. 125.

11. Arpad Haraszthy and Nesfield, *California Grapes and Wine,* 17 (bottles all imported from France); Simon, *Champagne,* 146 (up to 1914 all Champagne bottles were handmade).

12. The French word cuvée literally means a tub-full or vat-full. In the production of sparkling wine, it refers to a blend of still wines used to produce a particular bottling. The blends will differ from bottling to bottling or year to year.

13. Arpad Haraszthy and Nesfield, *California Grapes and Wine,* 20 (loss between 10 and 20 percent); O'Connell, *Inner Man,* 132 (loss from breakage about 16 percent).

14. See Ray, *Vineyards in the Sky,* 73 (quoting Paul Masson); Arpad Haraszthy and Nesfield, *California Grapes and Wine,* 20 (bottles explode with a report like that of artillery).

15. Mendelson, *From Demon to Darling,* 6–49, describes the growth and evolution of the temperance movement before the adoption of national prohibition.

16. Lapsley, *Bottled Poetry,* 4–5, points out that the quality of the state's vine stocks suffered seriously during prohibition, as better grape varieties were replaced with "poorer quality varieties that could withstanding shipping," or with "varieties with deeper pigmentation or astringency, such as Alicante Bouschet or Petite Sirah, that could stand dilution with water." When prohibition was repealed, these grapes were ill-suited to the production of good wines and, as Lapsley states, produced "a chronic statewide oversupply of poor-quality grapes, which reduced grape and wine prices for years to come." Mendelson, *From Demon to Darling,* 64–78, describes exceptions to the prohibition laws.

17. Wetmore, "Prominent Wine Men," 11.

18. U.S. Passport Applications, 1795–1905, 1855–1861, National Archives and Records Service, M1372.

19. Wetmore, "Prominent Wine Men," 11.

20. Emparan, *Vallejos of California,* 358.

21. For discussion, see Chapters 5 and 6.

22. Wetmore, "Prominent Wine Men," 11.

1. THE SON OF HIS FATHER

1. Wetmore, "Prominent Wine Men," 10.

2. Ibid.

3. "European Vines," *San Francisco Bulletin,* May 14, 1885, 4.

4. Ibid. For the controversy surrounding Arpad's claims about his father's introduction of Zinfandel to California, see discussion in Chapters 5 and 6.

5. Baptismal Register, Terézváros parish, Budapest, August 30, 1812.

6. Baptismal Register, Belváros parish, Szeged, November 19, 1789. McGinty, *Strong Wine,* 481–82nn11, 12.

7. John Paget, *Hungary and Transylvania,* new ed., (London: John Murray, 1855), I: 415 (Tekintetes Úr); when his first son (Géza) was baptized on January 2, 1834, Agoston was described in the Parish Register of Hegyes as "Spectabilis Dominus Augustinus Haraszti [*sic*] de Mokcsa." Baptismal Register, Parish of Kishegyes (also known as Hegyes), January 2, 1834.

8. Marriage Register, Parish of Futtak, January 6, 1833.

9. "Vine Culture" by "C. H.," *San Francisco Daily Alta California,* November 18, 1856, 1.

10. Baptismal Register, Parish of Kishegyes (also known as Hegyes), January 2, 1834.

11. Baptismal Register, Parish of Szenttamás, April 20, 1835.

12. McGinty, *Strong Wine,* 51–59.

13. "The Haraszthy Family," MS, typewritten p. 2. This manuscript is indispensable to serious Haraszthy studies, yet glaringly unreliable in particulars.

14. McGinty, *Strong Wine,* 98.

15. Ibid., 68–83.

16. Ibid., 77–78.

17. Ibid., 84–106.

18. Baptismal Register, Parish of Futtak, June 28, 1840.

19. McGinty, *Strong Wine,* 106.

20. Ibid., 81–82.

21. "The Haraszthy Family," MS, typewritten p. 14.

22. McGinty, *Strong Wine,* 71.

23. "The Haraszthy Family," MS, typewritten p. 14; Arpad Haraszthy, "Colonel Agoston Haraszthy," 6; Gärtner, "Tagebuch der röm. katholischen Missionen in Nord-America," MS, St. Norbert Abbey, De Pere, Wisconsin; McGinty, *Strong Wine,* 112.

24. McGinty, *Strong Wine,* 109.

25. Baptismal Register, St. Norbert Parish, December 14, 1848; Gärtner, "Tagebuch der röm. katholischen Missionen in Nord-America," MS, St. Norbert Abbey, De Pere, Wisconsin, 59, 242–43.

26. Baptismal Register, St. Aloysius Parish, Sauk City.

27. McGinty, *Strong Wine,* 139–76.

28. Hayes, "Diary of Judge Benjamin Hayes' Journey," MS, pp. 172, 174.

29. Brainard, "Journal of the Walworth Co. Mutual Mining Company," MS; McGinty, *Strong Wine,* 158.

30. McGinty, *Strong Wine,* 182–83.

31. Ibid., 190–91.

32. Ibid., 187–89, 226–27.

33. "A Remarkable Career," *New York Times,* February 27, 1870, 3.

34. McGinty, *Strong Wine,* 252–53.

35. Ibid., 252–54. For further discussion of the relations between Agoston Haraszthy, Arpad Haraszthy, and Lázár Mészáros, see Chapter 6.

36. "The Haraszthy Family," MS, typewritten p. 24.

37. "Arrival of the Golden Gate," *Supplement to the Daily Alta California,* April 30, 1857, 1, lists "A. F. Haraszthy" as a passenger from Panama. The Hungarian John Xánthus, who arrived in San Francisco on the same ship, said that he traveled from New York with Agoston Haraszthy's "brother." Madden, "California for Hungarian Readers," 130. But this was an obvious error for "son," since Agoston had no brother and Arpad was returning from the East at this time.

38. San Francisco (California) Deeds, Book 9, pp. 620, 621.

39. McGinty, *Strong Wine,* 249–51.

40. Ibid., 249–58, 288, 296.

41. Ibid., 262.

42. See McGinty, *Haraszthy at the Mint,* for the full story of the prosecution and trial.

43. Arpad Haraszthy, "Early Viticulture in Sonoma," 77.

44. McGinty, *Strong Wine,* 297–98, 304–305.

45. Ibid., 300–302, 327.

46. Arpad Haraszthy, "Early Viticulture in Sonoma," 77; "The Haraszthy Family," MS, handwritten p. 2.

47. See Chapters 5 and 6.

48. "The Haraszthy Family," MS, typewritten p. 24.

49. Ibid.

50. Ibid., typewritten pp. 24–25.

51. Ibid., typewritten p. 25.

52. *San Francisco Daily Alta California,* May 20, 1861, 1.

53. Agoston Haraszthy, *Grape-Culture, Wines, and Wine-Making,* 34.

54. McGinty, *Strong Wine,* 338–39.

55. Ibid., 323–27.

56. Agoston Haraszthy, "Report on Grapes and Wines of California," 311–29.

57. "The Importation of Foreign Vines and Fruits," *San Francisco Daily Alta California,* May 26, 1861, 2.

58. Ibid.

59. Agoston Haraszthy, *Grape Culture, Wines, and Wine-Making,* 34.

60. McGinty, *Strong Wine,* 357.

61. Ibid.

62. "Letter from Mr. Haraszthy," February 8, 1862, in *Appendix to Journals of Senate and Assembly* (1862).

63. *San Francisco Daily Alta California,* February 15, 1862, 2.

64. McGinty, *Strong Wine,* 359–69.

65. Appendix I to "Supplementary Report of Charles A. Wetmore," in *Appendix to the Journals of the Senate and Assembly* (1881), 184.

66. McGinty, *Strong Wine,* 376.

67. The book was Agoston Haraszthy, *Grape-Culture, Wines, and Wine-Making,* published by Harper and Brothers in 1862.

68. *San Francisco Daily Alta California,* February 2, 1863, 2; *New York Times,* May 10, 1862, 5.

69. Arpad Haraszthy, "Bottling Red Wine," *California Farmer,* June 21, 1861, 129.

70. These letters are listed in the bibliography.

71. *California Farmer,* June 14, 1861, 121.

72. Arpad Haraszthy, "Make Pure Wine—No Imitations," *California Farmer,* July 18, 1862, 129.

73. "European Vines," *San Francisco Bulletin,* May 14, 1885, 4.

74. Agoston Haraszthy, "Report on Grapes and Wines of California," 324.

75. "The Haraszthy Family," MS, typewritten p. 25.

76. In 1871, Arpad wrote that "almost every wine-growing country in the Old World owes its first plantation of vines to the monks." He named a dozen of the greatest wines of Europe (including Champagne) and said that they were attributable "to their [the monks'] labors alone," then added: "And what the monks did for the Old World, that did the Fathers for California. They planted the first vine, and they made our first wine." See Arpad Haraszthy, "Wine-Making in California," *Overland Monthly* 7, no. 6 (1871): 489.

77. Fredericksen, "One Hundred Years of American Champagne," 24; Teiser and Harroun, *Winemaking in California,* 65–66.

78. Fredericksen, "One Hundred Years of American Champagne," 24.

79. Pedro [*sic*] Sainsevain to Arpad Haraszthy, June 22, 1886, typescript copy in "The Haraszthy Family," MS.

80. "The Haraszthy Family," MS, typewritten p. 26.

81. McGinty, *Strong Wine,* 395–97.

82. Emparan, *The Vallejos of California,* 308, 311, 353.

83. "A Trip to the Vineyards of Sonoma Valley," *San Francisco Daily Alta California,* July 28, 1863, 1.

84. Ibid.

85. "Our Letter from Sonoma," *San Francisco Daily Alta California,* September 21, 1863, 1.

86. "A Trip to Sonoma Valley," *California Wine, Wool, and Stock Journal* (May 1863), 78.

87. These are listed in the bibliography.

88. "Wine-Making in California," *Harper's New Monthly Magazine* 29 (June 1864): 22–30. *Harper's* attributed this article to "A. Haraszthy," thus leading at least one wine historian to conclude that Agoston Haraszthy wrote it. See Pinney, *A History of Wine in America,* 281. But frequent internal references to "Mr. Haraszthy" as the founder and proprietor of Buena Vista, which would make no sense if Agoston was the author, strongly suggest that it was the work of Arpad Haraszthy.

89. Baptismal Register, 1840–1908, St. Francisco Solano Church, Sonoma; "The Haraszthy Family," MS, typewritten p. 32. Agostine Haraszthy was born on April 11, 1864.

90. "The Haraszthy Family," MS, typewritten p. 26.

91. McGinty, *Strong Wine,* 401–402.

2. TO MAKE THE WINE SPARKLE

1. See McGinty, *Strong Wine,* 323–29.

2. Arpad Haraszthy, "Early Viticulture in Sonoma," 77–79.

3. Muster Roll, Company B, 18th N.Y. Cavalry, National Archives Microfilm Publications, Compiled Records Showing Service of Military Units in Volunteer Union Organizations (Washington, D.C.: National Archives, 1964), roll 110.

4. Peninou, Unzelman, and Anderson, *History of the Sonoma Viticultural District,* 65.

5. Hyatt, *Hyatt's Hand-Book of Grape Culture,* 210.

6. "The Haraszthy Family," MS, typewritten p. 26.

7. *California Farmer,* October 7, 1864, 80; October 14, 1864, 89.

8. Hyatt, *Hyatt's Hand-Book of Grape Culture,* 210 (emphasis in original).

9. *San Francisco Daily Alta California,* March 27, 1865, 2; April 13, 1865, 1, 2.

10. "The Haraszthy Family," MS, typewritten p 26.

11. Hyatt, *Hyatt's Hand-Book of Grapes and Wine,* 210, says: "Mr. Arpad Haraszthy assures us that himself and partner made 30,000 gallons one season for their neighbors in Sonoma . . . for 8 cents per gallon, and they consider they made a profit of 100 per cent."

12. McGinty, *Strong Wine,* 401, 440.

13. "Prominent Wine Men: Sketch No. 16, I. Landsberger, of Landsberger & Son, San Francisco," *Pacific Wine and Spirit Review,* January 21, 1892, 21; "Obituary, Isador [*sic*] Landsberger," *Pacific Wine and Spirit Review,* August 31, 1904, 63.

14. "The Haraszthy Family," MS, typewritten p. 27.

15. *San Francisco Daily Alta California,* December 11, 1866, 1; McGinty, *Strong Wine,* 435–36.

16. "The Haraszthy Family," MS, typewritten p. 27.

17. "California Sparkling Wines," *San Francisco Daily Evening Bulletin,* November 9, 1867, 5.

18. "The Haraszthy Family," MS, typewritten p. 27.

19. The modern practice is to freeze the neck of the bottle before disgorgement. This could not be done in Arpad Haraszthy's time, when a successful disgorgement depended solely on the cellar worker's skill in handling the bottle, the cork, and the effervescent wine.

20. "California Sparkling Wines," *San Francisco Daily Evening Bulletin,* November 9, 1867, 5.

21. Stoll, "Over the Sparkling Wine Cup," 15; Stoll, "Haraszthy's 'Eclipse' Champagne," 10; Stoll, "History of Champagne Making in California," 4.

22. "California Sparkling Wines," *San Francisco Daily Evening Bulletin,* November 9, 1867, 5.

23. Ibid.

24. "Sparkling Californian Wine," *San Francisco Daily Alta California,* November 11, 1867, 1.

25. *Transactions of the California State Agricultural Society during the Years 1866 and 1867,* 172–73, 223–25.

26. Act of July 13, 1866, Sec. 36, 14 Stats. 98, imposed a tax of six dollars per dozen on "all wines, liquors, or compounds known or denominated as wine, made in imitation of sparkling wine or champagne, and put up in bottles in imitation of any imported wine, or with the pretence of being imported wine, or wine of foreign growth or manufacture."

27. "California Sparkling Wine," *San Francisco Daily Evening Bulletin,* November 9, 1867, 5.

28. In 1868, Congress revised the law taxing wines "made in imitation of sparkling wine or champagne" by limiting it to wines "not made from grapes grown in the United States." Act of July 20, 1868, An Act imposing taxes on distilled spirits and tobacco, and for other purposes, Secs. 48, 105, 15 Stats. 125.

29. *Daily Alta California San Francisco,* November 11, 21, 24, 26, 30, 1867, p. 1.

30. "Sparkling Californian Wine," *San Francisco Daily Alta California,* November 11, 1867, 1.

31. McGinty, "Angelica," 33–37; see Arpad Haraszthy, "Wine-Making in California," *Overland Monthly* 6, no. 1 (1871): 491 (describing Angelica as a "grape *liqueur,* for a wine it certainly cannot correctly be called").

32. "Best Glasses and Best Articles to Fill Them," *San Francisco Daily Alta California,* July 1, 1868, 2 (gold medal for Sparkling Sonoma wine awarded by Board of Managers of State Agricultural Society); advertisement in same issue (claiming gold medal from Board of Agriculture for sparkling wine awarded June 24, 1868).

33. *San Francisco Directory for the Year Commencing October, 1868* (San Francisco: Henry G. Langley, 1868), lix.

34. Arpad Haraszthy, "The Vintage in Sonoma," *San Francisco Daily Alta California,* November 21, 1868, 2.

35. McGinty, *Strong Wine,* 325–26, 329, 392, 422, 439–40, 459.

36. Arpad Haraszthy, "The Vintage in Sonoma," *San Francisco Daily Alta California,* November 21, 1868, 2.

37. *Report of the Committee on Culture of the Grape,* 12.

38. "Sparkling California," *San Francisco Daily Alta California,* March 9, 1869, 2.

39. Simon, *Champagne,* 28.

40. Ibid., 26.

41. "Sparkling California," *San Francisco Daily Alta California,* March 9, 1869, 2.

42. "California Wines: Landsberger & Co.," *California Farmer,* July 1, 1869, 180.

43. *San Francisco Daily Alta California,* October 10, 1869, 1 (Finke, Lachman & Jacobi); McGinty, *Strong Wine,* 429, 440, 449 (BVVS).

44. Appendix, "Production of Wine in California," in *Reports of the United States Commissioners to the Paris Universal Exposition, 1867,* 27.

45. "Progress of I. Landsberger & Co.'s Champagne Making," *California Farmer,* July 22, 1869, 4.

46. "California Champagne," *San Francisco Call,* April 16, 1871.

47. "The Haraszthy Family," MS, typewritten p. 32.

48. Arpad Haraszthy, "Wine-Making in California," *Overland Monthly* 7, no. 6 (1871): 489–97; 8, nos. 1, 2, 5 (1872): 34–41, 105–109, 393–98.

49. Arpad Haraszthy, "Wine-Making in California," *Overland Monthly* 7, no. 65 (1871): 494–95.

50. Arpad Haraszthy, "Wine-Making in California," *Overland Monthly* 8, no. 5 (1872): 395.

51. Ibid., 396.

52. Arpad Haraszthy, "Wine-Making in California," *Overland Monthly* 8, no. 2 (1872): 40.

53. Arpad Haraszthy, "Wine-Making in California," *Overland Monthly* 7, no. 6 (1871): 489.

54. McGinty, *Strong Wine,* 445–47.

55. Ibid., 461.

56. Ibid., 458–59.

57. Ibid., 461–62.

58. Ibid., 461–64.

59. Ibid., 465–66.

60. "Colonel Auguston [*sic*] Haraszthy," *San Francisco Daily Alta California,* August 27, 1869, 2.

61. "A Remarkable Career," *New York Times,* February 27, 1870, 3.

62. See discussion in Chapter 6.

63. Charles L. Sullivan, a prolific historian of California wine, led this effort with his article, "A Viticultural Mystery Solved: The Historical Origins of Zinfandel in California" (*California History* 57 (Summer 1978): 114–29). Thomas L. Pinney followed Sullivan's lead in his *History of Wine in America.* Both Sullivan and Pinney stressed Arpad's controversial recollections about the origins of Zinfandel in California. See discussion in Chapters 5 and 6.

64. See Sullivan, *Companion to California Wine,* 148 ("Arpad made the promotion of Agoston as the 'father of the California wine industry' a part of his attempts to keep his own business afloat") ; Sullivan, *Zinfandel,* 58 (Arpad's claim that Agoston was the "father" as "laughable,"' 61 (Arpad a "desperate man"), 63 (Arpad "lying"), 67 (Arpad peddling "historical nonsense"); Pinney, *A History of Wine in America,* 284 ("we should no longer take seriously the legend that has grown up about him [Agoston Haraszthy].

3. ECLIPSE EXTRA DRY

1. See *San Francisco Daily Alta California,* October 10, 1869, 1 (Riesling wine, Sonoma white and red wine, Sonoma Port and California Vermouth); *California Farmer,* July 1, 1869, 180 (Sparkling Muscatel); *Report of the Committee on Culture of the Grape,* 13 (Riesling).

2. Simon, *Champagne,* 91–93.

3. Ibid., 93–98.

4. Emparan, *The Vallejos of California,* 354.

5. Teiser and Harroun, "Introduction" to *Wine-Making in California,* by Arpad Haraszthy, 5.

6. Vizetelly, *History of Champagne,* 111.

7. Joe Drape, ed., *To the Swift: Classic Triple Crown Horses and their Race for Glory* (New York: St. Martin's Press, 2008), 296.

8. Emparan, *The Vallejos of California,* 354, asserts that toasts were drunk in Eclipse when the Palace Hotel was opened.

9. McGinty, *The Palace Inns,* 63–72.

10. *San Francisco Daily Alta California,* December 1, 1875, 1.

11. "Philadelphia," *San Francisco Daily Alta California,* June 3, 1876, 1. McCabe, *Illustrated History of the Centennial Exhibition,* 480.

12. McCabe, *Illustrated History of the Centennial Exhibition,* 480.

13. Ibid.

14. "California Wines," *San Francisco Daily Alta California,* October 22, 1876, 1 (see also advertisement, "Centennial Award," on p. 2).

15. "California Wines," *San Francisco Daily Alta California,* October 22, 1876, 1.

16. "The Wine Awards," *San Francisco Daily Alta California,* October 22, 1876, 2.

17. "An Award for California Champagne," *San Francisco Daily Alta California,* November 16, 1876, 1.

18. Wait, *Wines and Vines of California,* 94

19. "Brevities," *San Francisco Daily Alta California,* September 26, 1876, 1.

20. Wait, *Wines and Vines of California,* 94.

21. "Native Wines," *San Francisco Daily Alta California,* December 10, 1877, 2 (quoting *Bonfort's Wine and Liquor Circular*); Wait, *Wines and Vines of California,* 94.

22. "Dissolution of Partnership," *San Francisco Daily Alta California,* August 3, 1874, 3.

23. *Wine Dealers' Gazette* [San Francisco], July 1876, advertisement for I. Landsberger & Co., listing names of I. Landsberger, Arpad Haraszthy, and Edward Vollmer.

24. *San Francisco Directory for the Year Commencing December, 1869* (San Francisco: Henry G. Langley, 1869), 55, 223, 276, lists Louis Gross & Co. and Edward Vollmer & Co. of Belmont, Nevada, as the manufacturers of IXL Bitters. Belmont, Nevada, was then a thriving silver mining town; it has since become a ghost town. Henry and Simon Epstein then lived at 335 Eddy Street in San Francisco.

25. *General Index of the Official Gazette and Monthly Volumes of Patents of the United States Patent Office, 1872* (Washington, D.C.: Government Printing Office, 1873), 386.

26. *Wine Dealers' Gazette* [San Francisco], July 1876, advertisement for I. Landsberger & Co.

27. *San Francisco Directory for the Year Commencing April, 1876* (San Francisco: Henry G. Langley, 1876), 481.

28. *Transactions of the California State Agricultural Society during the Years 1868 and 1869,* 116.

29. *San Francisco Directory for the Year Commencing December, 1869* (San Francisco: Henry G. Langley, 1869), 55, 223, 276.

30. *San Francisco Directory for the Year Commencing April, 1871* (San Francisco: Henry G. Langley, 1871), 236; *San Francisco Directory for the Year Commencing April, 1876* (San Francisco: Henry G. Langley, 1876), 481.

31. Collins, "The Man Who Ate, and Drank, California: Major Benjamin C. Truman," 14–18.

32. "California's Vintage," *New York Times,* January 7, 1877, 1.

33. Ibid.

34. Ibid.

35. "California Viniculture," *San Francisco Daily Evening Bulletin,* January 20, 1877, 4.

36. Ibid.

37. Ibid.

38. "Installation of the New Officers of Excelsior Lodge," *San Francisco Daily Alta California,* December 31, 1874, 1.

39. *Bohemian Club,* 105.

40. Ibid., 9.

41. Hart, *In Our Second Century,* 327–67; for Bosqui, see Starr, "Introduction" to *Grapes and Grape Vines of California* (unnumbered pages).

42. In a letter to Charles Warren Stoddard written from Davos, Switzerland, in December 1880, Stevenson said: "Remember me to [Frank] Unger, [Julian] Rix, [Arpad] Haraszthy, and, last but not least, my brother Scot, [Joe] Austin." Ernest Mehew, ed., *Selected Letters of Robert Louis Stevenson* (New Haven: Yale University Press, 1998), 176–77. After Stevenson settled in Samoa, Arpad sent him shipments of Eclipse from San Francisco. See Chapter 7.

43. Bosqui, *Memoirs of Edward Bosqui,* 127.

44. Driesbach, *Bountiful Harvest,*12–37; Perry, *Pacific Arcadia,* 74–75.

45. O'Connell, *The Inner Man,* 133.

46. Ibid., 160.

47. Swanberg, *Citizen Hearst,* 72; Morris, *Ambrose Bierce*, 159; Saunders, *Ambrose Bierce,* 53.

48. Swanberg, *Citizen Hearst,* 72; Morris, *Ambrose Bierce*, 159; Saunders, *Ambrose Bierce,* 53.

49. Coblentz, *Ambrose Bierce,* unnumbered p. 9.

50. Bromley, *The Long Ago,* 84–85.

51. *Bohemian Club,* 110.

52. "The Bohemian's Founders Meet Around the Table for Annual Dinner," *San Francisco Call,* March 11, 1900, 21.

53. The words "society" and "association" were apparently used interchangeably.

54. "The Haraszthy Family," MS, typewritten p. 32.

55. See, e.g., Charles A. Wetmore, "Native Wines," *San Francisco Daily Alta California,* December 10, 1877, 2.

56. "Grapes and Grapevines of California Illustrated," *San Francisco Daily Alta California,* December 9, 1877, 1 (reprinting article from *National Republican* of Washington, D.C.).

57. "The Haraszthy Family," MS, typewritten p. 31.

58. *Grapes and Grape Vines of California.*

59. "The Zinfandel," unnumbered page, in *Grapes and Grape Vines of California.*

60. See discussion in Chapters 5 and 6.

61. *Grapes and Grape Vines of California: A Facsimile of the Original Edition of 1877*, with an Introduction by Kevin Starr (San Francisco: J. Windle, 1980); *Grapes and Grape Vines of California* (New York: Harcourt Brace Jovanovich, 1980).

62. Adams, "An Historical Note on Grapes and Grape Vines of California," unnumbered page.

63. Starr, "Introduction" to *Grapes and Grape Vines of California: A Facsimile of the Original Edition of 1877*, unnumbered page.

64. I examined the very rare copy preserved in the Special Collections department of the Shields Library at the University of California, Davis.

65. Apponyi, *The Libraries of California*, 232.

66. Emparan, *The Vallejos of California*, 352.

67. Ibid., 357–60.

68. "An Impressive Ceremony," *San Francisco Daily Alta California*, July 17, 1879, 1.

4. ARPAD HARASZTHY & CO.

1. "The Haraszthy Family," MS, typewritten p. 27.

2. "Copartnership Notice," *San Francisco Daily Alta California*, July 11, 1880, 4.

3. "Isador [*sic*] Landsberger," *Pacific Wine and Spirit Review*, August 31, 1904, 63.

4. Bancroft, *History of Nevada, Colorado, and Wyoming*, 185.

5. *San Francisco Directory for the Year Commencing December, 1869* (San Francisco: Henry G. Langley, 1869), 223.

6. Ibid., 276.

7. *San Francisco Directory for the Year Commencing April, 1871* (San Francisco: Henry G. Langley, 1871), 236, 319; *San Francisco Directory for the Year Commencing March, 1872* (San Francisco: Henry G. Langley, 1872), 233, 724.

8. *San Francisco Directory for the Year Commencing March, 1875* (San Francisco: Henry G. Langley, 1875), 271.

9. Ibid.; *New City Annual Directory of San Francisco, 1875* (San Francisco: D. M. Bishop & Company, 1875), 343, 768.

10. *San Francisco Directory for the Year Commencing April, 1879* (San Francisco: Francis Valentine & Company, 1879), 303, 954.

11. Peninou, *History of the Orleans Hill Vineyard*, 16.

12. Arpad Haraszthy and Nesfield, *California Grapes and Wine*, 25.

13. Ibid., 24–26.

14. "Statement of Orleans Hill Vinicultural Society," in *Transactions of the California State Agricultural Society during the Years 1870 and 1871,* 300.

15. Ibid.

16. "History of the Orleans Hill Vineyard and its Diseases by J. Knauth, Sacramento, Cal., 1880," Appendix D in *Appendix to the Journals of the Senate and Assembly of the Twenty-fourth Session of the Legislature of the State of California.* The joint stock company was sometimes called the Orleans Hill Vinicultural Association and sometimes the Orleans Hill Vinicultural Society.

17. University of California—College of Agriculture, *Report of the Viticultural Work,* 192.

18. For description of the Orleans vine and grapes, see University of California—College of Agriculture, *Report of the Viticultural Work,* , 192; see also Amerine and Winkler, "Composition and Quality of Musts and Wines of California Grapes," 658.

19. "History of the Orleans Hill Vineyard and its Diseases by J. Knauth," 112.

20. "Statement of Orleans Hill Vinicultural Society," in *Transactions of the California State Agricultural Society during the Years 1870 and 1871,* 301.

21. Ibid.

22. Peninou, *History of the Orleans Hill Vineyard,* 10 (Orleans and Riesling); "California Viniculture," *San Francisco Daily Evening Bulletin,* January 20, 1877, 4 (Zinfandel).

23. Peninou, *History of the Orleans Hill Vineyard,* 9–11, 17. Peninou p. 17 says that Epstein transferred the property to himself and Arpad Haraszthy & Co. for nineteen thousand dollars in 1882. My own examination of the real property records in Yolo County did not reveal any recorded transfer from Epstein to Arpad Haraszthy & Co., thus suggesting that Epstein retained title to the land but transferred an equitable interest in the property to Arpad Haraszthy & Co.

24. McGinty, *Strong Wine,* 430-31, 437–38, 470–71.

25. "History of the Orleans Hill Vineyard and its Diseases by J. Knauth, 112.

26. Real property records in Yolo County reveal that legal title to the Orleans Vineyard property remained in the name of Henry Epstein and Jenny Epstein, his wife, until it was transferred to the California Wine Association in 1894. Book 52 of Deeds, Yolo County, p. 110. See discussion in Chapter 7. It would thus appear that the interest of Arpad Haraszthy & Co. in the property arose out of a contract (oral or written) between the partners. No written contract has been found.

27. At Esparto, which is three miles from the Orleans Vineyard site, average temperatures tend to be in the seventies in the summer and in the forties in the winter (both on the Fahrenheit scale). The warmest month is July, with an

average maximum temperature of 96.4° F. The coldest month is December, with an average minimum temperature of 34.2° F. The average annual precipitation is 17.86 inches, which is fairly evenly distributed throughout the year. "Esparto, CA, weather," accessed October 6, 2009, http://www.idcide.com/weather/ca/esparto.htm.

28. "California Viniculture," *San Francisco Daily Evening Bulletin*, January 20, 1877, 4.

29. "Orleans Hills Vineyard," *Sacramento Daily Union*, November 30, 1872, 5.

30. See Arpad Haraszthy, "Wine-Making in California," *Overland Monthly* 8, no. 5 (1872): 395; "The Culture of the Grape: Statements of Professor Eugene Hilgard and A. Haraszthy Upon the Wine and Grape Industries of the State, Made before the Committee on Culture and Improvement of the Grapevine, February ___ [*sic*], 1880," in *Appendix to the Journals of the Senate and Assembly of the Twenty-third Session of the Legislature of the State of California*, vol. 5, 4, 6–7. For Agoston Haraszthy's views on irrigation, see McGinty, *Strong Wine*, 314–15.

31. Peninou, *History of the Orleans Hill Vineyard*, 18. Peninou depicted the Orleans Vineyard site as a near wasteland, afflicted by oppressively hot temperatures in the summer, and said that the decision of Arpad Haraszthy and Henry Epstein "to choose these dry, hot sun-swept foothills as the site for the planting of choice grape varieties to be used for the production of fine still wines and champagne is unexplainable." Ibid., 17. He apparently believed that the site was in the Capay Valley, for he included lengthy descriptions of the Capay Valley in his history of the vineyard and stated that "nature never intended that grapes for champagne, or any other dry wine, should be grown in the hot foothills of the Capay Valley." Ibid., 23. In fact, however, the Orleans Vineyard site is not in the Capay Valley, but approximately a mile and a half south of the mouth of that valley, in the foothills of the much larger Sacramento Valley. In 2003, Charles Sullivan adopted Peninou's characterization of the Orleans Vineyard site, saying that the site was "desertlike" and agreeing that "the purchase by a supposedly knowledgeable leader of the wine industry [Arpad Haraszthy]" was "unexplainable." Sullivan, *Zinfandel*, 60–61. Sullivan stated flatly that "the land was not suited to viticulture." Sullivan, *Companion to California Wine*, 148. But the directory of grape growers and winemakers published by the Board of State Viticultural Commissioners in 1888 listed the names of more than a hundred viticulturists in Yolo County, with twenty (including Arpad Haraszthy & Co.) listed in the Madison District in which the Orleans Vineyard was located. See *Directory of the Grape Growers and Wine Makers of California Compiled by the Secretary of the Board of State Viticultural Commissioners* (Sacramento: J. D.

Young, Supt. State Printing, 1888), 61–62. Rainfall figures in the area are greater than those of a desert (generally defined as an area with less than ten inches of annual rainfall). In the late twentieth and early twenty-first centuries, the federal government designated two nearby sites (Capay Valley and Dunnigan Hills) as American Viticultural Areas, signifying that they are known to be distinct areas in which grapevines are grown, and wineries produced wines in both districts. Notwithstanding all of this, Dr. James Lapsley, who has experience both as a commercial winemaker in Yolo County and as a member of the viticulture and enology faculty at Davis, believes that, at best, it would have been extremely difficult to raise wine grapes at the Orleans Vineyard site by dry-farming (i.e., without irrigation). He suspects that the average daytime temperatures are in the high eighties and low nineties and points out that the rainfall is not normally received during the growing season (April through October). He believes that the vineyardists in the Madison District in 1888 grew grapes for table use, not for wine production, and many may have done so on flat land adjacent to creeks, where ground water was available. This is not true of the foothills where the Orleans Vineyard was located. In Lapsley's judgment, the Orleans Vineyard site is not a desert, but it is "desert-like" during the growing season. Lapsley to author, February 22 and March 11, 2010.

32. Peninou, *History of the Orleans Hill Vineyard,* 17.

33. *Woodland Democrat,* as quoted in *San Francisco Daily Alta California,* October 8, 1885, 2.

34. King, *King's Handbook of the United States,* 84.

35. Peninou, *History of the Orleans Hill Vineyard,* 20; Arpad Haraszthy and Nesfield, *California Grapes and Wine,* 26.

36. Peninou, *History of the Orleans Hill Vineyard,* 22.

37. *Arpad Haraszthy, Henry Epstein, Arpad Haraszthy &Co. "Eclipse Champagne," Extra Dry. American Industry Again Triumphant* (N.p., n.d.). Although this brochure bears no date, internal evidence indicates that it was published in 1882 or 1883.

38. Arpad Haraszthy and Nesfield, *California Grapes and Wine,* 23.

39. *Arpad Haraszthy, Henry Epstein, Arpad Haraszthy &Co. "Eclipse Champagne."*

40. "California Wines: What an Enterprising Californian Firm Has Done for the Champagne Trade," *San Francisco Merchant,* April 13, 1888, 5. The same cuvées were described in Benjamin Truman's article, "The Wines of California," *New York Times,* April 6, 1887, 4.

41. "California Wines: What an Enterprising Californian Firm Has Done for the Champagne Trade," *San Francisco Merchant,* April 13, 1888, 5.

42. Ibid.

43. See McGinty, *Strong Wine,* 335–44, 376–78, 382–83, 385.

44. *Statutes of California, Passed at the Twelfth Session of the Legislature, 1861,* 677 (Concurrent Resolution, No. 25, adopted March 2, 1861); see McGinty, *Strong Wine,* 339.

45. For an early assessment of state efforts to promote the California wine industry, see "How the State Created the Wine Industry," *Pacific Rural Press* 97, no. 6 (February 8, 1919): 169, 187, which states that the commission of 1861 was the first such effort and the creation of the State Board of Viticultural Commissioners in 1880 was the second.

46. Collins, "Portrait of the Artist as a Young Bulldog," 31.

47. "The Culture of the Grape: Statements of Professor Eugene Hilgard and A. Haraszthy," Vol. 5, 3–11.

48. At the Golden Eagle meeting, Hilgard said that a mixture of sulfur and charcoal would eradicate the phylloxera. French scientists had proven that applications of carbon bisulphide would kill the phylloxera. But carbon bisulphide is volatile, expensive, and difficult to use. It vaporizes at room temperature; when mixed with air it becomes explosive; to achieve practical results, it must be applied repeatedly with elaborate equipment; and at high levels it is toxic to the men who use it. Grafting ultimately proved to be the best solution to the phylloxera infestation.

49. "The Culture of the Grape: Statements of Professor Eugene Hilgard and A. Haraszthy," Vol. 5, 9–12.

50. Ibid., Vol. 5, 8, 10.

51. *Statutes of California, 1880,* Chapter 62, An Act for the promotion of the viticultural industries of the State.

52. "Viticultural Commissioners," *San Francisco Daily Alta California,* May 27, 1880, 1; "The Viticultural Commissioners," *San Francisco Daily Alta California,* May 27, 1880, 2.

53. Teiser and Harroun, *Winemaking in California,* 103–104.

54. *Statutes of California, 1881,* An Act to define and enlarge the duties and powers of the Board of State Viticultural Commissioners, and to authorize the appointment of certain officers, and to protect the interests of horticulture and viticulture, approved March 4, 1881.

55. *Report of Arpad Haraszthy, President of the California State Board of Viticultural Commissioners, to His Excellency, R. W. Waterman, Governor of the State of California, San Francisco, April 11th, 1888,* 7.

56. *Statutes of California, 1881,* An Act to define and enlarge the duties and powers of the Board of State Viticultural Commissioners, and to authorize the

appointment of certain officers, and to protect the interests of horticulture and viticulture, approved March 4, 1881.

57. *Report of Arpad Haraszthy . . . to His Excellency,* 6.

58. Ibid., 27.

59. "That Viticultural Bill," *San Jose Daily Herald,* February 9, 1885, 2.

60. *San Diego Union,* August 29, 1883, 3.

61. *Pacific Rural Press,* February 16, 1884, quoting *San Diego Union.*

62. "Wine Making in San Diego County," *Sacramento Daily Record-Union,* December 15, 1883, 1.

63. "El Cajon Land Company," *Pacific Rural Press,* February 16, 1884, quoting *San Diego Union.*

64. Geraci, "The El Cajon, California, Raisin Industry: An Exercise in Gilded Age Capitalism," 329–54, tells the story of the raisin industry in the El Cajon Valley.

65. *Laws and Resolutions Passed by the Legislature of 1883–1884 at its Extra Session, Convened March 24, 1884,* Chapter 10, An Act to enlarge the duties of the Board of State Viticultural Commissioners, Approved February 26, 1885.

66. Statutes of California, 1887, Chapter 36, An Act to prohibit the sophistication and adulteration of wine, and to prevent fraud in the manufacture and sale thereof, Approved March 7, 1887.

67. Ex Parte Kohler, 74 *California Supreme Court Reports* 38, 43–45 (1887).

68. "The Work at Washington" and "American Wine-Makers in Convention, *San Francisco Merchant,* June 4, 1886, 53.

69. Ben C. Truman, "The Wines of California," *New York Times,* April 6, 1887, 4.

5. THE ZINFANDEL CONNECTION

1. Husmann, *Grape Culture and Wine-Making,* 152.

2. Adams, *Wines of America,* 547.

3. Four-page manuscript in handwriting of Arpad Haraszthy, attached to "The Haraszthy Family," MS. See discussion in McGinty, *Strong Wine,* 254–55.

4. Arpad Haraszthy, "Early Viticulture in Sonoma," 77. See discussion in McGinty, *Strong Wine,* 300–301.

5. *San Francisco Bulletin,* May 14, 1885, 4.

6. Hyatt, *Hyatt's Handbook of Grape Culture,* 210.

7. "Sparkling California," *San Francisco Daily Alta California,* March 9, 1869, 2.

8. Arpad Haraszthy, "Wine-Making in California," *Overland Monthly* 7, no. 6 (1871): 494–95.

9. "California Viniculture," *Daily Evening Bulletin,* January 20, 1877, 4.

10. Unnumbered page in article on "Zinfandel" in *Grapes and Grape Vines of California.*

11. *Transactions of the California State Agricultural Society during the Year 1879,* 146; see Pinney, *A History of Wine in America*, 282.

12. Wetmore, *Propagation of the Vine,* 20.

13. McGinty, *Strong Wine,* 324.

14. Four-page, handwritten manuscript by Arpad Haraszthy attached to "The Haraszthy Family," MS. Hittell's *Commerce and Industries of the Pacific Coast,* 246, stated that, at Crystal Springs in 1853, Agoston "set out a strawberry-patch, an orchard, and a large number of vines obtained for him from the Eastern States and Europe through General L. Meszaros, one of his Hungarian compatriots. . . . Among the foreign vines which he imported in that year was the Zinfandel, then first introduced into California. He appreciated its merits, and ever after recommended it as the best grape for wine."

15. Peninou, *History of the Orleans Hill Vineyard,* 17.

16. *Arpad Haraszthy, Henry Epstein, Arpad Haraszthy & Co. "Eclipse Champagne."*

17. Robert A. Thompson was a Virginia native and a graduate of the University of Virginia. He settled in Sonoma County in 1852. He and his brother Thomas L. Thompson were editors of the Sonoma and Santa Rosa *Democrat.* He was elected Sonoma County clerk in 1877 and held the office for three terms. At the time of his death, he was preparing a history of California for publication. This was not published. See "Pen Is Laid Aside," *Press Democrat,* August 5, 1903, 2.

18. "The Zinfandel Grape," San Francisco *Evening Bulletin,* May 1, 1885, 2.

19. Ibid.

20. *California Farmer,* April 23, 1859, 92; May 20, 1859, 10; *California Culturist,* July 1860, 41. See discussion in McGinty, *Strong Wine,* 321–23.

21. *California Farmer,* September 21, 1860, 28; McGinty, *Strong Wine,* 322.

22. "The Zinfandel Grape," San Francisco *Evening Bulletin,* May 1, 1885, 2.

23. Ibid.

24. "The Zinfandel Grape," *St. Helena Star,* July 10, 1884, 1; "The Zinfandel Grapevine," San Francisco *Evening Bulletin,* May 5, 1885, 2.

25. "Reply to Arpad Haraszthy," *St. Helena Star,* June 8, 1885, 1.

26. *Transactions of the California State Agricultural Society during the Year 1858,* 243.

27. Ibid.

28. *California Culturist,* November 15, 1858, advertisement; *California Farmer,* November 26, 1858, 131 (reprinted in subsequent editions through February 25, 1859).

29. "The Zinfandel Grape," *St. Helena Star,* July 10, 1884, 1.

30. "Reply to Arpad Haraszthy," *St. Helena Star,* June 8, 1885, 1.

31. "Viticulture in Napa County" (letter dated May 4, 1885), *St. Helena Star,* May 18, 1885, 1, reprinted from San Francisco *Bulletin.*

32. "European Vines" (letter dated May 11, 1885), *San Francisco Bulletin,* May 14, 1885, 4; reprinted in *St. Helena Star,* May 21, 1885, 2.

33. "European Vines" (letter dated May 11, 1885), *San Francisco Bulletin,* May 14, 1885, 4; reprinted in *St. Helena Star,* May 21, 1885, 2.

34. "European Vines" (letter dated May 11, 1885), San Francisco *Bulletin,* May 14, 1885, 4; reprinted in *St. Helena Star,* May 21, 1885, 2.

35. "Reply to Arpad Haraszthy" (letter dated May 25, 1885), *St. Helena Star,* June 8, 1885, 1, 4.

36. "The Zinfandel," *San Jose Daily Herald,* May 20, 1885, 3.

37. "Viticultural: A Mammoth Enterprise," *St. Helena Star,* March 5, 1885, 3.

38. "Los Gatos," *San Jose Daily Herald,* March 17, 1885, 3.

39. "Viticultural Convention," *San Jose Daily Herald,* June 4, 1885, 2.

40. *San Francisco Merchant,* July 3, 1885, 82.

41. "The Viticulturists," *San Jose Daily Herald,* May 28, 1885, 3.

42. Ibid.

43. Arpad Haraszthy, "Early Viticulture in Sonoma," 77–78.

44. "Sonoma County and Russian River Valley Illustrated," *San Francisco Daily Alta California,* July 9, 1888, 2.

45. "Arpad Haraszthy's claims were generally repeated by leaders of the industry in the years after his death. . . . Astonishing as it may seem, not one twentieth-century wine writer or historian, amateur or professional, prior to the 1970s ever wrote a word about the heated debate of the 1880s from which the legend had been distilled." Sullivan, *Zinfandel,* 71.

46. Sullivan, *Zinfandel,* 70, writes that Thompson and Boggs "did not have the endurance, the resources, or the moxie to keep the fight going." But what "endurance" or "resources" would have been necessary to write letters to the newspapers, as they had done previously?

47. Husmann, *Grape Culture and Wine-Making in California,* 152.

48. Ibid., 243.

49. "The Grape in California," *Pacific Rural Press,* August 3, 1889, 95.

6. HIS CUP OF CONTENT

1. Sullivan, *Zinfandel*, 4.

2. Sullivan posited four possible ways in which the Zinfandel could have been introduced into California. See Sullivan, "A Viticultural Mystery Solved," 120–23.

3. Sullivan chose to focus on Macondray's introduction because it could be "traced in the contemporary historical record and because in the 1880s those who could recall the confused horticultural events of the 1850s in California chose to award the palm to this adventurous and entrepreneurial sea captain." Sullivan, *Zinfandel*, 29.

4. "[I]n discussing the introduction of the Zinfandel to California, it must be acknowledged that many nurserymen, far more than mentioned here, imported the standard New England grape collection to California in the 1850s . This roster would of course include the name of Agostin [*sic*] Haraszthy." Sullivan, "A Viticultural Mystery Solved," 123–24.

5. Sullivan, *Zinfandel*, 148.

6. Ibid., 4, 67.

7. Sullivan, *Companion to California Wine*, 148.

8. Sullivan, *Zinfandel*, 59, 61, 63.

9. Sullivan, "Zinfandel: A True Vinifera," 75.

10. Sullivan, "A Viticultural Mystery Solved," 115, 118.

11. "[W]hen these events took place, Arpad was a teenager, studying either on the East Coast or in France." Sullivan, *Zinfandel*, 62. His "years on the continent did not qualify him to make 'eyewitness' statements on the spread of Zinfandel in California between 1852 and 1862." Sullivan, "A Viticultural Mystery Solved," 117.

12. Pinney, *History of Wine in America*, 284.

13. "European Vines" (letter dated May 11, 1885), *San Francisco Bulletin*, May 14, 1885, 4; reprinted in *St. Helena Star*, May 21, 1885, 2.

14. See *Transactions of the California State Agricultural Society for 1858*, 243; *California Culturist*, November 15, 1858, advertisement; *California Farmer*, November 26, 1858, 131 (reprinted in subsequent editions through February 25, 1859); see also discussion in Chapter 5.

15. Sullivan, *Zinfandel*, 69.

16. Kenyeres, Ágnes, ed., *Magyar Életrajzi Lexikon*, Vol. 2 (Budapest: Ákadémiai Kiadó, 1969), 197.

17. "Gen. Meszaros [*sic*]—An Appeal to the Public," *New York Times* of September 16, 1853. In this letter, Mészáros briefly recapitulated his military career,

which began during the Napoleonic Wars in 1813–15, noted his participation in the Hungarian war for independence in 1848 and 1849, and mentioned his relocation to the United States (which he called the "Giant Republic" and "this powerful Union").

18. Letter of December 25, 1853, in Mészáros, *Külföldi levelei és életirata,* 54, 69.

19. Letter of December 7, 1852, in Mészáros, *Külföldi levelei és életirata,* 19.

20. Letters of April 14 and September 14, 1854, in Mészáros, *Külföldi levelei és életirata,* 54, 69.

21. Letter of March 12, 1854, in Mészáros, *Külföldi levelei és életirata,* 53–54.

22. Prince, *A Treatise on the Vine,* 343.

23. Letters from October 15, 1855, to September 14, 1858, in Mészáros, *Külföldi levelei és életirata,* 85–131.

24. Letter of April 14, 1854, in Mészáros, *Külföldi levelei és életirata,* 57.

25. Letter of September 14, 1854, in Mészáros, *Külföldi levelei és életirata,* 69.

26. Letter of December 17, 1857 (written in Flushing), in Mészáros, *Külföldi levelei és életirata,* 132.

27. See Lambert-Gocs, "Shedding Light on the Zinfandel Name," 54, for interesting speculation as to how Mészáros could have obtained vines from any of "several varietal collections established by Hungarians in the early 19th century."

28. Sullivan stated that it was "impossible, of course," for Agoston to have imported Hungarian vines in February, 1852, because he was then in the Legislature. Sullivan, *Zinfandel,* 68.

29. Book 9 of Deeds, San Francisco, 620–21; see McGinty, *Strong Wine,* 243.

30. "European Vines" (letter dated May 11, 1885), *San Francisco Bulletin,* May 14, 1885, 4; reprinted in *St. Helena Star,* May 21, 1885, 2.

31. Arpad Haraszthy, "Early Viticulture in Sonoma," 77.

32. "Introduction of the Zinfandel," *Pacific Wine and Spirit Review,* January 5, 1892, p. 20.

33. Sullivan, *Zinfandel,* 69.

34. Sullivan, "Zinfandel: A True Vinifera," 86n55.

35. Arpad Haraszthy, "Wine-Making No. 9," *California Wine, Wool, and Stock Journal* 2 (1864): 53–54. In February 2010, I consulted a research librarian at the Boston Public Library, who gave me a detailed recapitulation of the contents of the Boston Public Library Collection of the *California Wine, Wool, and Stock Journal.* None of Arpad's articles are missing from that collection.

36. Four-page, handwritten manuscript by Arpad Haraszthy attached to "The Haraszthy Family," MS. For discussion, see Chapter 5.

37. In his "Report on Grapes and Wine of California," published in 1858 by the California State Agricultural Society, Agoston urged the U.S. government to instruct its consuls throughout the world to collect cuttings from the widest possible varieties of vines and send them to the U.S. Patent Office, which would plant them in a suitable place and distribute them to those sections of the country in which the climate and soil were most suitable for vine growing. Agoston Haraszthy, "Report on Grapes and Wine of California," in *Transactions of the California State Agricultural Society during the Year 1858,* 328. In a second report submitted to the State Agricultural Society in 1858, Agoston wrote: "No man can fully comprehend yet what fine wines we will be able to make, when we have once the proper assortments of the different qualities of foreign grapes. . . . [T]ake the proper variety of them and you will make a splendid wine." *Transactions of the California State Agricultural Society during the Year 1858,* 246. See McGinty, *Strong Wine,* 310–11.

38. Carole P. Meredith, "Science as a Window into Wine History" (2002), accessed June 30, 2011, http://www.amacad.org/publications/bulletin/winter 2003/ wine.pdf. See Sullivan, *Zinfandel,* 163.

39. Antonio Calò, Angelo Costacurta, Vesna Maras, Stefano Meneghetti and Manna Crespan, "Molecular Correlation of Zinfandel (Primitivo) with Austrian, Croatian, and Hungarian Cultivars and Kratosija, and Additional Synonym," *American Journal of Enology and Viticulture* 59 (2008): 205–209.

40. See, e.g., Charles Nordhoff, *California for Health, Pleasure, and Residence* (1872), 217, ("father of wine-culture in this State"); John S. Hittell, *The Commerce and Industries of the Pacific Coast of North America* (1882), 247, ("father of the vine in California"); Frona Eunice Wait, *Wines and Vines of California* (1889), 91, ("father of the wine industry in this state"); Hubert H. Bancroft, *History of California* (1890), 7:44 ("father of viniculture in California"); Edward R. Emerson, *The Story of the Vine* (1902), 225 ("father of the wine industry as it is in California today"); Idwal Jones, *Vines in the Sun* (1949), 84 ("father of modern California viticulture"); Vincent P. Carosso, *The California Wine Industry* (1951), 38 ("father of the modern California wine industry"); John Melville, *Guide to California Wines* (1955), 59 ("father of modern California viticulture"); Leon D. Adams, *The Commonsense Book of Wine* (1958), 126 ("father of modern California viticulture"); M. F. K. Fisher, *The Story of Wine in California* (1962), 5 ("father of modern wine growing in California"); Frank Schoonmaker, *Frank Schoonmaker's Encyclopedia of Wine* (1964), 162, ("often and quite fairly called the 'father of California viticulture'"); Alexis Lichine, *Alexis Lichine's Encyclopedia of Wine and Spirits* (1967), 78 ("recognized as the father of California viticulture"); Robert Lawrence Balzer, *Wines of California* (1978), 90, ("the father of

California viticulture"); Ruth Teiser and Catherine Harroun, "Introduction" to *Winemaking in California* by Arpad Haraszthy (1983), 36 ("'father of California viticulture' and 'father of modern viticulture in California'"); Ernest P. Peninou, *A History of the Orleans Hill Vineyard & Winery of Arpad Haraszthy & Company* (1983), 12 ("father of California viticulture"); David S. Lavender, *California, Land of New Beginnings* (1987), 281 ("father of the California wine industry"); Hugh Johnson, *Vintage: The Story of Wine* (1989), 362 ("known as the 'father of wine-growing'" in California); James Laube, *California's Great Chardonnays* (1990), 25 ("father of California viticulture"). Of course, these statements do not prove that Agoston was *in fact* the "father of California viticulture," merely that he was generally regarded as such for well over a century.

41. In the twentieth century, Charles Sullivan stated that Charles Kohler was "the 'father' of the California wine industry" or "the father of California's commercial wine industry," and that, "during his lifetime," Kohler was "generally recognized" as such. Sullivan, *Companion to California Wine*, 49, 132, 171. Sullivan has provided no quotations from early wine pioneers, or later wine writers or historians, to substantiate his assertion. On February 6, 2010, I conducted a Google search of the internet to compare the number of internet references to Haraszthy and Kohler in this regard. On that date, there were 51,100 hits to Haraszthy and "father of California wine" and only 4 to Kohler and "father of California wine." There were 23,500 hits to Haraszthy and "father of the California wine industry" and only 4 to Kohler and "father of the California wine industry." There were 3,330 hits to Haraszthy and "father of California viticulture" and only 9 to Kohler and "father of California viticulture." A search of Google Books on the same date produced fewer hits, although the preponderance in favor of Haraszthy over Kohler was similarly lopsided. For example, there were 140 Google Book hits to Haraszthy and "father of California viticulture" and none to Kohler and "father of California viticulture." There were 124 hits to Haraszthy and "father of California wine" and only 3 to Kohler and "father of California wine." Examination of some of the hits to "Kohler" and these search terms revealed that the sources did not acknowledge Kohler as "the father," but merely mentioned Kohler in the same article in which Haraszthy was acknowledged as "the father." None of this is cited to minimize Charles Kohler's important contributions to the early history of winemaking in California, which both Agoston and Arpad Haraszthy acknowledged. They merely cast doubt on Sullivan's assertion that Kohler was "generally" recognized as "the father."

42. Letter from Charles Sullivan to Brian McGinty, September 27, 1979.

43. Sullivan, "A Man Named Agoston Haraszthy," 18.

44. Sullivan, *Zinfandel*, 51.

45. Ibid., 58.

46. Ibid.

47. McGinty, *Strong Wine,* 7–8.

48. James Beard, "Shopping for California Wines," *House and Garden,* August, 1956, 94.

49. "Viticultural Commission," *San Francisco Daily Alta California,* April 19, 1888, 8; "The State Viticulturists," *San Diego Union,* April 19, 1888, 1.

50. *San Francisco Merchant,* April 13, 1888, 8.

51. "Arpad Haraszthy," *San Diego Union,* April 17, 1888, 5.

52. "Viticultural Commission," *San Francisco Daily Alta California,* April 14, 1888, 2.

53. *San Francisco Merchant,* April 27, 1888, 34.

54. *San Francisco Merchant,* June 8, 1888, 72.

55. "The Cruiser Charleston," *San Francisco Daily Alta California,* August 2, 1888, 1.

56. "California Wine: A Grand Banquet in Honor of Arpad Haraszthy," *San Francisco Call,* August 3, 1888, 7.

57. Ibid.

58. "The Festal Board: Complimentary Banquet Tendered to Arpad Haraszthy," *San Francisco Daily Alta California,* August 2, 1888, 8; "California Wine: A Grand Banquet in Honor of Arpad Haraszthy," *San Francisco Call,* August 3, 1888, 7; "Haraszthy Honored," *San Francisco Merchant,* August 3, 1888, 136.

59. See "Honors to Haraszthy," *Pacific Rural Press* 36, no. 6 (August 11, 1888): 112 ("The company continued at the tables until the hands of the clock began to point out the small hours of the coming morn").

7. THE LAST ECLIPSE

1. "Death of A. F. Haraszthy," *San Francisco Morning Call,* February 3, 1888, 8.

2. "History of the Discovery of the Phylloxera Vastatrix and Its Ravages in Sonoma Valley by H. Appleton," Appendix C to *First Annual Report of the Board of State Viticultural Commissioners,* 25–30.

3. "Death of A. F. Haraszthy," *San Francisco Morning Call,* February 3, 1888, 8; Lynch, *Sonoma Valley Story,* 304 (A. F. Haraszthy's term as mayor from April 21, 1884, to April 16, 1888).

4. Wetmore, *Propagation of the Vine,* 2.

5. Court records in Estate of Attila F. Haraszthy, deceased, Sonoma County Clerk's Office, Santa Rosa, California.

6. "Death of Major Gaza Haraszthy," *San Francisco Daily Alta California,* January 28, 1879, 1.

7. "The Strickland-Haraszthy Wedding," *San Francisco Call,* April 16, 1888, 3.

8. *Langley's San Francisco Directory for the Year commencing May, 1888* (San Francisco: Francis, Valentine & Company, 1888), 565; *Register of the University of California, 1884–1885* (Berkeley: Published by the University) (Carlos Haraszthy as matriculate in Toland College of Medicine in University of California).

9. "Carlos J. Haraszthy," *San Francisco Call,* February 14, 1892, 13.

10. *Langley's San Francisco Directory for the Year commencing May, 1888* (San Francisco: Francis, Valentine & Company, 1888), 565.

11. "The Viticulturists," *San Francisco Daily Alta California,* March 11, 1888, 1; "Index to Some of the Reports of the Board of State Viticultural Commissioners," *San Francisco Merchant,* May 11, 1888, 34–36.

12. Arpad Haraszthy, "How to Drink Wine," 184.

13. Ibid., 186.

14. Ibid.

15. Ibid., 196.

16. Ibid., 191.

17. Ibid., 194.

18. Ibid., 197. Arpad habitually used "drank" where modern grammarians would use "drunk." The usage was correct in 1888.

19. Arpad Haraszthy, "How to Drink Wine," 198–99.

20. Ibid., 198.

21. *Report of the Sixth Annual State Viticultural Convention,* 183–200; Wait, *Wines and Vines of California,* Chapter 4, "How to Drink Wine."

22. "Viticultural Interests," *San Francisco Daily Alta California,* August 2, 1888, 2.

23. *Report of Arpad Haraszthy . . . to His Excellency,* 12–13.

24. "Condition of the Vines," *Merchant and Viticulturist,* July 22, 1889, 155; "The Brandy Union," *Merchant and Viticulturist,* August 8, 1889, 161–62; "The Convention," *Merchant and Viticulturist,* August 22, 1889, 178; "The Surplus Wine Question," *San Francisco Daily Alta California,* August 23, 1889, 1.

25. "The Vintage and the Vines," *Merchant and Viticulturist,* September 8, 1889, 9.

26. "Trade Notes," *Pacific Wine and Spirit Review,* October 5, 1891, 13; "Humbugged with Wine," *Pacific Wine and Spirit Review,* November 20, 1891, 24.

27. "Trade Notes, Etc.," *Pacific Wine and Spirit Review,* June 6, 1894, 19.

28. "Trade Notes," *Pacific Wine & Spirit Review,* March 21, 1892, 15.

29. "Co-operation," *Merchant and Viticulturist,* June 21, 1889, 115.

30. Ibid.

31. "Mumm's Mean Lies," *Merchant and Viticulturist,* June 21, 1889, 118 (quoting *American Analyst*).

32. "How It Was Done," *Pacific Wine and Spirit Review,* May 20, 1891, 8.

33. "Cantin at Work," *Pacific Wine and Spirit Review,* September 20, 1891, 3.

34. In California, Harrison received 118,027 popular votes to Cleveland's 118,174.

35. After the election, Eugene J. Cantin was quoted as saying that California wine producers contributed to Harrison's defeat. *Pacific Wine and Spirit Review,* November 21, 1892, 17.

36. "Press Club Wines," *Pacific Wine and Spirit Review,* January 21, 1892, 16.

37. "Champagne Making," *Pacific Wine and Spirit Review,* August 21, 1891, 11.

38. "Never Learns, Never Forgets," *Pacific Wine and Spirit Review,* May 20, 1891, 10 (quoting from *Bonfort's*).

39. "The Paris Exposition," *Merchant and Viticulturist,* September 8, 1889, 2; "Twenty-Seven Medals," *Merchant and Viticulturist,* October 22, 1889, 11.

40. "Prize Wines," *Merchant and Viticulturist,* October 22, 1889, 8.

41. "The Dublin Awards," *Pacific Wine and Spirit Review,* October 20, 1892, 10.

42. "Trade Notes," *Pacific Wine and Spirit Review,* February 20, 1893, 17.

43. "Triumphant Again" (advertisement), *Pacific Wine and Spirit Review,* February 24, 1896, 8.

44. "At the Mechanics' Fair," *Pacific Wine and Spirit Review*, September 7, 1895, 25.

45. "At the Pavilion," *San Francisco Daily Alta California,* October 5, 1887, 8; "Drawing to a Close," *San Francisco Daily Alta California,* October 7, 1887, 8.

46. "The Mechanics' Fair," *San Francisco Daily Alta California,* September 14, 1888, 4 (this work was the same as the "Champagne Galop" by Lumbye published as his Opus 14 in 1854).

47. *Faust Souvenir, Tivoli Opera House, Admission Day, September 9, 1895.*

48. "Trade Notes," *Pacific Wine and Spirit Review,* October 5, 1891, 13.

49. For a description of Arpad's workload in December 1889, see his letter to M. G. Vallejo dated December 28, 1889, in Emparan, *Vallejos of California*, 363.

50. *Langley's San Francisco Directory for the Year commencing May, 1889* (San Francisco: Francis, Valentine & Company, 1889), 624 .

51. Guinn, *History of California,* Vol. 1, 820.

52. Ibid.

53. Emparan, *Vallejos of California,* 363, 386, 388, 390; *San Francisco Daily Alta California,* December 11, 1890, 5; *Langley's San Francisco Directory for the Year commencing May, 1889* (San Francisco: Francis, Valentine & Company, 1889) 1296 (listed as N. P. Vallejo, traveling salesman).

54. *Langley's San Francisco Directory for the Year commencing May, 1891* (San Francisco: Geo. B. Wilbur, 1891), 653 (listed as Augustin Haraszthy); *Langley's San Francisco Directory for the Year commencing May, 1892* (San Francisco: Geo. B. Wilbur, 1892), 672 (listed as A. F. Haraszthy); *Langley's San Francisco Directory for the Year commencing May, 1893* (San Francisco: Geo. B. Wilbur, 1893), 669 (listed as A. F. Haraszthy).

55. *Langley's San Francisco Directory for the Year Commencing May, 1893* (San Francisco: Geo. B. Wilbur, 1893), 669 (listed as Charles Haraszthy).

56. The *Call* reported in February 1892 that Carlos Haraszthy had gone to New York "with the intention of taking his degrees at Bellevue College of Medicine, and he expects to take his doctor's degree next March." "Carlos J. Haraszthy," *San Francisco Call,* February 14, 1892, 13. Bellevue Hospital Medical College was later absorbed into the NYU School of Medicine, which maintains records for the earlier institution. In 2009, I checked with Colleen Bradley-Sanders, archivist, who informed me that records maintained by NYU do not show that anyone named Haraszthy graduated from the Bellevue Hospital Medical College.

57. Emparan, *Vallejos of California,* 363; "General Vallejo Buried," *San Francisco Chronicle,* January 22, 1890, 6 (Agoston F. Haraszthy identified as "Guste" [*sic*] Haraszthy).

58. "Wines at Chicago," *Pacific Wine and Spirit Review,* June 21, 1892, 13; "Viticulture Exhibitors Meet," *Pacific Wine and Spirit Review,* December 20, 1892, 21.

59. *Final Report of the California World's Fair Commission,* 77; "World's Fair: California at the Fair," *Pacific Rural Press,* August 5, 1893, 107.

60. "Chicago Department," *Pacific Wine and Spirit Review,* June 6, 1893, 13.

61. *Final Report of the California World's Fair Commission,* 120–21.

62. Wetmore, *Treatise on Wine Production,* 54–55.

63. "Viticultural Palace," *Pacific Wine and Spirit Review,* April 20, 1894, 15.

64. "Instructions to the Jury of Awards Midwinter Fair," *Pacific Wine and Spirit Review,* July 20, 1894, 27; "Viticultural Palace Reports," *Pacific Wine and Spirit Review,* Sept. 20, 1894, 26.

65. "Instructions to the Jury of Awards Midwinter Fair," *Pacific Wine and Spirit Review,* July 20, 1894, 27.

66. "A Viticultural Banquet," *Pacific Wine and Spirit Review,* July 6, 1894, 13.

67. "Trade Notes, Etc.," *Pacific Wine and Spirit Review,* May 5, 1894, 19.

68. Henry Epstein and Jenny Epstein, his wife, to California Wine Association, a corporation, Book 52 of Deeds, Yolo County, p. 110.

69. *California Wine Association, Minute Book,* vol. 1, 212, 225–40.

70. "What the C.W.A. Is Doing," *Pacific Wine and Spirit Review,* October 5, 1894, 13.

71. *California Wine Association, Minute Book,* vol. 1, 176, 185–88, 193, 210.

72. Ibid., Vol. 1, 225–40.

73. "Trade Circulars," *Pacific Wine and Spirit Review,* May 7, 1895, 22.

74. "Arpad Haraszthy's New Position," *Pacific Wine and Spirit Review,* May 7, 1895, 10.

75. "Trade Notes, Etc.," *Pacific Wine and Spirit Review,* August 30, 1894, 17.

76. "Exhibit in Berlin," *Pacific Wine and Spirit Review,* October 8, 1895, 12.

77. *Statutes of California,* 1895, Chapter 189, An Act to repeal, etc.; "College of Practical Viticulture," *Pacific Wine and Spirit Review,* December 9, 1895, 12; "New Viticultural College," *San Francisco Call,* January 15, 1896, 7; "College of Practical Viticulture," *Pacific Wine and Spirit Review,* April 23, 1896, 12.

78. "College of Practical Viticulture," *Pacific Wine and Spirit Review,* December 9, 1895, 12; "College of Practical Viticulture," *Pacific Wine and Spirit Review,*" April 23, 1896, 12.

79. "The New Viticultural College," *San Francisco Call,* January 15, 1896, 7.

80. *Statutes of California,* 1895, Chapter 189, An Act to repeal, etc., Sec. 3.

81. "Haraszthy Arpad [*sic*]," *Pacific Wine and Spirit Review,* May 7, 1896, 10.

82. "Notes and Personals," *Pacific Wine and Spirit Review,* February 6, 1897, 24.

83. "Viticultural Convention," *Pacific Wine and Spirit Review,* February 22, 1897, unnumbered page (faces page 18).

84. "Personal and Trade Notes," *Pacific Wine, Spirit and Tobacco Review,* November 30, 1898, 9.

85. "Midwinter Fair Awards," *Pacific Wine and Spirit Review,* August 6, 1894, 27.

86. "Prices Current," *Pacific Wine and Spirit Review,* August 20, 1892, 33.

87. "Olson Co. Grocers" (advertisement), *San Francisco Call,* September 23, 1900, 25.

88. Advertisement for the Emporium, *San Francisco Call,* September 2, 1900, 25.

89. Advertisement for Leo Metzger & Co., *Pacific Wine and Spirit Review,* July 31, 1899, 10.

90. "The Bohemian's Founders Meet Around the Table for Annual Dinner," *San Francisco Call,* March 11, 1900, 21.

91. "One of the Fortunates," *Arizona Republican,* October 6, 1900, 3.

92. "Arpad Haraszthy's Death a Shock," *San Francisco Bulletin,* November 6, 1900, 2.

93. Paolo De Vecchi was a notable man in his own right. Born in 1847 near Turin, Italy, he received his medical degree from the University of Turin in 1872. He fought with Giuseppe Garibaldi in the struggle for the unification of Italy and with Italian troops in the Franco-Prussian War. After spending some time in South America, he came to San Francisco around 1880, and remained to practice medicine there for twenty-five years. In 1900, his office was in the Crocker Building on Market Street. He was, among other things, founder of San Francisco's St. Joseph's Hospital, president of the Italian Swiss Colony (an important vine-growing and wine-producing operation in Sonoma County), one of the founders of the Sierra Club, and a member of the Bohemian Club. He is credited with having introduced the Lister method of antisepsis to the Pacific Coast. He retired in 1905 and, in 1910, moved to New York City, where he died in 1931. He was the author of published monographs on medical, surgical, and other subjects. See "Dr. Paolo De Vecchi," *Bulletin of the New York Academy of Medicine* 7, no. 6 (June 1931): 483–85.

94. "Young Haraszthy Was Hero of the Romance," *San Francisco Call,* November 18, 1900, 25.

95. "Romance Brightens Haraszthy's Old Age," *San Francisco Call,* November 17, 1900, 9.

96. "Funeral Services of Arpad Haraszthy," *San Francisco Bulletin,* November 18, 1900, 28.

97. The bodies of Arpad and Jovita Haraszthy rested in Calvary Cemetery until 1940 or 1941, when they were removed to Holy Cross Cemetery in Colma, south of San Francisco. The removal was in compliance with a decision by the San Francisco Board of Supervisors that cemetery land in the city limits should be cleared and made available to development. Nearly all of the graves in San Francisco were removed to Colma before 1941. Thanks to Kathleen Mino, Family Service Counselor of the Catholic Cemeteries of the Archdiocese of San Francisco for locating the Haraszthy gravesites through cemetery records in March 2010.

AFTERWORD

1. "Arpad Haraszthy's Death a Shock," *San Francisco Bulletin,* November 16, 1900, 2.

2. "Romance Brightened Haraszthy's Old Age," *San Francisco Call,* November 17, 1900, 9.

3. "Sudden Death of Arpad Haraszthy," *San Francisco Chronicle,* November 17, 1900, 14.

4. "Arpad Haraszthy's Interesting Career," *San Francisco Examiner,* November 17, 1900, 6.

5. "Death of A. Haraszthy," *Santa Rosa Republican,* November 17, 1900, 1.

6. "Death Strikes Arpad Haraszthy," *Pacific Wine and Spirit Review,* November 30, 1900, 29

7. In *Strong Wine: The Life and Legend of Agoston Haraszthy* (Stanford University Press, 1998), I have written at length on what I call the "Haraszthy Legend," refuting the many erroneous elements that compose it, but affirming the solid accomplishments of most of Agoston Haraszthy's extraordinary life.

8. An Act for preventing the manufacture, sale, or transportation of adulterated or misbranded or poisonous or deleterious foods, drugs, medicines, and liquors, and for regulating traffic therein, and for other purposes. June 30, 1906. 34 Stat. 768.

9. An advertisement for Olson Brothers, 915 Market Street, appeared in the *San Francisco Call,* July 11, 1904, at page 3, advertising Arpad Haraszthy's Eclipse at thirty-five cents per bottle (regularly fifty cents) and $3.50 per dozen.

10. The block of buildings that had comprised Arpad's cellars was occupied in 1906 by A. P. Hotaling & Co., a whiskey warehouse with offices at 429–437 Jackson Street, and the Swiss-American Wine Co., with offices at 530 Washington. Although these buildings sustained little or no damage during the earthquake, they were threatened by the fire that followed the earthquake. Thousands of buildings in San Francisco were destroyed, including twenty-five of the twenty-eight commercial wine establishments in the city. Hotaling and the Swiss-American premises were saved by a combination of luck and water that was pumped into them from the excavation site for the new U.S. Custom House across Sansome Street. See "How 'Old Kirk' was Saved," *Pacific Wine and Spirit Review,* 48, nos. 6–7 (combined issues for April and May, 1906, denominated the "Calamity Edition"), 23. See also "What Fire Did to the San Francisco Wine and Liquor Trade," (ibid., 9) and letter to editor from Swiss-American Wine Co., May 15, 1906 (ibid., 11).

11. Peninou and Unzelman, *The California Wine Association and Its Member Wineries, 1894–1920,* is a full history of the CWA.

12. "Wine and Vine News of the State," *Pacific Wine and Spirit Review,* October 31, 1902, 54.

13. "Died," *Petaluma Daily Courier,* September 19, 1903, 1.

14. "Report on the Competition for Women Photographers," *The Photo-Miniature* 10 (1911): 481; "Notes," *The Craftsman* 18 (1910): 142; Sadakichi Hartman, "A Review of the Picture Exhibit at the Philadelphia Convention, *The Photographic Times* 44 (1912), 330; "Society at Home and Abroad, *New York Times,* May 19, 1912, X1.

15. Court file in Estate of Arpad Haraszthy, Deceased, No. 11, 534, Superior Court, San Francisco.

16. Thanks to Gail Unzelman for relaying this information, which derived from a visit she made with Ernest Peninou to the Washington Street building.

17. The debts that present-day producers owe to their predecessors extend not only to methods of production that remain classic and timeless despite the advances of modern mechanization (see discussion in the introduction). They also include the attitudes, business decisions, and sheer determination that made the old-time producers successful and that, adopted today, help modern-day makers achieve similar successes.

BIBLIOGRAPHY

GOVERNMENT DOCUMENTS

Annual Report of the Board of State Viticultural Commissioners for 1887. Sacramento: J. D. Young, Supt. State Printing, 1888.

Appendix to the Journals of the Senate and Assembly of the Twenty-third Session of the Legislature of the State of California. Vol. 5. Sacramento: J. D. Young, Supt. State Printing, 1880.

Appendix to the Journals of the Senate and Assembly of the Twenty-fourth Session of the Legislature of the State of California. Vol. 2. Sacramento: J. D. Young, Supt. State Printing, 1881.

Directory of the Grape Growers and Wine Makers of California Compiled by the Secretary of the Board of State Viticultural Commissioners. Sacramento: J. D. Young, Supt. State Printing, 1888.

Final Report of the California World's Fair Commission, Including a Description of All Exhibits from the State of California, Collected and Maintained under Legislative Enactments, at the World's Columbian Exposition, Chicago, 1893. Sacramento: A. J. Johnston, Supt. State Printing, 1894.

First Annual Report of the Board of State Viticultural Commissioners. San Francisco: Edward Bosqui & Co., 1881.

Laws and Resolutions Passed by the Legislature of 1883–84 at Its Extra Session, Convened March 24, 1884. Sacramento: James J. Ayers, Supt. State Printing, 1885.

Laws and Resolutions Passed by the Legislature of 1885–86 at Its Extra Session, Convened July 20, 1886. Sacramento: P. L. Shoaff, Supt. State Printing, 1887.

Report of Arpad Haraszthy, President of the California State Board of Viticultural Commissioners, to His Excellency, R. W. Waterman, Governor of the State of California, San Francisco, April 11th, 1888. San Francisco: E. C. Hughes, Printer, 1888.

Report of the Committee on Culture of the Grape, on the Cultivation of the Grape, and the Production of Wines and Brandies in California. Sacramento: D. W. Gelwicks, State Printer, 1870.

Report of the Sixth Annual State Viticultural Convention, Held at Pioneer Hall, San Francisco, March 7, 8, 9, 10, 1888, under the Auspices of the Board of State Viticultural Commissioners of California. Sacramento: J. D. Young, Supt. State Printing, 1888.

Reports of the United States Commissioners to the Paris Universal Exposition, 1867. Washington, D.C.: Government Printing Office, 1870.

Statutes of California and Amendments to the Codes Passed at the Twenty-Fifth Session of the Legislature, 1881. Sacramento: James J. Ayers, Supt. State Printing, 1883.

Statutes of California and Amendments to the Codes Passed at the Twenty-Seventh Session of the Legislature, 1887. Sacramento: P. L. Shoaff, Supt. State Printing, 1887.

Statutes of California and Amendments to the Codes Passed at the Twenty-Eighth Session of the Legislature, 1889. Sacramento: J. D. Young, Supt. State Printing, 1889.

Statutes of California and Amendments to the Codes Passed at the Twenty-Ninth Session of the Legislature, 1891. Sacramento: A. J. Johnston, Supt. State Printing, 1891.

Statutes of California and Amendments to the Codes Passed at the Thirtieth Session of the Legislature, 1893. San Francisco: Bancroft-Whitney Company, 1893.

Statutes of California, Passed at the Twelfth Session of the Legislature, 1861. Sacramento: Charles T. Botts, State Printer, 1861.

Statutes of California Passed at the Twenty-Third Session of the Legislature, 1880. Sacramento: J.D. Young, Supt. State Printing, 1880.

Statutes of California Passed at the Twenty-Fourth Session of the Legislature, 1881. San Francisco: A. L. Bancroft, 1881.

Transactions of the California State Agricultural Society during the Year 1858. Sacramento: John O'Meara, State Printer, 1859.

Transactions of the California State Agricultural Society during the Years 1866 and 1867. Sacramento: D. W. Gelwicks, State Printer, 1868.

Transactions of the California State Agricultural Society during the Years 1868 and 1869. Sacramento: D. W. Gelwick, State Printer, 1870,

Transactions of the California State Agricultural Society during the Years 1870 and 1871. Sacramento: T. A. Springer, State Printer, 1872.

Transactions of the California State Agricultural Society during the Year 1879. Sacramento: J. D. Young, Supt. State Printing, 1880.

University of California—College of Agriculture. *Report of the Viticultural Work during the Seasons 1887–93, with Data Regarding the Vintages of 1894.* Sacramento: A. J. Johnston, Superintendent State Printing, 1896.

MANUSCRIPTS

Brainard, David. "Journal of the Walworth Co. Mutual Mining Company, Commencing March the 20th, 1849. By David Brainard." Bancroft Library, University of California, Berkeley.

Gärtner, Maximilian. "Tagebuch der röm. katholischen Missionen in Nord-America für Joh. Stef. Maximilian Gärtner[,] regul. Chorherrn des Praemonstrat. Stiftes Wilten in Tirol, A.D. 1846 (Diary of the Roman Catholic Missions in North America by Johann Stefan Maximilian Gartner, Canon Regular of the Praemonstratensian Abbey of Wilten in Tyrol, A.D. 1846). St. Norbert Abbey, De Pere, Wisconsin. English translation by Stephan Klopfer in Archive of Archdiocese of Milwaukee, Milwaukee, Wisconsin. Film copy of English translation in Stiftsarchiv Wilten, Wilten Abbey, Innsbruck, Austria.

Haraszthy, Arpad. "Colonel Agoston Haraszthy." State Historical Society of Wisconsin, Madison.

———. Eleven letters relating to viticulture in Europe and California, 1861–1863. James L. Warren Papers. Bancroft Library, University of California, Berkeley.

The Haraszthy Family. Bancroft Library, University of California, Berkeley. Forty-eight-page typescript dated July 1, 1886, with handwritten corrections by Arpad Haraszthy, plus four pages of handwritten manuscript in the hand of Arpad Haraszthy and ten pages of handwritten notes extracted from the account book of Agoston Haraszthy. Prepared by Arpad Haraszthy, or at his direction, for Hubert Howe Bancroft.

Hayes, Benjamin. "Diary of Judge Benjamin Hayes' Journey Overland from Socorro to Warner's Ranch from October 31, 1849, to January 14, 1850." Bancroft Library, University of California, Berkeley.

Minute Books of the California Wine Association. North Baker Library, California Historical Society Library, San Francisco.

BROCHURES

Arpad Haraszthy, Henry Epstein, Arpad Haraszthy & Co. "Eclipse Champagne," Extra Dry. American Industry Again Triumphant. N.p., n.d. Folded brochure of one sheet with twelve panels. Only known copy in the Special Collections Research Center at the Henry Madden Library, California State University, Fresno. N.d., but internal evidence indicates it was published in 1882 or 1883.

California Big Tree Joint Wine Exhibit: C. Carpy & Co., J. Gundlach & Co., Arpad Haraszthy & Co., Napa Valley Wine Co.: San Francisco. World's Columbian Exposition, Chicago, 1893. Folded brochure of one sheet with six panels. Brian McGinty collection.

NEWSPAPERS

Arizona Republican (Phoenix)
New York Times
Petaluma Daily Courier
Sacramento Daily Bee
St. Helena Star
San Francisco Chronicle
San Francisco Daily Alta California
San Francisco Daily Evening Bulletin
San Francisco Examiner
San Francisco Morning Call
San Jose Daily Herald
Santa Rosa Press Democrat
Santa Rosa Republican
San Diego Union

BOOKS AND ARTICLES

Adams, Leon D. *The Commonsense Book of Wine.* New York: David McKay, 1958.

———. "A Historical Note on Grapes and Grape Vines of California," in *Grapes and Grape Vines of California.* New York: Harcourt Brace Jovanovich, 1980.

———. *The Wines of America.* 3rd ed. New York: McGraw-Hill, 1985.

Amerine, M. A., and A. J. Winkler. "Composition and Quality of Musts and Wines of California Grapes." *Hilgardia* 15 (February 1944): 493–673.

Apponyi, Flora Haines. *The Libraries of California: Containing Descriptions of the Principal Private and Public Libraries throughout the State.* San Francisco: A. L. Bancroft, 1878.

Balzer, Robert Lawrence. *Wines of California.* New York: Harry N. Abrams, 1978.

Bancroft, Hubert H. *History of California.* 7 vols. San Francisco: History Company, 1886–90.

———. *History of Nevada, Colorado, and Wyoming, 1540–1888.* San Francisco: History Company, 1890.

Bohemian Club: History, Officers and Committees, Incorporation, Constitution, By-Laws and Rules, Former Officers, Members, In Memoriam. San Francisco: The Bohemian Club, 1960.

Bosqui, Edward. *Memoirs of Edward Bosqui.* Oakland, Calif.: Holmes Books Co., 1952.

Bromley, George Tisdale. *The Long Ago and the Later On, or Recollections of Eighty Years.* San Francisco: A. M. Robertson, 1904.

Carosso, Vincent P. *The California Wine Industry, 1830–1895: A Study of the Formative Years.* Berkeley and Los Angeles: University of California Press, 1951.

Coblentz, Edmond D. *Ambrose Bierce, Stepfather of the Family: Address by E. D. Coblentz delivered in the Grove of Turning Leaves, Family Farm, August 31, 1958.* Twelve-page pamphlet. N.p., n.d.

Collins, Marvin. "How California Got its First Great Wine Book: Edward Bosqui's *Grapes and Grape Vines of California*, 1877." *Wayward Tendrils Quarterly* 18, no. 3 (July 2008): 1–7.

———. "The Man Who Ate, and Drank, California: Major Benjamin C. Truman." *Wayward Tendrils Quarterly* 16, no. 2 (April 2006): 15–20; 16, no. 3 (July 2006): 1–6.

———. "Portrait of the Artist as a Young Bulldog: The Paris Letters and the Rise of Charles A. Wetmore." *Wayward Tendrils Quarterly* 16, no. 4 (October 2006): 25–37.

Darlington, David. *Angels' Visits: An Inquiry into the Mystery of Zinfandel.* New York: Henry Holt, 1991.

———. *Zin: The History and Mystery of Zinfandel* (a reprint of *Angel's Visits* with a new epilogue by the author). New York: Da Capo Press, 2001.

Davies, Jack L. "Sparkling Wines." Chap. VI.8 in *The University of California/Sotheby Book of California Wine*, edited by Doris Muscatine, Maynard A. Amerine, and Bob Thompson. Berkeley and Los Angeles: University of California Press/Sotheby Publications, 1984.

Driesbach, Janice T. *Bountiful Harvest: 19th Century California Still Life Painting.* Sacramento: Crocker Art Museum, 1991.

Elite Directory for San Francisco and Oakland, The. San Francisco: Argonaut Publishing Co., 1879.

Emerson, Edward R. *The Story of the Vine.* New York: G. P. Putnam's Sons, 1902.

Emparan, Madie Brown. *The Vallejos of California.* San Francisco: Gleeson Library Associates, 1968.

Final Report of the California World's Fair Commission. Sacramento: A. J. Johnston, Supt. State Printing, 1894.

Fisher, M. F. K. *The Story of Wine in California.* Berkeley and Los Angeles: University of California Press, 1962.

Francisco, Cathleen. *Zinfandel: A Reference Guide to California Zinfandel.* San Francisco: Wine Appreciation Guild, 2001.

Fredericksen, Paul. "One Hundred Years of American Champagne." *Wine Review* (June 1947), 22–24, (July 1947), 14–16.

Geraci, Victor W. "The El Cajon, California, Raisin Industry: An Exercise in Gilded Age Capitalism." *Southern California Quarterly* 74, no. 4 (Winter 1992): 329–54.

Grapes and Grape Vines of California. Published under the Auspices of the California State Vinicultural Association. Oleographed by Wm. Harring from Original Water Color Drawings by Miss Hannah Millard. San Francisco: Edward Bosqui & Co., 1877.

Guinn, J. M. *A History of California and an Extended History of Its Southern Coast Counties.* Vol. 1. Los Angeles: Historic Record Co., 1907.

Haraszthy, Agoston. *Grape Culture, Wines, and Wine-Making, with Notes upon Agriculture and Horticulture.* New York: Harper & Brothers, 1862.

———. "Report on Grapes and Wines of California, by Col. A. Haraszthy, of Buena Vista, Sonoma County, California." In *Transactions of the California State Agricultural Society during the Year 1858.* Sacramento: John O'Meara, State Printer, 1859, 311–29.

Haraszthy, Arpad. "Bottling Red Wine." *California Farmer,* June 21, 1861, 129.

———. "The Castle of Johannisberg, and the Famed Johannisberg Wine." *California Farmer,* December 27, 1861, 89.

———. "Drawing Off Wine." *California Farmer,* July 3, 1862, 114.

———. "Early Viticulture in Sonoma." In *Sonoma County and Russian River Valley Illustrated.* San Francisco: Bell and Heymans, 1888, 77–79. Reprinted in *San Francisco Merchant* 20 (1888): 113–14.

———. "Fermenting Vats." *California Wine, Wool, and Stock Journal* 1 (1863): 93–96.

———. "Frost in the Vineyards of France." *California Farmer,* September 6, 1861, 4.

———. "Grapes and Wine Better than Gold Mines: The Coming Leading Agricultural Interest of California." *The Daily Bee* (Sacramento), December 24, 1880, p. 1.

———. "How to Drink Wine." In *Report of the Sixth Annual State Viticultural Convention, Held at Pioneer Hall, San Francisco, March 7, 8, 9, 10, 1888, under the Auspices of the Board of State Viticultural Commissioners of California.* Sacramento: J. D. Young, Supt. State Printing, 1988, 183–200. Reprinted in

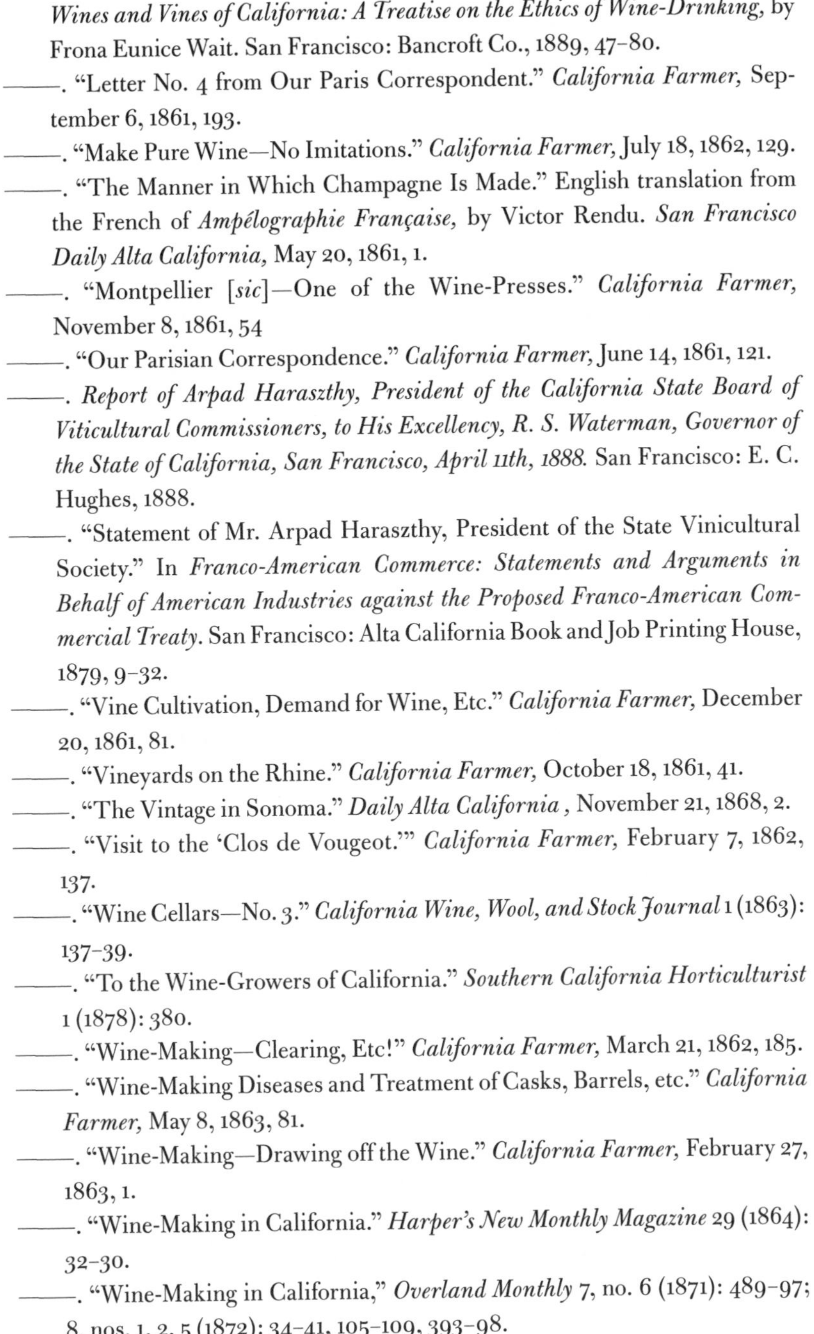

Wines and Vines of California: A Treatise on the Ethics of Wine-Drinking, by Frona Eunice Wait. San Francisco: Bancroft Co., 1889, 47–80.

———. "Letter No. 4 from Our Paris Correspondent." *California Farmer,* September 6, 1861, 193.

———. "Make Pure Wine—No Imitations." *California Farmer,* July 18, 1862, 129.

———. "The Manner in Which Champagne Is Made." English translation from the French of *Ampélographie Française,* by Victor Rendu. *San Francisco Daily Alta California,* May 20, 1861, 1.

———. "Montpellier [*sic*]—One of the Wine-Presses." *California Farmer,* November 8, 1861, 54

———. "Our Parisian Correspondence." *California Farmer,* June 14, 1861, 121.

———. *Report of Arpad Haraszthy, President of the California State Board of Viticultural Commissioners, to His Excellency, R. S. Waterman, Governor of the State of California, San Francisco, April 11th, 1888.* San Francisco: E. C. Hughes, 1888.

———. "Statement of Mr. Arpad Haraszthy, President of the State Vinicultural Society." In *Franco-American Commerce: Statements and Arguments in Behalf of American Industries against the Proposed Franco-American Commercial Treaty.* San Francisco: Alta California Book and Job Printing House, 1879, 9–32.

———. "Vine Cultivation, Demand for Wine, Etc." *California Farmer,* December 20, 1861, 81.

———. "Vineyards on the Rhine." *California Farmer,* October 18, 1861, 41.

———. "The Vintage in Sonoma." *Daily Alta California* , November 21, 1868, 2.

———. "Visit to the 'Clos de Vougeot.'" *California Farmer,* February 7, 1862, 137.

———. "Wine Cellars—No. 3." *California Wine, Wool, and Stock Journal* 1 (1863): 137–39.

———. "To the Wine-Growers of California." *Southern California Horticulturist* 1 (1878): 380.

———. "Wine-Making—Clearing, Etc!" *California Farmer,* March 21, 1862, 185.

———. "Wine-Making Diseases and Treatment of Casks, Barrels, etc." *California Farmer,* May 8, 1863, 81.

———. "Wine-Making—Drawing off the Wine." *California Farmer,* February 27, 1863, 1.

———. "Wine-Making in California." *Harper's New Monthly Magazine* 29 (1864): 32–30.

———. "Wine-Making in California," *Overland Monthly* 7, no. 6 (1871): 489–97; 8, nos. 1, 2, 5 (1872): 34–41, 105–109, 393–98.

———. *Wine-Making in California.* With an introduction by Ruth Teiser and Catherine Harroun. San Francisco: Book Club of California, 1978.

———. "Wine-Making in France." *California Farmer,* August 20, 1861, 161.

———. "Wine-Making No. 4." *California Wine, Wool, and Stock Journal* 1 (1863): 161–64.

———. "Wine-Making No. 5." *California Wine, Wool, and Stock Journal* 1 (1863): 193–96.

———. "Wine-Making No. 6." *California Wine, Wool, and Stock Journal* 1 (1863): 241–44.

———. "Wine-Making No. 7." *California Wine, Wool, and Stock Journal* 2 (1864): 13–15.

———. "Wine-Making No. 8." *California Wine, Wool, and Stock Journal* 2 (1864): 44–45.

———. "Wine-Making No. 9." *California Wine, Wool, and Stock Journal* 2 (1864): 53–54.

———. "Wine-Making No. 10." *California Wine, Wool, and Stock Journal* 2 (1864): 77–79.

———. "Wine-Making No. 11." *California Wine, Wool, and Stock Journal* 2 (1864): 113–15.

———. "Wine-Making No. 12." *California Wine, Wool, and Stock Journal* 2 (1864): 137–38.

———. "Wine-Making on the Close de Vougeot." *California Farmer,* February 14, 1862, 145.

———. "Wine Presses—No. 2." *California Wine, Wool, and Stock Journal* 1 (1864): 113–16.

———, and David W. C. Nesfield. *California Grapes and Wine and The Vine Land of the West, or, Champagne and Its Manufacture.* San Francisco: Bosqui Engraving and Printing Co., 1883.

[Haraszthy, Charles.] "Vine Culture by C. H." *San Francisco Daily Alta California,* November 18, 1856, 1.

Hardy, Thomas. *Notes on Vineyards in America and Europe.* Adelaide, Australia: L. Henn & Co., 1885.

Hart, Jerome A. *In Our Second Century: From an Editor's Notebook.* San Francisco: Pioneer Press, 1931.

Heintz, William F. "The Woes of Early Champagne Making." *Wines and Vines* 60, no. 6 (June 1979): 93–94.

Hitchcock, David. *Zinfandel.* Pasadena, Calif.: Weather Bird Press, 1980.

Hittell, John S. *The Commerce and Industries of the Pacific Coast of North America.* San Francisco: A. L. Bancroft & Co., 1882.

Husmann, George. *Grape Culture and Wine-Making in California: A Practical Manual for the Grape-Grower and Wine-Maker.* San Francisco: Payot, Upham and Co., 1888.

Hutton, Ian George. *The Zinfandel Trail: A Guide to the Wine and the Wineries that Produce It.* Esher, Surrey, UK: IGH Publications, 1998.

Hyatt, T. Hart. *Hyatt's Hand-Book of Grape Culture.* San Francisco: H. H. Bancroft, 1867.

Johnson, Hugh. *Vintage: The Story of Wine.* New York: Simon and Schuster, 1989.

Jones, Idwal. *Vines in the Sun: A Journey through the California Vineyards.* New York: William Morrow, 1949.

King, Moses, ed. *Kings's Handbook of the United States.* With text by M. F. Sweetser. Buffalo, N.Y.: Moses King Corporation, 1891–92.

Knoll, Alfred Phillip. "Champagne." *International and Comparative Law Quarterly* 19 (1970): 309–16.

Lambert-Gocs, Miles. "Shedding Light on the Zinfandel Name." *Wines and Vines* 87, no. 4 (April 2006): 54.

Lapsley, James T. *Bottled Poetry: Napa Winemaking from Prohibition to the Modern Era.* Berkeley and Los Angeles: University of California Press, 1996.

Laube, James. *California's Great Chardonnays.* San Francisco: Wine Spectator Press, 1990.

Lavender, David S. *California, Land of New Beginnings.* Lincoln: University of Nebraska Press, 1987.

Lichine, Alexis, in collaboration with William Fifield and with the assistance of Jonathan Bartlett and Jane Stockwood. *Alexis Lichine's Encyclopedia of Wines & Spirits.* New York: Alfred A. Knopf, 1967.

Lynch, Robert M. *The Sonoma Valley Story: Pages through the Ages, Sonoma Valley Through the Eyes of the* Sonoma Index-Tribune *family and Staff.* Sonoma, Calif.: Sonoma Index-Tribune, 1997

Madden, Henry Miller. "California for Hungarian Readers: Letters of János Xánthus, 1857 and 1859." *California Historical Society Quarterly* 28 (1949): 125–42.

Master Hands in the Affairs of the Pacific Coast, Historical, Biographical and Descriptive: A Resumé of the Builders of Our Material Progress. San Francisco: Western Historical and Publishing, 1892.

McCabe, James D. *The Illustrated History of the Centennial Exhibition Held in Commemoration of the One Hundredth Anniversary of American Independence.* Philadelphia: National Publishing Co., 1876.

McGinty, Brian. "Angelica: An Old California Tradition." *Vintage Magazine* 5, no. 5 (October 1975): 33–37.

——. *Haraszthy at the Mint.* Famous California Trials Series, Vol. 10. Los Angeles: Dawson's Book Shop, 1975.

——. *The Palace Inns: A Connoisseur's Guide to Historic American Hotels.* Harrisburg, Pa.: Stackpole Books, 1978.

——. *Strong Wine: The Life and Legend of Agoston Haraszthy.* Stanford: Stanford University Press, 1998.

——. "A Toast to Eclipse." *Wine World* 3 (September–October, 1974), 41–43.

Melville, John. *Guide to California Wines.* San Carlos, Calif.: Nourse Publishing Co., 1955–60.

Mendelson, Richard. *From Demon to Darling: A Legal History of Wine in America.* Berkeley and Los Angeles: University of California Press, 2008.

Mészáros, Lázár. *Külföldi levelei és életirata (The Foreign Letters and Autobiography of Lázár Mészáros).* Pest: Ráth Mór, 1867.

Morris, Roy, Jr. *Ambrose Bierce: Alone in Bad Company.* New York: Crown Publishers, 1995.

Nordhoff, Charles. *California for Health, Pleasure, and Residence: A Book for Travellers and Settlers.* New York: Harper & Brothers, 1872.

O'Connell, Daniel. *The Inner Man: Good Things To Eat and Drink and Where To Get Them.* San Francisco: Bancroft Co., 1891.

Peninou, Ernest P. *A History of the Orleans Hill Vineyard & Winery of Arpad Haraszthy & Company.* Winters, Calif.: The Winters Express, 1983.

——, and Gail G. Unzelman. *The California Wine Association and Its Member Wineries, 1894–1920.* Santa Rosa, Calif.: Nomis Press, 2000.

——, and Sidney S. Greenleaf. *A Directory of California Wine Growers and Wine Makers in 1860: With Biographical and Historical Notes and Index.* Berkeley: Tamalpais Press, 1967.

——, assisted by Gail G. Unzelman and Michael M. Anderson. *History of the Sonoma Viticultural District: The Grape Growers, the Wine Makers, and the Vineyards.* Santa Rosa, Calif.: Nomis Press, 1998.

Perry, Claire. *Pacific Arcadia: Images of California, 1600–1915.* New York: Oxford University Press; Stanford, Calif.: Iris & B. Gerald Cantor Center for Visual Arts, Stanford University, 1999.

Pinney, Thomas. *A History of Wine in America: From the Beginnings to Prohibition.* Berkeley and Los Angeles: University of California Press, 1989.

Prince, William Robert, aided by William Prince. *A Treatise on the Vine.* New York: T. & J. Swords, 1830.

Ray, Eleanor, with Barbara Marinacci. *Vineyards in the Sky: The Life of Legendary Vintner Martin Ray.* Aptos, Calif.: Mountain Vines Publishing, 1993.

Resource Guide to Zinfandel. Rough and Ready, Calif.: Zinfandel Advocates and Producers, 2002.

Saunders, Richard. *Ambrose Bierce: The Making of a Misanthrope.* San Francisco: Chronicle Books, 1985.

Schoonmaker, Frank. *Frank Schoonmaker's Encyclopedia of Wine.* New York: Hastings House, 1964, 1965.

Simon, André L. *Champagne.* With a chapter on American Champagne by Robert J. Misch. New York: McGraw-Hill, 1962.

Starr, Kevin. "Introduction" to *Grapes and Grape Vines of California,* published under the Auspices of the California State Vinicultural Association. New York: Harcourt Brace Jovanovich, 1980.

Stewart, Rhoda. *A Zinfandel Odyssey: A Tale of California's Most Captivating Wine Grape.* San Rafael, Calif.: PWV, Inc., 2001.

Stoll, Horatio P. "Agostin [*sic*] Haraszthy's Eventful Career." *Wines and Vines* 18, no. 1 (January 1937): 16–17.

———. "California Champagne's First Triumph." *Wines and Vines* 18, no. 12 (December 1937): 4.

———. "California Wine Exhibits for Fifty Years." *Wines and Vines* 19, no. 12 (December 1938): 6, 8, 10.

———. "Haraszthy's 'Eclipse' Champagne." *Wines and Vines* 17, no. 12 (December 1936): 10.

———. "History of Champagne Making in California: Notable Achievements in the Pre-Prohibition Era." *California Grape Grower* 15, no. 3 (March 1934): 4–5.

———. "Over the Sparkling Wine Cup." *Pacific Wine and Spirit Review,* 52, no. 7 (May 31, 1910): 14–15.

Street, Richard Steven. *Beasts of the Field: A Narrative History of California Farmworkers, 1769–1913.* Stanford, Calif.: Stanford University Press, 2004.

Sullivan, Charles L. "By the Late 1880's, Arpad Haraszthy Was Producing 250,000 Bottles of Eclipse." *California Winelands* (January 11, 1986): 9.

———. *A Companion to California Wine: An Encyclopedia of Wine and Winemaking from the Mission Period to the Present.* Berkeley and Los Angeles: University of California Press, 1998.

———. "A Man Named Agoston Haraszthy." Part 1, *Vintage Magazine,* February 1980, 18–19; Part 2, *Vintage Magazine,* March 1980, 23–25; Part 3, *Vintage Magazine,* April 1980, 11–17.

———. "A Viticultural Mystery Solved: The Historical Origins of Zinfandel in California. *California History* 57 (Summer 1978): 114–29.

——. *Zinfandel: A History of a Grape and Its Wine.* Berkeley and Los Angeles: University of California Press, 2003.

——. "Zinfandel: A True Vinifera." *Vinifera Wine Growers Journal* 9, no. 2 (Summer 1982): 71–86.

Swanberg, W. A. *Citizen Hearst: A Biography of William Randolph Hearst.* New York: Charles Scribner's Sons, 1961.

Teiser, Ruth, and Catherine Harroun. "Introduction" to *Wine-Making in California,* by Arpad Haraszthy. San Francisco: Book Club of California, 1978.

——. *Winemaking in California: The Account in Words and Pictures of the Golden State's Two-Century-Long Adventure with Wine.* New York: McGraw-Hill Book Company, 1983.

Truman, Ben. C. *See How It Sparkles.* Los Angeles: George Rice and Sons, 1896.

Vizetelly, Henry. *A History of Champagne with Notes on the Other Sparking Wines of France.* London: Henry Sotheran & Co., 1882.

Wait, Frona Eunice. *Wines and Vines of California: A Treatise on the Ethics of Wine-Drinking.* San Francisco: Bancroft Company, 1889. Reissued: Berkeley, Calif.: Howell-North Books, 1973, with an introduction by Maynard A. Amerine.

Walters, Dean. "Illustrated California Wine History: Buena Vista & the Mercurial 'Count'." *Wayward Tendrils Quarterly* 20, no. 1 (January 2010): 1–9.

Wetmore, Charles A. *Ampelography of California.* San Francisco: Merchant Publishing Co., 1884.

——. "Prominent Wine Men: Sketch No. 11, Arpad Haraszthy of San Francisco." *Pacific Wine and Spirit Review,* September 20, 1891, 10–11.

——. *Propagation of the Vine.* San Francisco: San Francisco Merchant, 1880.

——. *Propagation of the Vine: How to Regulate Vineyards by the Use of Seedlings: A Treatise Illustrating the Superiority of Constitutionally Perfect Roots, Also an Essay on the Physical and Moral Influence of the Vine.* 2nd ed. with appendix. San Francisco: San Francisco Merchant, 1880.

——. *Treatise on Wine Production and Special Reports on Wine Examinations, the Tariff and Internal Revenue Taxes, and Chemical Analyses.* Appendix B to the Report of the Board of State Viticultural Commissioners for 1893–94. Sacramento: A. J. Johnston, Supt. State Printing, 1894.

ACKNOWLEDGMENTS

My researches into the Haraszthys and their wines began so many years ago that I cannot now remember the names of all those who gave me insights or helped me gather information. My memories of my grandfather Agoston F. Haraszthy (1869–1943)—son of Attila Haraszthy (1835–1888) and grandson of the original Agoston Haraszthy (1812–1869)—are warm but indistinct, for he died when I was only six years old. He did not speak to me about Eclipse, but he did tell my mother much about the years he worked in his Uncle Arpad's champagne cellars in San Francisco, and she informed me of the enthusiasm with which he spoke of the exacting process by which Eclipse was made and sent forth to delight the city and the world. I first ventured into the wine cellars at Buena Vista during the time that Frank and Antonia Bartholomew held sway there. They fell heir to the Haraszthy legacy when they purchased the core of Agoston Haraszthy's old Buena Vista Estate in 1943. They restored the stone cellars, damaged in the great earthquake of 1906 and unused since then, and began once again to produce wines bearing the Buena Vista label. After Bart's death, Antonia realized their dream of reconstructing the neo-Pompeiian house that served as Agoston's headquarters during his time at Buena Vista. During the years that my uncle Jan Haraszthy and his loving wife, my aunt Mianna Haraszthy, lived at Buena Vista, I visited often.

But warm memories and recollected stories are not enough to build a history on. I have researched the Haraszthy story on the ground in Hungary, Wisconsin, and California. I have visited archives, solicited recollections from old pioneers, consulted the pages of crumbling books in dusty libraries, and buried my head in countless newspapers and journals. The result is this story of Arpad Haraszthy and Eclipse, a sequel to my biography, *Strong Wine: The Life and Legend of Agoston Haraszthy,* published by Stanford University Press in 1998. This volume overlaps in part with the earlier book—but only in a very limited way, for the story of Arpad and Eclipse is strong enough to stand on its own. My researches in recent years have brought me in contact with men and women who share my enthusiasm for the Haraszthy story and were generous with their time and efforts in helping me with my research. I am happy to name some of them—though I will inevitably forget the names of some others.

Dr. James T. Lapsley, historian of California wine, member of the faculty at the University of California, Davis, and a practical winemaker in Yolo County; Dr. Victor Geraci, wine historian and Associate Director of the Regional Oral History Office at the Bancroft Library; Dr. Richard Grant Peterson, legendary winemaker and scholar, whose rich background in California wine includes practical experience in the manufacture of sparkling wine; and Dr. James J. Rawls, California historian whose knowledge of the history of the Golden State knows no bounds, all read drafts of the manuscript and offered suggestions for improvement, correction of errors, and words of encouragement. I have tried to follow all of their suggestions, though I may have fallen short in one particular or another.

Scott Shields of the Crocker Art Museum in Sacramento, Robin Doolin of the Oakland Museum of California, Alfred Harrison of the North Point Gallery in San Francisco, Dean Walters of Vintage Antiques in San Anselmo, Patricia Keats of the Society of California Pioneers, Diane Smith of the Sonoma Valley Historical Society, Peter Hanff and Susan Snyder of the Bancroft Library, and Gail Unzelman, wine book collector and editor extraordinaire of *Wayward Tendrils Quarterly,* helped me locate art work related to Arpad and Eclipse. Marvin Collins offered insights gathered in the course of his almost encyclopedic research into California wine history of the late nineteenth century. Ann Foley Scheuring of Rumsey, California, author of *Valley Empires: Hugh Glenn and Henry Miller in the Shaping of California* and other books, offered insights into the geography of the Capay Valley and environs gathered from her years of residence there. Elizabeth Kane of the Sonoma State Historic Parks helped me run down Sonoma leads, including one (perhaps the only) surviving bottle of Eclipse, now preserved in the museum in General Vallejo's home at Lachryma Montis. Kathleen Mino, Family Service Counselor of the Catholic Cemeteries of the Archdiocese of San Francisco, helped me locate the final burial places of Arpad and Jovita Haraszthy in Colma, south of San Francisco.

My research efforts were helped at various times by Colleen Bradley-Sanders of the Ehrman Medical Library, NYU School of Medicine; Doug Cisney of the Sonoma County Library in Petaluma; Lara Michels of the Judah L. Magnes Museum in Berkeley; Tammy Lau of the Special Collections Research Center in the Madden Library at California State University, Fresno; the staffs of the Bancroft Library in Berkeley, the California State Archives in Sacramento, the California Room at the State Library in Sacramento, the Shields Library at the University of California, Davis, the Yolo County Archives in Woodland, the California Historical Society in San Francisco, the Boston Public Library, and the Library of Congress.

At the University of Oklahoma Press, Chuck Rankin and Bob Clark gave the book a very good home, and Emily Jerman and Jo Ann Reece edited it with close and loving care.

To all of these—and those whose names I should have remembered but didn't—my sincere thanks.

INDEX